AUTHENTICITY

FOUNTAINHEAD PRESS V SERIES

Edited by
Shane Borrowman

FOUNTAINHEAD
PRESS

Our green initiatives include:

Electronic Products
We deliver products in non-paper form whenever possible. This includes pdf downloadables, flash drives, and CDs.

Electronic Samples
We use Xample, a new electronic sampling system. Instructor samples are sent via a personalized web page that links to pdf downloads.

FSC Certified Printers
All of our printers are certified by the Forest Service Council, which promotes environmentally and socially responsible management of the world's forests. This program allows consumer groups, individual consumers, and businesses to work together hand-in-hand to promote responsible use of the world's forests as a renewable and sustainable resource.

Recycled Paper
Most of our products are printed on a minimum of 30% post-consumer waste recycled paper.

Support of Green Causes
When we do print, we donate a portion of our revenue to green causes. Listed below are a few of the organizations that have received donations from Fountainhead Press. We welcome your feedback and suggestions for contributions, as we are always searching for worthy initiatives.
Rainforest 2 Reef
Environmental Working Group

INTRODUCTION TO THE FOUNTAINHEAD PRESS V SERIES

By Brooke Rollins and Lee Bauknight
Series Editors

The *Fountainhead Press V Series* is a new collection of single-topic readers that take a unique look at some of today's most pressing issues. Designed to give writing students a more nuanced introduction to public discourse—on the environment, on food, and on digital life, to name a few of the topics—the books feature writing, research, and invention prompts that can be adapted to nearly any kind of college writing class. Each *V Series* textbook focuses on a single issue and includes multi-genre and multimodal readings and assignments that move the discourse beyond the most familiar patterns of debate—patterns usually fettered by entrenched positions and often obsessed with "winning."

The ultimate goal of the series is to help writing students—who tend to hover on the periphery of public discourse—think, explore, find their voices, and skillfully compose texts in a variety of media and genres. Not only do the books help students think about compelling issues and how they might address them, they also give students the practice they need to develop their research, rhetorical, and writing skills. Together, the readings, prompts, and longer assignments show students how to add their voices to the conversations about these issues in meaningful and productive ways.

With enough readings and composing tasks to sustain an entire quarter or semester, and inexpensive enough to be used in combination with other rhetorics and readers, the *Fountainhead Press V Series* provides instructors with the flexibility to build the writing courses they want and need to teach. An instructor interested in deeply exploring environmental issues, for example, could design a semester- or quarter-long course using *Green*, the first of the *V Series* texts. At the same time, an instructor who wanted to teach discrete units on different issues could use two or more of the *V Series* books. In either case, the texts would give students ample opportunity—and a variety of ways—to engage with the issues at hand.

The *V Series* uses the term "composition" in its broadest sense. Of course, the textbooks provide students plenty of opportunities to write, but they also include assignments that take students beyond the page. Books in the series encourage students to explore other modes of communication by prompting them: to design websites, to produce videos, posters, and presentations; to conduct primary and secondary research; and to develop projects with community partners that might incorporate any number of these skills. Ultimately, we have designed the *Fountainhead Press V Series* to work for teachers and students. With their carefully chosen readings, built-in flexibility, and sound rhetorical grounding, the *V Series* books would be a dynamic and user-friendly addition to any writing class.

TABLE OF CONTENTS

INTRODUCTION
Fraud and Fundamental Misunderstandings

By Shane Borrowman

What I was seeing didn't make any sense.

I was teaching an online writing class, and students were required to take part in regular discussions of the essays we were reading, responding to a question and then responding to one another, all within the same virtual thread of conversation. It didn't take me long to get a sense of people from their posts: James was a no-nonsense sort of guy, answering the question in exactly the number of required words. No more, no less. Lisbon took the same approach when she responded to her peers, quoting their original answers in well-chosen snippets and then explaining, in exacting detail, why she agreed or disagreed. Randi was playful, taking a teasing tone but always staying on task. Chris wandered away from the question and the reading and often had to be asked pointed questions by his peers, just to clarify the meaning of his posts. Some folks didn't use any capital letters or punctuation, so reading required an extra act of translation, at least at first.

There was always baseline consistency. James sounded like James, whether he was answering questions about "Resurrecting the Champ" or responding to Lisbon's rough draft of her memoir. Randi was always Randi—joking with Chris about his negative feelings toward boxing during a discussion of "Who Killed Benny Paret?" or gently chiding herself for struggling to punctuate properly when coordinating conjunctions separated complete sentences.

But Tina sounded different—not different from James or Lisbon or Randi or Chris but different from Tina. Responding to an essay about the need for greater regulation of sports involving animals—such as greyhound racing—Tina might engage with the text in a careful, insightful way, noting how the argument that was presented was weak because of its heavy reliance on emotional appeals. Responding to another student's writing, she might be dismissive and callous, ignoring both the strong features of the text and the feelings of its writer. But stress happens in all lives, and everyone responds differently. I assumed that the erratic responses were a reaction to the stress of our class and possibly stresses beyond class—and other students made this same assumption, responding to Tina in consistent and professional ways across the weeks and the work.

Then Jerry changed everything. In a discussion of "The Men We Carry in Our Minds," Tina's post was short, vague, and off task. Responding to Tina's discussion post, Jerry noted that it would have been possible to write such a string of generalizations without even reading the essay. Tina exploded: "I don't care what you think about me since you have two kids and no job and no man." Tina had the facts straight in her insult; Jerry, when she introduced herself, told everyone that she was unmarried, unemployed, and the mother of two children. But this post was inappropriate and unprofessional, and it violated the school's policy regarding how students could and could not interact with each other.

I contacted Tina, noting that she'd agreed to abide by all of the relevant policies by enrolling in the course and explaining that I was required to file an Incident Report (which would have no effect on her grade in the class, unless a pattern of such interactions was established).

My email was met with silence, and the Incident Report prompted no outburst. I assumed (despite knowing what happens when assumptions are made) that the matter was closed. The class continued, and the discussions went on.

Then Tina submitted an essay that was plagiarized from an easily identifiable online source.

I contacted her again, explaining the process I'd followed to establish that plagiarism was committed, explaining the consequences, and explaining her rights to appeal the matter. While plagiarism was more serious than unprofessional/combative postings to discussion forums, the incident still affected only her grade on this specific assignment. She could, I assured her, still pass the class.

"Thank you," Tina responded, "for informing me of this matter. I have been working extra hours at work, and my husband and daughter have been doing my classes for me. I didn't know that this essay had been plagiarized."

Suddenly, I was at the center of a perfect storm.

Tina's posts in class discussions were erratic from the start because Tina wasn't Tina at all. She was Tina's Husband and Tina's Daughter. Her essay was from an online source, plagiarized by either the husband or daughter. And she'd just confessed to me that she wasn't doing any of the work at all, although her "Thank you" seemed to imply that she'd be fixing the plagiarism issue soon.

But plagiarism had become only part of the issue. Tina was defrauding the school, enrolling in classes but not actually taking them—at least in this case. She was lying to her classmates by presenting "Tina" to them—when "Tina" was truly a corporate being made up of at least Tina, the daughter, and the husband. She—or her daughter/husband—was stealing content from an online source and presenting it as her/their own writing—an act of fraud aimed squarely at me, specifically, the members of the class, and the school, generally. Tina's existence in the class had all the truth of a padded resume, an exaggerated dating profile, a ghost-written book. Less, really. A padded resume would still include facts—just facts that were stretched to (and maybe slightly beyond) the breaking point. An exaggerated dating profile still represents a real person in most ways—just a polished version of that person, a version crafted to be more appealing to potential partners. And a ghost-written book would exist within a long tradition of ghost writing, one where it's understood that John F. Kennedy had only nominal involvement with his *Profiles in Courage* and, at the other end of the spectrum, a reality television star incapable of speaking in complete sentences could publish her/his autobiography within only weeks of becoming famous.

There was no authentic level on which Tina, her participation in the class, or her enrollment at the school could be understood or even verified—beyond the existence of a birth certificate and Social Security number, neither of which is universally accepted in America as proof of legitimate existence. Even Tina's tuition was being paid in a fraudulent way, given that she'd taken out loans to cover the education that she was/wasn't earning. She was obtaining loans that, at a minimum, required her to attend the classes the money was paying for—and if she stopped attending at any point, she was legally required to pay back a portion of her loan amount. But how could anyone, ever, determine if Tina had attended the class at all? I did what a corporate structure calls for in a situation with so many variables: I forwarded the whole matter to my supervisor—who passed it to her supervisor, along with a ton of supporting documentation of "Tina" and her/their work—and Tina was suspended for a year. After the suspension was complete, she could petition for re-admittance.

Tina's final email to me and to the Dean of Students was concise and clear: "Fuck you. Fraud." I'm not sure if that came from her, her daughter, or her husband, though.

To me, the response was irrelevant, ultimately, and is memorable only because of its absurdity and childishness. Except for that last single-word accusation: "Fraud." Who? Me or the Dean? How? Since a fraud is someone who deceives in order to achieve an advantage, this seems like an unlikely charge for Tina to level against either me or the dean who suspended her. What advantage did either of us seek at this intersection of online education, false representation, and plagiarism?

What my mind goes back to again and again, year after year, is the underlying question, though: "Why would Tina tell me this?" After more than two decades of teaching, I can't imagine a student coming to my office to tell me, face-to-face, that they had not done any of the work, had relied on others to do all of the work, and had created circumstances where plagiarism would or could be committed in their name.

For Tina to feel that such an admission could be made to me, a fundamental misunderstanding of our relationship, and of the entire situation, had to occur. Tina was a student at a reputable for-profit university, one that took its educational role seriously and designed its classes to demand much of the students. But Tina, I think, saw herself first and foremost as a customer—one of many customers, in fact. According to the Federal Government, by 2008 nearly 1.8 million students were enrolled annually at for-profit post-secondary schools. Tina applied for and received student loans, using them to pay her tuition at a school that she may never have attended—literally, in the sense that it existed only in virtual space, and metaphorically, in the sense that she may not have done any of the work required in the classes in which she was enrolled.

Tina bought an education, for all intents and purposes, in the same way she would have financed a used Buick. Except she probably would have driven the Buick herself.

The virtual space of the university was an authentic one—placing demands on students and holding them to high standards. But Tina used the possibilities of online space to enlist the direct assistance of her husband and daughter who, quite literally, stood in for her (attending class, in the sense of participating in class discussions as "Tina" rather than themselves).

But the misunderstanding went beyond the corporate creation of "Tina" as a student. For her to confess to me, she had to deeply misread the relationship between us, the relationship between professor and student. I was there to instruct, to mentor, to guide, and to grade. She was there, well, to be instructed, mentored, guided, graded. We were there to work together toward a shared goal: making Tina a more successful writer. I was, of course, also charged by the corporation with enforcing course and school policies—regarding student conduct, plagiarism, and significant acts of academic dishonesty.

It would never, ever have occurred to me that Tina—that anyone—could misunderstand this, but, of course, the matter is easily misunderstood when it's reframed. In a face-to-face educational setting, Tina would have been more likely to see me as the representative of the educational system (along with other things, including her seeing my role as helper, hopefully). But in a for-profit, online setting, I suddenly became someone charged not with enforcing policies but with delivering product. Without my knowledge, at least initially, Tina changed the nature of our relationship by allowing "Tina" to do her work for her, but she assumed that this wasn't a problem. She paid for the class, negotiated her non-participation with the aid of her husband and daughter, and thanked me for calling her attention to the fact that they weren't living up to their part of this devil's bargain.

But "Tina" left me to consider my own authenticity in the online space. My students knew only what I told them, such as vague statements about where I lived—northern Nevada, at the time—and what I liked to do in my spare time (yard work). They knew I had twins but didn't know I was struggling desperately to manage my role as stay-at-home father, a struggle I felt I was losing daily. They knew I liked to work around the home—painting and making small improvements—but didn't know that I'd given this work up almost entirely, once my home, purchased for $233,000, was revalued at $70,000 in the collapsed housing market. And they didn't know that they were, all of them, spread thin on my plate of professional responsibility.

I was teaching more than twenty students in the class "Tina" was attending. I was teaching another twenty in a second class for that same school. I was also working for two other online for-profit universities, and I was teaching a total of thirteen classes at a time. The amount of work I was putting into any one class—or any one student—was negligible. I sat at my desk for as many as fifteen hours at a stretch, responding to hundreds of student papers, emails, etc. I was presenting a professional face to all of these students, and I was doing almost nothing behind that facade—nothing that would truly qualify as teaching. I was delivering prescribed course content in prescribed ways, and I was making no effort at all to go beyond that. For each school, I located the basement of expectations, the absolute lowest level at which I could function without being fired, and I set up my office there.

My class, like "Tina," was only a real class in the most general sense. Students did almost all of the learning on their own, with me providing only the required amount of feedback. Failure rates were spectacularly high (in my class and across each university), and plagiarism occurred in more than half of assignments, according to one often-whispered statistic.

Despite all of these factors, some students did succeed. They learned to write, learned to be better readers, learned to think critically about their sources as they performed research. Many of those students thanked me for helping them so much. Some even praised me as one of the best online teachers they'd ever had.

I felt like a fraud. I'm pretty sure I was a fraud, at least by my own definitions of professional responsibility. I rationalized my situation financially: Teaching so many classes for so many schools was the only way I could make enough money to support my family. It was an irrationalization at the worst, scant comfort at best.

I negotiated a fictional "Dr. Borrowman" in every class, for every school, to every student—one no more related to my real abilities than "Tina" was related to the actual student in her class.

These sorts of negotiations and (mis)representations are at the heart of *Authenticity*, beginning with "In Business," an unpublished manuscript by famed author Norman Maclean. In his most highly regarded work, the novella "A River Runs Through It," Maclean tells the story of his family, specifically the story of his murdered brother, Paul. He tells the truth as he lived it and as he wants readers to experience it—the truth of the experience and its familial fallout; his story is all the stronger for his infidelity to facts. In "In Business," written much earlier in Maclean's career and never completed, he considers the legend of George Armstrong Custer, arguing that tourism and beer sales combined and conspired to make the fallen cavalry officer a legend, despite any reality to the contrary.

The readings in *Authenticity* go well beyond the legend of Custer and his last stand, naturally. Matters of authenticity are matters of accuracy, matters of truthfulness, matters of reliability and legitimacy. These are the issues discussed here—in a range of contexts. While *Authenticity* begins with Custer and questions about his legend's reliability (when tourists and saloon patrons are being rhetorically targeted), it moves through issues of creativity and nonfiction, ghostwriting and grade inflation, padded resumes and online dating.

Beyond its readings, *Authenticity* includes a range of research, invention, and composing prompts that will guide you through aspects of the prewriting, writing, and rewriting processes—all designed to help you hone both your critical thinking

and critical writing skills in relation to matters of fact versus fiction, reality vs. fantasy, truth vs. Truth. To begin this process of analysis and investigation, consider the exploration activity that follows this introduction, an activity that asks you to consider something you know...and how it might be right or wrong.

Consider a memorable event from your past—the birthday party when you turned eighteen, a wedding ceremony, a family reunion, etc. Regardless of the memory you choose, be sure to select something that at least two other people are likely to remember.

In writing, describe the memory in as much detail as possible. What came before the event you've chosen? What happened after? Who was present and how did they look and act? What did you and others who were there say to one another? Tell the story of this memory, start to finish.

After you have written your description of this memory, discuss it with one or more classmates. Tell them the story. Read aloud what you've written, but be sure to make notes of any other details you add as you speak to your peers. Often, the act of writing and then speaking will lead to more details, more nuances, more substance. Jot these additions down before you lose them.

Later, call someone else who was present in the specific memory you described in writing and to your peers. Do not share your writing (at first). Instead, ask this person to describe the event you've chosen. What do they remember?

Be sure to take notes on how this person remembers the event you described. It's fine to tell them that you're doing this as a class assignment, and it's fine to share your writing after they have had a chance to respond. But don't read your description first, as that will influence how this other person's memory of the event is communicated.

Before returning to class, describe how this other participant in the memory remembers the event you chose. Where did their memory align with yours? What differences were there between the ways the two of you remembered the event? What do you think might account for the similarities and differences in how the two of you remember the same event?

As you consider these questions, remember that memory is rarely a matter of being right or wrong. More often than not, every participant in a given event has their own memories, some of which align with "what actually happened" and some of which are flawed—because, for example, people tend to remember best the moments that are their worst (thus over-emphasizing moments where they were embarrassed or where they did something that they now regret or find painful).

After all this writing and discussing, what aspects of your own memory of the event do you now worry may be inauthentic in some way?

As a class, generate a list of major events that have occurred during your lifetimes—from Superbowl victories to natural disasters. In small groups, select one event and take ten minutes for each member to describe, in writing, what they remember about this event. Then share your writing: Where do your memories of the event coincide? Where do they diverge?

AUTHENTICITY

According to the University of Chicago Press, "In his eighty-eight years, Norman Maclean (1902–90) played many parts: fisherman, logger, firefighter, scholar, teacher. But it was a role he took up late in life, that of writer, that won him enduring fame and critical acclaim—as well as the devotion of readers worldwide. Though the 1976 collection A River Runs Through It and Other Stories was the only book Maclean published in his lifetime, it was an unexpected success, and the moving family tragedy of the title novella—based largely on Maclean's memories of early twentieth-century Montana—has proved to be one of the most enduring American stories ever written." The chapter that follows is a part of Maclean's never-published, never-finished historical and cultural analysis of the Battle of the Little Bighorn—where, in late June of 1876, Lt. Col. George Armstrong Custer led the 7th Cavalry to a spectacular defeat (in which his 276 troops attacked several thousand Lakota and Cheyenne warriors). Several more chapters from this unpublished work appear in O. Alan Weltzien's collection The Norman Maclean Reader.

IN BUSINESS

By Norman Maclean

There is no balance-sheet that tells whether the debt Gen. Custer owes Anheuser-Busch, Inc., is greater than the debt the corporation owes the General, who was a teetotaler. The General's debt is not reduced by the fact that, when the business connection was first established, the memory of the General was a national asset and the company was still pretty much a local brewery. In the long run, they have done very well by each other.

There is some correlation between the profits of this world and its lasting memories. Although the dead are not allowed to take it with them, the dead who continue to live in this world generally go on making money. In a way, they have to earn their keep. Why not? Sometimes business rescues individuals from near oblivion and makes them weekly heroes on TV, as it has done with Wyatt Earp and Bat Masterson. Sometimes it immortalizes a whole class of men by industrializing them. The cowboy, for instance. Apart from Westerns on movie and TV, apart from rodeos and dude ranches and adult consumption altogether, it would take quite an audit to calculate the annual profit in children's cowboy boots, pants, belts, hats, toy revolvers, etc. More frequently, of course, business capitalizes on well established reputations but its investment in them raises the valuation of their stock and adds to their security as well as to that of the investor. So Prudential Insurance advertisements increase our feeling of security about Prudential and even about the Rock of Gibraltar.

1.

Custer's Last Stand has been a big money maker. How much it has made would be impossible to calculate, and it is undoubtedly proper that something should remain misty about the economics of the dead. There are, for instance, small local profits starting with the Black Hills where there is a Custer State Park and a town of Custer that has grown into a motel city famous because Custer's command first discovered gold near there in 1874. In the Black Hills, State Park lodges, souvenir shops, etc., sell Ed Ryan's story of how at Gen. Custer's request he remained behind with a sick buddy, and in the summer Ed dispenses autographs to eastern pilgrims.[1] Just a few miles from Custer, a massive sculptor makes a hard-earned living from the private contributions and admission fees of those who came to watch him change a mountain into a statue of Crazy Horse.[2] North of the Black Hills, in Medora, North Dakota, the Eaton brothers started one of the first dude ranches, the Custer Trail Ranch. From here on west to the Battlefield the trade picks up—the town of Custer, Montana, the General Custer Hotel in Billings and a mounting number of Custer motels and restaurants (some not too good). Who knows how many cars choose the Custer Battlefield Highway because it has this tradename and not just a number? One hundred and thirty thousand people visit the Field annually, even though they have to turn off an east-west transcontinental road to get there; and it is an important source of income for the permanent residents who live near by in Crow Agency and even in Hardin. This is small stuff, but it all adds up.

As a source of national income, writers have profited from it more than any other large group of investors. Some of these returns have been small—quick articles and stories, novels with rapidly fading royalties, etc.; it has been a natural for the fast-buck writer. But it has also been turned into steady income, even a few historians having made small nest eggs out of the Battle. And when it gets into the movies and TV, as it has done almost since the beginning of screen history, it gets into Big Money. Of course, as we all know, its biggest business affiliation has been with Budweiser beer.

---

1 See above, [incomplete].
2 See below, [incomplete].

2.

"Custer's Last Fight" began its advertising career at an important moment in the history of advertising and American business in general. Lithographs of it made their first barroom appearances soon after Mr. Busch acquired the Adams' painting[3] and therefore in the very late 80's or early 90's. During the 80's, according to Frank Presbrey, standard authority on the subject, only four American companies (Sapolio, Royal Baking Powder, Pear's Soap and Ivory Soap) advertised on a large scale and "in the highest sense,"[4] but during the 90's, especially after the depression of '93, advertisement and business fast became Big Business. "How pregnant the advertising '90's were with the future of American business may be put with the statement that it was in this period that the foundation was laid with large-scale advertising for such present-day establishments as the Eastman Kodak Company, Sears, Roebuck & Co., the Quaker Oats Company, the Shredded Wheat Company, Postum Cereal Company, H.L. Heinz (which bought Mulvany's painting, 'Custer's Last Rally'), Gold Dust, the National Biscuit Company and others of similar size and prestige...."[5]

Presbrey points out certain general developments in advertising during the 90's that help to explain the early commercial success of the lithograph, "Custer's Last Fight." "By 1896 illustrations had become so much a characteristic of the advertisement that the Western Druggist ventured a prophecy that 'when the history of advertising is written, the present will be known as "the picture period."'"[6] Moreover, because of rapid improvements in methods of reproduction, the "picture" advertisements of the '80s changed from "relatively lifeless" outlines to "the naturalness and greater emotiveness of the half-tone reproduction of humans in action."[7] The concurrent development of another important advertising device, the slogan, gave trademarks to other companies, and to other beers, including "The Beer That Made Milwaukee Famous"; but in the public mind Anheuser-Busch became identified with a picture full of "motiveness" and "humans in action."

---

3 Don Russell, "Sixty Years in Bar Rooms; or 'Custer's Last Fight,'" p. 62.
4 *The History and Development of Advertising* (New York, 1929), p. 338.
5 P. 360.
6 P. 356.
7 P. 382.

It is hardly possible that Mr. Adolphus Busch could have known what an important step he was taking in the history of his company's relations with the public when he first distributed lithographs of "Custer's Last Fight" to bars handling his beer. He had first-hand evidence, of course, for believing that they would stir up some interest for a time, since the Adams' painting had evidently attracted a good deal of attention while it was hanging in the St. Louis saloon. But within a few years he presented the Adams' painting to the 7th Cavalry in a gesture characteristic of early advertisement much of which was a projection of the owner's personality, and in a gesture, too, characteristic of the patriotism and generosity of Mr. Busch who had his company wire $100,000 to San Francisco at the time of the earthquake.[8] But the gesture also probably indicates that "Mr. Busch assumed interest in the lithographs had been exhausted," and it is Don Russell's conjecture that, when the interest increased instead, Mr. Busch had to commission Mr. Becker, foreman of the department issuing his lithographs, to make a painting "after" the departed original.[9] Who knows at the time, even in business, which of his gestures is going to be taken as his public image?

"About one million copies have been distributed to bars and taverns through the years."[10] In addition, the success of "Custer's Last Fight" must have entered into the thinking of company officials when later they commissioned Oscar E. Beringhaus "to paint a series of oils depicting the romantic growth and expansion of America," a series so notable that "even ardent prohibitionists" acclaimed its art.[11] But it is "Custer's Last Fight" that has become America's best known object of art. At present, about 25,000 copies of it are issued annually, and, significantly, many of these are sent to customers who want to hang them in their recreation and rumpus rooms.[12]

8 Roland Krebs and Percy J. Orthwein, *Making Friends Is Our Business: 100 Years of Anheuser-Busch* (Cuneo Press, 1953), pp. 1–2.
9 Don Russell, pp. 62–63.
10 For this and other information I am indebted to the advertising agency handling the Budweiser account, the D'Arcy Advertising Company, and in particular to Robert B. Irons who is manager of their account with Standard Oil Company (Indiana) and to James B. Orthwein, vice-president of the agency and son of one of the co-authors of *Making Friends Is Our Business: 100 Years of Anheuser-Busch*. Their responses to my queries were always immediate, full and friendly. Information obtained from them will be acknowledged hereafter simply as "Irons-Orthwein."
11 *Making Friends Is Our Business*, pp. 337, 4.
12 Irons-Orthwein.

3.

In these days of high-powered research into consumer-motivation, it seems natural to want to make a few friendly speculations concerning the causes of the happy business relations that have long existed between "Custer's Last Fight" and Budweiser beer. Since much of this study deals with the general causes of the Battle's appeal to the public everywhere, these speculations focus on the Battle's barroom success. They are speculations of friends, all of whom are familiar with American art, advertising, the West and, in varying degrees, with barrooms.

Joshua Taylor, historian of American art, says that we should start by recalling a period when a saloon was one thing and a barroom another—the barroom with goboons [spittoons] and sawdust on the floors, and walls of the fancy saloon crowded with good to not-so-good examples of what the carriage-trade regarded as the latest style in painting. It is true that, although some pictures early had been given to bars by wholesalers, Anheuser-Busch was the first brewery to specialize in this kind of advertisement,[13] and, in so doing, according to Taylor's theory, helped to make the barroom into a poor man's saloon. Andrew Armstrong, ad man and amateur painter, has much the same theory. He thinks that the lithograph of "Custer's Last Fight" may be an early example of what would now be called "tone-up" advertisement (a distributor walks into a retail establishment and says if you'll use our product we'll give you a fancy lamp and turn this place into a cocktail lounge). John Jamieson says that, when his advertising agency used to handle beer accounts, they always tried to think of something "controversial" to hang on the tavern walls. According to his theory, a customer has a few drinks, points to "Custer's Last Fight," and then announces to the customer next to him, "Do you know that happened out in Nebraska and every son-of-a-bitch was killed and scalped?" The adjacent customer or the one down from him says, "You're crazy. That happened in Colorado where I was born, and my uncle was in it and used to tell me all about it when I was a kid."

One thing for sure, it is an odd advertisement for beer. In the first place, it is the only national event that has become a trademark in the public mind for a large American business. A good many companies have identified themselves with national heroes, for instance the Franklin Life Insurance Company, but this identification is generally based on some quality of the hero, like thrift,

13 Irons-Orthwein.

which the customer is supposed to link with the company. Other companies, of course, have used historical events in their advertising, but these have generally been related to the company's own history, as the Pennsylvania Railroad's calendars (by Dean Cornwell) depicting important events in the history of transportation and the calendars of western railroads depicting scenes from the history of westward-ho. On the surface at least, it is not easy to see the relations that have proved most lasting between a historical event and a big business—the relations between "Custer's Last Fight" and beer—even when the fact that the General was an ardent teetotaler is set aside.

Perhaps a recent development in advertising may give us a glimpse into some of the underlying relations. According to the motivational ad men, advertisement should present not so much the objective merits of the product as the feelings the customer should have in using it. Although "Custer's Last Fight" has no visible relations to beer as a product, it may give general expression to the feelings of the consumer of the product—heroic, on a high eminence, free of family and full of pro patria, ready to fight through all encirclements or, just as good or even better, to be carried out in the attempt.

The attitude of the D'Arcy Agency, which handles the Budweiser advertising account, is perhaps the most illuminating of all. They do not like to get very analytical about the success of "Custer's Last Fight," and about such success it does seem more decent to be reverential than analytical. Reverence itself, however, can be slightly analyzed and divided into at least two elements—a reverence of the holy origins of the mystery and a reverence of its continuing practical efficacy. When asked for an explanation of the success of "Custer's Last Fight," those who should know best are likely to say, "Mr. Busch did it for the 7th Cavalry—and it sells beer."

4.

In attempting to make some rough estimate of the size of the after-image of Gen. Custer and his Last Stand, we may have come across some of the secular although none of the spectral answers to the question of what are the necessary conditions for enduring life in the world as we know it. Although the question is directed only to the lower world, it has overtones that suggest it should be asked in catechetical form.

QUESTION:

How can a man lose his own life and gain immortality, at least in this world?

ANSWER:

History can temporarily elevate this or that man above others, but when the history of the moment floats from under him he will be secure only if he has mingled with our enduring dreams, "dreams" here being used in a modern sense as images not only of romantic desires and longings but of fears, resentments and perversities as well. And it further appears that the living do not remain deeply involved with the dead unless the living imagine that they see in the dead parts of their own lives—and deaths.

To this should be added, not cynically on the whole, that the dead increase their security here by making good business connections. Immortality on earth, then, seems to depend on three factors: history, our private lives, and business.

Invent

The Battle of the Little Bighorn is among the most famous—or infamous—stories of American death and defeat, sharing company with historical narratives surrounding the Japanese attack on Pearl Harbor and the Mexican siege of The Alamo, for example. Why are stories of defeat in the face of impossible odds so compelling to audiences? These stories—like that of Custer's ill-fated 7th Cavalry, which would suffer another crushing defeat in the Battle of the Ia Drang Valley during the Vietnam War—capture the imaginations of nearly every generation. Why? What makes a story of predictable defeat a story that can be told again and again, year after year?

Collaborate

With your peers, watch two different film versions of Custer's Last Stand (ideally, films produced at least several years, or even decades, apart)—perhaps *The Great Sioux Massacre* (1965) and the appropriate episode of *Son of the Morning Star* (1991). How do the literal depictions of the events of the battle differ? How do the portrayals of the characters—both Custer and the Native Americans—differ?

What might account for these differences? How do you, as a member of a modern viewing audience, react to each of these versions? How do you think your reactions differ from those of the original viewing audience? Why?

Early in his essay, Maclean writes, "Custer's Last Stand has been a big money maker." Pick one other historical event or person and describe how that event or person has been profitable across time. Be sure to explain your choice in full detail and for whom this event or person has been profitable.

Stephen Glass was a reporter for The New Republic *and a contributor to publications ranging from* Rolling Stone *to* Harpers. *A series of questionable choices led to his firing from* The New Republic *and a virtual expulsion from the world of journalism. Glass studied law at Georgetown University Law Center. Because of his past misdeeds, however, Glass is virtually locked out of his newly chosen profession, as he is unable to pass the "good moral character" portion of any state Bar Exam.*

HACK HEAVEN

By Stephen Glass

Ian Restil, a 15-year-old computer hacker who looks like an even more adolescent version of Bill Gates, is throwing a tantrum. "I want more money. I want a Miata. I want a trip to Disney World. I want X-Man comic [book] number one. I want a lifetime subscription to *Playboy*, and throw in *Penthouse*. Show me the money! Show me the money!" Over and over again, the boy, who is wearing a frayed Cal Ripken Jr. t-shirt, is shouting his demands. Across the table, executives from a California software firm called Jukt Micronics are listening—and trying ever so delicately to oblige. "Excuse me, sir," one of the suits says, tentatively, to the pimply teenager. "Excuse me. Pardon me for interrupting you, sir. We can arrange more money for you. Then, you can buy the [comic] book, and then, when you're of more, say, appropriate age, you can buy the car and pornographic magazines on your own."

It's pretty amazing that a 15-year-old could get a big-time software firm to grovel like that. What's more amazing, though, is how Ian got Jukt's attention—by breaking into its databases. In March, Restil—whose nom de plume is "Big Bad Bionic Boy"—used a computer at his high school library to hack into Jukt. Once he got past the company's online security system, he posted every employee's salary on the company's website alongside more than a dozen pictures of naked women, each with the caption: "the big bad bionic boy has been here baby." After weeks of trying futilely to figure out how Ian cracked the security program, Jukt's engineers gave up. That's when the company came to Ian's Bethesda, Maryland, home—to hire him.

And Ian, clever boy that he is, had been expecting them. "The principal told us to hire a defense lawyer fast, because Ian was in deep trouble," says his mother, Jamie Restil. "Ian laughed and told us to get an agent. Our boy was definitely right." Ian says he knew that Jukt would determine it was cheaper to hire him—and pay him to fix their database—than it would be to have engineers do it. And he knew this because the same thing had happened to more than a dozen online friends.

Indeed, deals like Ian's are becoming common—so common, in fact, that hacker agents now advertise their commissions on websites. Computer Insider, a newsletter for hackers, estimates that about 900 recreational hackers were hired in the last four years by companies they once targeted. Ian's agent, whose business card is emblazoned with the slogan "super-agent to super-nerds," claims to represent nearly 300 of them, ages nine to 68. A failed basketball agent, Joe Hiert got into the industry when one of his son's friends, 21-year-old Ty Harris, broke into an Internet security firm three years ago and came to him for advice. The software maker paid Harris $1 million, a monster truck, and promised "free agency"—meaning he can quit and work for a competitor at any time.

Of course, a cynic might say hacker schemes look an awful lot like protection rackets. That's an awfully nice computer network you got there. It'd be a shame if somebody broke into it.... Law-enforcement officials, in particular, complain that deals between companies and their online predators have made prosecution of online security breaches impossible. "We are basically paralyzed right now," explains Jim Ghort, who directs the Center for Interstate Online Investigations, a joint police project of 18 states. "We can't arrest or prosecute most hackers, because corporate victims are refusing to come forward. This is a huge problem."

In March, Nevada law-enforcement officials got so desperate they ran the following radio advertisement: "Would you hire a shoplifter to watch the cash register? Please don't deal with hackers." The state took to the airwaves shortly after a hacker broke into a regional department store's computer system and instructed it to credit his Visa card about $500 per day. According to Nevada officials, the boy racked up more than $32,000 in credit before he was caught—but the store wouldn't press charges. It let him keep the money, then threw in a $1,500 shopping spree—all in exchange for showing them how to improve their security.

Little wonder, then, that 21 states are now considering versions of something called the Uniform Computer Security Act, which would effectively criminalize immunity deals between hackers and companies—while imposing stiff penalties on the corporations who make such deals. "This is just like prostitution," says Julie Farthwork of the anti-hacker Computer Security Center, which helped draft the legislation. "As a society, we don't want people making a career out of something that's simply immoral."

Not surprisingly, hackers hate the proposed legislation. They see themselves as "freelance security investigators," and they even have their own group— the National Assembly of Hackers—to lobby against the new law. "Really, hackers have to put in a lot of sunk costs before they find the one that's broken and get paid," says Frank Juliet, the group's president. "So, it's definitely a large community service that we are doing."

Less predictable, however, is the opposition of companies that have been hacked. It seems they don't like the proposed law, either, because they're worried they'll be stuck with no legal way to patch holes in their security systems. The Association of Internet-based Businesses has actually formed a task force with the National Assembly of Hackers to lobby against the law.

It remains to be seen who will win, but, until new laws are passed, hackers like Ian Restil will continue to enjoy a certain exalted status—particularly among their peers. At a conference sponsored by the National Assembly of Hackers last week, teenage hackers and graying corporate executives flocked to Ian, patting him on the back and giving him high-fives. "We're so proud of him," said Ian's mother. "He's doing such good things, and he's so smart and kind." At the formal dinner that followed, the emcee explained that Ian had just signed a contract for $81,000 in scholarship money—and a collection of rare comic books. The audience applauded wildly. Then, Ian stood on his chair and took a bow. He announced that he had hacked into a new company and frozen their bank account temporarily. "And now they're going to show me the money," he said, swirling his hips and shaking his fists. "I want a Miata. I want a trip to Disney World...."

As a writer, Stephen Glass was known, among other things, for writing detailed, engaging descriptions of people and events—bringing the facts of a story to life for his readers. Read through "Hack Heaven" and consider this: Where are the detailed descriptions most vivid for you? What is Glass doing, as a writer telling you about a topic, at each of these points that's causing you to react as you are?

At the time of its publication in 1998, the Internet was a very different place—or "place," perhaps—than it is today. Think about your own use of and interactions with the Internet on a daily basis—from visiting social-networking sites to performing research to television commercials that nearly beg you to visit the Web site of a company or product...possibly to receive something wonderful for nearly no price. How does the Internet as it is now differ from the Internet when you were younger? Put another way, what can you do now that you couldn't do before—from playing games to streaming movies or music to working? Using a variety of research methods—from online searches to interviewing older friends and relations—learn more about the Internet in the late 1990s. How does the Internet from 1998 contrast with the Internet today?

According to his personal web site (www.penenberg.com), Adam L. Penenberg, a journalism professor at New York University, "wrote the department's journalism handbook for students, which received unanimous faculty approval and the ethics pledge, which all students must sign—and teaches multimedia, magazine writing, and hard news and investigative reporting." He is the author of three books: Spooked: Espionage in Corporate America, Tragic Indifference: One Man's Battle With the Auto Industry Over the Dangers of SUVs, and Viral Loop: From Facebook to Twitter, How Today's Smartest Businesses Grow Themselves.

LIES, DAMN LIES AND FICTION

BY ADAM L. PENENBERG

It's tough proving a negative. It is even tougher proving that something or someone does not exist.

That was the challenge after *The New Republic* story, "Hack Heaven," which appeared in the May 18 issue, proved to be unverifiable. At first it appeared that Forbes Digital had been scooped by a weekly political publication.

"Hack Heaven" detailed the exploits of Ian Restil, a 15-year-old computer hacker who broke through the online security system of a "big-time software firm" called Jukt Micronics. Once inside, the cheeky youth posted every employee's salary on the company's web site alongside a bunch of nudie pictures, each bearing the caption "THE BIG BAD BIONIC BOY HAS BEEN HERE BABY."

But instead of calling in the Feds, Jukt executives, according to *The New Republic*, decided to hire the teenage hacker, who had obtained the services of an agent, Joe Hiert, described as a "super-agent to super-nerds." The magazine also claimed that such deals have thwarted efforts to prosecute hackers and that law enforcement officials in Nevada got so desperate that they ran radio advertisements: "Would you hire a shoplifter to watch the cash register? Please don't deal with hackers."

A frightening story. But not true.

The article was a complete and utter hoax perpetrated by one of the magazine's own associate editors, 25-year-old Stephen Glass.

Our first step was to plug Jukt Micronics into a bunch of search engines. We found no Web site, odd for a "big-time software firm." Our next step was to contact the Software Publishers Association of America. Nothing. Next on our list was the California Franchise Tax Board. An official from the Tax Board confirmed that Jukt Micronics had never paid any taxes. Further investigations revealed that Jukt Micronics, if it existed at all, was not listed under any of California's 15 area codes. Sarah Gilmer from the office of the California Secretary of State said there was no record of the company, "as a corporation, a limited liability or limited partnership."

A search of Lexis-Nexis' extensive database turned up only one reference to Jukt Micronics: Glass's *New Republic* story.

A frightening story. But not true.

What about Nevada's radio announcements? We were unable to locate a single law enforcement official in Nevada who could verify their existence. Neither the Las Vegas Metropolitan Police nor the Nevada State Highway Patrol had heard of this antihacker radio spot. We called four of the largest radio stations in the state and the city editors from both the *Las Vegas Sun* and the *Las Vegas Review-Journal*. Again, all were ignorant.

"I know nothing about a public service announcement radio campaign on hackers," Bob Harmon, Public Information Officer for the Nevada State Attorney General's Office, told Forbes Digital Tool, "and I'd certainly know about it."

Next on our checklist was the official-sounding "Center for Interstate Online Investigations," supposedly a joint police project in 18 states, and the "Computer Security Center," a supposed advocacy group. Both organizations had inside-the-Beltway bureaucratic names, but officials at the Justice Department, the FBI, the U.S. Customs Department and police departments in California and New Hampshire (both aggressive cybercrime fighters) had never heard of these organizations.

Wait. There's more.

Glass also cited an organization called the "National Assembly of Hackers," which he claimed had sponsored a recent hacker conference in Bethesda, Md. Surely this was real. But no. Despite our best efforts, we could not unearth a single hacker who had even heard of this outfit, let alone attended the conference.

Glass reported that 21 states were considering versions of the "Uniform Computer Security Act," which would "criminalize immunity deals between hackers and companies." Again, law enforcement officials were unaware of any such law, and the National Conference of Commissions on Uniform State Laws, based in Chicago, reported no knowledge of it.

In short, nothing in the story could be verified. Even Jukt Micronics' phone number turned out to be a cell phone.

"Steve has admitted to making up certain parts of it," Lane said on Sunday. "Based on my own investigations, I have determined to a moral certainty that the entire article is made up."

It is ironic that online journalists have received bad press from the print media for shoddy reporting. But the truth is, bad journalism can be found anywhere.

It is not the medium; it is the writer.

Consider the analysis of "Hack Heaven" and the charges against Stephen Glass that are made by Adam L. Penenberg. As a reader who has read and considered the strengths and weaknesses of Glass' article, how do you find yourself reacting? Is your instinct to defend Glass, to side with Penenberg, or something else entirely? Even though Glass fictionalized the entirety of his article, are computer hackers still dangerous enough that the article has worth? Why? In a brief essay, describe how you reacted, as a reader, to Glass, initially—and then describe how your reading of Glass has or has not been changed after weighing Penenberg's charges.

Stephen Glass published his article—and many, many others—in a respectable print publication, while the refutation of his article was published initially on the Web site affiliated with *Forbes* magazine. How might this difference in the place of publication have influenced readers—or how might it still influence them today, even? Is information in print viewed with more trust than information presented online? Why?

As a class, watch the film *Shattered Glass* (2003). While this movie is about the specific events surrounding the rise and fall of Stephen Glass, as a writer, it is also about the issue of accuracy in journalism—the very foundation of journalism, print or online. What issues does the film raise for you about whether or not information presented to you may or may not be accurate? Consider the ways you use information—even in a matter as simple as consulting the weather report online and then making weekend plans based on what you're "told". What happens when you begin to doubt that information's veracity?

Early in his journalism career, according to American Journalism Review, Jayson Blair was "driven" and "on fire"—the kind of dedicated young professional that people remember. He seemed to write with flair, with passion, with a moving style and grace that captured the essence of every story he covered. While working at The New York Times, Blair suffered a string of professional setbacks that derailed his promising career.

RELATIVES OF MISSING SOLDIERS DREAD HEARING WORSE NEWS

BY JAYSON BLAIR

Gregory Lynch Sr. choked up as he stood on his porch here overlooking the tobacco fields and cattle pastures, and declared that he remained optimistic—even though a military official had just come by to warn him to brace himself, that even worse news could be coming any day now.

It is hard to imagine, he says, any worse news than what he learned on Sunday night: his 19-year-old daughter, Pfc. Jessica Lynch, had been in the Army convoy that was ambushed in southern Iraq.

Fifteen soldiers were missing, captured or killed and Private Lynch's fate was unknown, officials said at that time. But Mr. Lynch said today that the official told him five of the soldiers in the unit, not including his daughter, could be seen alive on a videotape broadcast on an Arab television network. Two other soldiers could be identified and were dead in one room, Mr. Lynch said the official told him, but there were also several other bodies—six or more—that could be seen in another room.

If all the additional bodies of those soldiers are from the 507th Maintenance Company and there were only six of them, in the brutal equation running through Mr. Lynch's mind, there is still a chance his eldest daughter is alive.

"She is listed as missing; we still believe she is missing," he said.

Since that ambush on Sunday, much of the nation's attention has focused on the five members of the 507th, whose frightened images appeared on Iraqi television and later in news broadcasts here.

And in recent days the families of the prisoners of war have expressed hope that their loved ones would be returned safely once the fighting ends. But for the families of the eight members of the 507th whom the Pentagon lists as "whereabouts unknown," there is an extra degree of dread in their wait.

"We don't know anything. Not knowing anything is so hard," said Ruben Estrella, whose 18-year-old son, Pvt. Ruben Estrella-Soto of El Paso, is among the members of the 507th listed as missing. "I can't take this waiting."

Mr. Lynch seemed distracted as he stood on the porch of his hilltop home here looking into the tobacco fields and pastures. He talked about the satellite television service that brought CNN and other cable news networks into his home, his family's long history of military service and the poor condition of the local economy.

It was almost as if he wanted to talk about anything —anything other than his elder daughter. He took a deep breath and stared nervously at his wife, Deadre—her eyes red and watery—and then looked at their 17-year-old daughter, Brandi, as he recounted the events of Sunday night.

That was when he found out that his elder daughter was missing, along with the 14 other soldiers from the 507th Maintenance Company who had been ambushed in southern Iraq. The family was watching television that afternoon when they were jolted by the news that an Army maintenance unit had been ambushed early that morning. Then they heard that an Arab television network was broadcasting images of soldiers who had been captured. Then they heard that one of the prisoners of war was a woman. They found some relief, though, when they heard that the woman was black.

"I told my wife that we should not worry because no news is good news and we hadn't heard anything," Mr. Lynch said, explaining his relief.

But then the knock came.

An Army officer in a green full-dress uniform was at the door to deliver the message that his daughter's company had been ambushed and no one knew where she was. Several soldiers had been captured, the officer said, and others had been killed. But, Mr. Lynch recalled, the officer said she was not among them and was nowhere to be found.

"He told us that the Army had no idea where she was and that she was being listed as missing in action," Mr. Lynch said.

The waiting and wondering have taken their toll, creating an emotional upheaval in each family member's life.

Jessica's older brother, Gregory Jr., who is in the West Virginia National Guard, was flown home from Fort Bragg, N.C. Brandi, a senior at Wirt County High School, where Jessica graduated less than two years ago, has hardly left her mother's side.

For a while, they watched television, flipping from channel to channel, for a tidbit about Private Lynch. But it was turned off after a reporter asked the White House press secretary, Ari Fleischer, "Does the president think that the Iraqi Army has somehow changed to avoid raping of female prisoners?"

Since finding out her daughter was missing, Deadre Lynch says, she has not been able to sleep much. When she has been able to catch a few minutes of sleep, she says, she has dreamed that her daughter ran away from her unit before the attack to help some Iraqi child. The last time the family heard from their daughter was in an e-mail message from Kuwait two weeks ago. She wrote about her dreams of becoming an elementary school teacher and her discomfort with any order not to stop to help any children because it could be a decoy or a trap.

At the Pentagon today, Defense Department officials announced for the first time the names of the confirmed dead from the 507th, as well as those who are still classified as missing. The prisoners of war had already been identified by military officials and relatives who had seen their television images.

The dead were listed as Specialist Jamaal R. Addison, 22, of Roswell, Ga., and Pfc. Howard Johnson II, 21, of Mobile, Ala.

The missing were listed as Private Lynch; Private Estrella-Soto; Master Sgt. Robert J. Dowdy, 38, of Cleveland; and Specialist James M. Kiehl, 22, of Des Moines, as well as Chief Warrant Officer Johnny Villareal Mata, 35, of

El Paso, and Pfc. Lori Ann Piestewa, 23, of Tuba City, Ariz. Pvt. Brandon Ulysses Sloan, 19, of Bedford, Ohio, and Sgt. Donald Ralph Walters, 33, of Salem, Ore., were also listed as missing.

Part of what has made the circumstances of the 507th so striking is that most of its members were young and in noncombat roles. The unit had been sent to supply soldiers on the front lines on Sunday when the lead vehicle made a wrong turn, taking them off a highway and across a bridge. The unit—made up of mechanics, supply clerks, a cook—was trapped by two buses, Iraqi irregular forces and tanks. The unit keeps trucks rolling, fixes generators and maintains other equipment, said Jean Offutt, a spokeswoman at Fort Bliss, the base in western Texas.

A firefight ensued where several members of the 507th, including its chief officer, were wounded and escaped. Marines who were sent in to look for the other members found only the remains of some of their vehicles.

Officials at Fort Bliss asked relatives of the members of the 507th not to speak to the news media today, citing concerns that Iraqi forces would use the interviews to coerce information against those who are prisoners.

Stacie Walters, 27, who learned that her husband, Sgt. Donald Walters, was among the missing, said that part of his job during the first Persian Gulf war had been to guard captured Iraqi soldiers. His sister, Kimberly Cieslak, who lives in Salem, Ore., said that her brother "came back pretty traumatized from that experience," adding that during that war he had seen "too many dead people."

Pentagon officials also said Specialist Gregory P. Sanders, 19, of Indiana, an Army infantryman, was killed in combat in Iraq on Monday. Mr. Sanders, the son of a Navy sailor, began wearing combat fatigues when he was 2 years old, relatives said. "He wanted to be a soldier," said Rick Knight, his uncle, who said Army officials told him that his nephew had been killed in a sniper shooting. "He was born to be a soldier."

Pentagon officials also said a second serviceman was killed in a grenade attack believed to have been carried out by another soldier at Camp Pennsylvania in Kuwait. The officials said Maj. Gregory Stone, 40, of Boise, Idaho, a member of the Air National Guard, died on Tuesday of injuries suffered in that attack.

The officials also said that two marines in an engineering unit, Cpl. Evan T. James, 20, of Hancock, Ill., and Sgt. Bradley S. Korthaus, 29, of Scott, Iowa, who disappeared near the Saddam Canal in southeastern Iraq on Monday, were being listed as missing in action.

In Iowa, Sergeant Korthaus's brother Steve said he had joined the Marines just after graduating from high school in 1992 and "would have been mad if he didn't get to go" to Iraq, even though he had just become engaged. "He wanted to be a marine since he was 10 years old," Mr. Korthaus said.

As terrible as it is to consider, the story of Pvt. Jessica Lynch, as narrated by Jayson Blair, is all-too-common during times of war: When an event occurs in a combat zone, reporters cover both the official angles, such as that handled by members of the press corps. who deal daily with the President and the official representatives of the White House Administration, and the less official angles, such as the "human interest" side of the tale related by Blair. Which "side" of the story seems most meaningful or important to you and why? Is it most important to hear the official words about an event, from military and political leaders, for example? Or is it most important to hear how events affect the lives of normal people—especially the ones directly involved in the story that's unfolding? Or is there some middle ground? And what is it about these stories that makes them important to the audience, few of whom have any direct connection with the events under discussion?

After reading "Relatives of Missing Soldiers Dread Hearing Worse News," what questions or concerns do you have regarding the capture of Pvt. Jessica Lynch and others? How and where does Blair lead you to feel this way? For example, if you are concerned about Pvt. Lynch's physical safety, reread the article and note the places where Blair nudges you toward feeling that way. Where does Blair attempt to make this story about more than Pvt. Lynch? How effectively is this expansion of the topic beyond Pvt. Lynch accomplished? In a short essay, explain your thoughts.

How does the story of Pvt. Jessica Lynch end? Jayson Blair delivers the opening of the tale, but, as so often happens, the story is incomplete—just one bit of news that comes across readers' minds and then falls away. So learn the rest of the story, and explain how you do so. When you want to know more about some relatively minor historical event—the capture of a single group of soldiers—what do you do? How do you verify that the version of the tale you're learning is the truth as it is widely understood?

Working with your peers, consider this question: How would you have reacted to this story if Jessica Lynch's first name was never given—or was given simply as Pvt. J. Lynch, with nothing to indicate her gender. Why is the story of a soldier missing in action different when that story is about a woman, or is the story no different at all?

FLAG RAISING ON IWO JIMA
FEBRUARY 23, 1945

Photo By National Archives

This photograph represents an iconic image of American victory in the Pacific Theatre during World War II. Using the Internet and resources available at your library, research the photo. Where was it taken, specifically? By whom? Who is featured in the photo? What questions exist about the authenticity of this image? How credible are the sources of criticism?

Searching online and in your library, locate another photograph from World War II. In an essay, describe your chosen photograph and give details of its history—from the name of the photographer to the original place of publication. What aspect of the war does it show to viewers? How much knowledge must a viewer bring to the photograph—regarding content and context—to make sense of what is shown?

This is an iconic image of American victory in World War II. But what photographs exist of Americans in World War II that represent defeat? Searching online and in your library, locate a photograph of the war that offers viewers a negative, rather than positive, interpretation. What images in the photograph make it negative? Is your chosen image more or less emotionally charged than the image of victory presented in this book? Why? As a group, discuss your photograph and present your conclusions.

Searching online and in your library, find the names of the men featured in this photograph. Profile each man in one or two paragraphs (making sure that you clearly cite your sources of information). How does your knowledge of each man's origins and ultimate fate affect your viewing of the photograph? Locate a copy of Johnny Cash's song "The Ballad of Ira Hayes" and consider it in relation to your own profile of this man. How does the information you found in your research compare and contrast with the profile Cash offers?

REBEL SHARPSHOOTER, GETTYSBURG
JULY 5, 1863
PHOTO BY NATIONAL ARCHIVES

Describe this picture in as much detail as possible. What do you see? Based on what you see, what can you infer about the context—the setting, the time period, the story that led to this moment in time?

The American Civil War was the first major war in the photographic age, the first war that took place when the technology of photography had developed to a point where it was portable and reasonably inexpensive. But photography, at that time, could not capture a moving image. The photographic subject had to remain very still in order for an image as crisp as this one to be produced. Thus portraits were common—as were pictures of the dead. Searching online, examine archives of photographs of warfare that has taken place since the 1860s. In what ways do you see the technology of photography changing? How might those changes affect the ways in which the subject is understood? Does the ability to photograph actions in progress change the way in which a viewer might respond? How?

While this image of a dead Confederate sniper at Gettysburg is striking, it is also embroiled in controversy: It may have been staged by the photographer. In groups, research this issue of staging of photographs during the American Civil War—and this image specifically. What elements of this photograph are alleged to be false? How might a definitive answer to the controversy be reached? In the end, does it matter if the photograph is staged? Is its impact lessened if it is not understood as a captured moment in time and instead a crafted work of art? Why?

In May of 2003, The New York Times *published this massive "correction" to address the situation created by reporter Jayson Blair—who committed plagiarism and other acts of fraud in more than half of the 73 articles he wrote for* The New York Times. *As the original byline reads, "This article was reported and written by Dan Barry, David Barstow, Jonathan D. Glater, Adam Liptak, and Jacques Steinberg. Research support was provided by Alain Delaquérière and Carolyn Wilder." Given the subject matter under discussion, this extensive co-authorship (with well documented support) was certainly a deliberate way to reassure readers of the factual nature of reporting in* The New York Times.

TIMES REPORTER WHO RESIGNED LEAVES LONG TRAIL OF DECEPTION

BY DAN BARRY, DAVID BARSTOW, JONATHAN D. GLATER, ADAM LIPTAK, AND JACQUES STEINBERG.

Research support was provided by Alain Delaquérière and Carolyn Wilder

A staff reporter for *The New York Times* committed frequent acts of journalistic fraud while covering significant news events in recent months, an investigation by *Times* journalists has found. The widespread fabrication and plagiarism represent a profound betrayal of trust and a low point in the 152-year history of the newspaper.

The reporter, Jayson Blair, 27, misled readers and *Times* colleagues with dispatches that purported to be from Maryland, Texas and other states, when often he was far away, in New York. He fabricated comments. He concocted scenes. He lifted material from other newspapers and wire services. He selected details from photographs to create the impression he had been somewhere or seen someone, when he had not.

And he used these techniques to write falsely about emotionally charged moments in recent history, from the deadly sniper attacks in suburban Washington to the anguish of families grieving for loved ones killed in Iraq.

In an inquiry focused on correcting the record and explaining how such fraud could have been sustained within the ranks of *The Times*, the *Times* journalists have so far uncovered new problems in at least 36 of the 73 articles Mr. Blair wrote since he started getting national reporting assignments late last October. In the final months the audacity of the deceptions grew by the week, suggesting the work of a troubled young man veering toward professional self-destruction.

Mr. Blair, who has resigned from the paper, was a reporter at *The Times* for nearly four years, and he was prolific. Spot checks of the more than 600 articles he wrote before October have found other apparent fabrications, and that inquiry continues. *The Times* is asking readers to report any additional falsehoods in Mr. Blair's work; the e-mail address is retrace@nytimes.com.

Every newspaper, like every bank and every police department, trusts its employees to uphold central principles, and the inquiry found that Mr. Blair repeatedly violated the cardinal tenet of journalism, which is simply truth. His tools of deceit were a cellphone and a laptop computer—which allowed him to blur his true whereabouts—as well as round-the-clock access to databases of news articles from which he stole.

The Times inquiry also establishes that various editors and reporters expressed misgivings about Mr. Blair's reporting skills, maturity and behavior during his five-year journey from raw intern to reporter on national news events. Their warnings centered mostly on the errors in his articles.

His mistakes became so routine, his behavior so unprofessional, that by April 2002, Jonathan Landman, the metropolitan editor, dashed off a two-sentence e-mail message to newsroom administrators that read: "We have to stop Jayson from writing for *The Times*. Right now."

After taking a leave for personal problems and being sternly warned, both orally and in writing, that his job was in peril, Mr. Blair improved his performance. By last October, the newspaper's top two editors—who said they believed that Mr. Blair had turned his life and work around—had guided him to the understaffed national desk, where he was assigned to help cover the Washington sniper case.

By the end of that month, public officials and colleagues were beginning to challenge his reporting. By November, the investigation has found, he was fabricating quotations and scenes, undetected. By March, he was lying in his articles and to his editors about being at a court hearing in Virginia, in a police chief's home in Maryland and in front of a soldier's home in West Virginia. By the end of April another newspaper was raising questions about plagiarism. And by the first of May, his career at *The Times* was over.

A few days later, Mr. Blair issued a statement that referred to "personal problems" and expressed contrition. But during several telephone conversations last week, he declined repeated requests to help the newspaper correct the record or comment on any aspect of his work. He did not respond to messages left on his cellphone, with his family and with his union representative on Friday afternoon.

The reporting for this article included more than 150 interviews with subjects of Mr. Blair's articles and people who worked with him; interviews with *Times* officials familiar with travel, telephone and other business records; an examination of other records including e-mail messages provided by colleagues trying to correct the record or shed light on Mr. Blair's activities; and a review of reports from competing news organizations.

The investigation suggests several reasons Mr. Blair's deceits went undetected for so long: a failure of communication among senior editors; few complaints from the subjects of his articles; his savviness and his ingenious ways of covering his tracks. Most of all, no one saw his carelessness as a sign that he was capable of systematic fraud.

Mr. Blair was just one of about 375 reporters at *The Times*; his tenure was brief. But the damage he has done to the newspaper and its employees will not completely fade with next week's editions, or next month's, or next year's.

"It's a huge black eye," said Arthur Sulzberger Jr., chairman of *The New York Times Company* and publisher of the newspaper, whose family has owned a controlling interest in *The Times* for 107 years. "It's an abrogation of the trust between the newspaper and its readers."

For all the pain resonating through the *Times* newsroom, the hurt may be more acute in places like Bethesda, Md., where one of Mr. Blair's fabricated articles described American soldiers injured in combat. The puzzlement is deeper, too, in places like Marmet, W. Va., where a woman named Glenda Nelson learned that Mr. Blair had quoted her in a news article, even though she had never spoken to anyone from *The Times*.

"*The New York Times*," she said. "You would expect more out of that."

THE DECEPTION

Reporting Process Riddled With Lies

Two wounded marines lay side by side at the National Naval Medical Center in Bethesda. One of them, Jayson Blair wrote, "questioned the legitimacy of his emotional pain as he considered his comrade in the next bed, a runner who had lost part of his leg to a land mine in Iraq."

The scene, as described by Mr. Blair in an article that *The Times* published on April 19, was as false as it was riveting. In fact, it was false from its very first word, its uppercase dateline, which told readers that the reporter was in Bethesda and had witnessed the scene. He had not.

Still, the image was so compelling, the words so haunting, that *The Times* featured one of the soldier's comments as its Quotation of the Day, appearing on Page 2. "It's kind of hard to feel sorry for yourself when so many people were hurt worse or died," it quoted Lance Cpl. James Klingel as saying.

Mr. Blair did indeed interview Corporal Klingel, but it was by telephone, and it was a day or two after the soldier had been discharged from the medical center. Although the corporal, whose right arm and leg had been injured by a falling cargo hatch, said he could not be sure whether he uttered what would become the Quotation of the Day, he said he was positive that Mr. Blair never visited him in the hospital.

"I actually read that article about me in *The New York Times*," Corporal Klingel said by telephone last week from his parents' home. "Most of that stuff I didn't say."

He is confident, for instance, that he never told Mr. Blair that he was having nightmares about his tour of duty, as Mr. Blair reported. Nor did he suggest that it was about time, as Mr. Blair wrote, "for another appointment with a chaplain."

Not all of what Mr. Blair wrote was false, but much of what was true in his article was apparently lifted from other news reports. In fact, his 1,831-word front-page article, which purported to draw on "long conversations" with six wounded servicemen, relied on the means of deception that had infected dozens of his other articles over the last few months.

Mr. Blair was not finished with his virtual visit to Bethesda. Sgt. Eric Alva, now a partial amputee, was indeed Corporal Klingel's roommate for two days. But the sergeant, who is quoted by Mr. Blair, never spoke to him, said Lt. Cmdr. Jerry Rostad, a medical center spokesman. And a hospitalman whom Mr. Blair describes as being down the hall, Brian Alaniz, was discharged five days before Corporal Klingel arrived.

"Our records indicate that at no time did Mr. Blair visit N.N.M.C. or interview patients," Commander Rostad said.

As he would do in other articles, Mr. Blair appears to have stitched this narrative by drawing at least partly on information available in the databases of various news organizations. For example, he describes Hospitalman Alaniz as someone who "not only lost his right leg, but also had a finger torn off, broke his left leg and took shrapnel in his groin and arms." His description seems to mirror one that had appeared in *The Washington Post*.

Mr. Blair's deceptive techniques flouted long-followed rules at *The Times*. The paper, concerned about maintaining its integrity among readers, tells its journalists to follow many guidelines as described in a memo on the newsroom's internal Web site. Among those guidelines: "When we use facts gathered by any other organization, we attribute them"; "writers at *The Times* are their own principal fact checkers and often their only ones"; "we should distinguish in print between personal interviews and telephone or e-mail interviews."

In addition, the newspaper uses a dateline only when a reporter has visited the place.

Mr. Blair knew that rule. In March of last year, an editors' note published in *The Times* about an article by another reporter prompted Mr. Blair to e-mail a colleague the entry in *The Times's* stylebook about "dateline integrity." In part, the stylebook explains that a dateline guarantees that the reporter whose name appears on the article "was at the specified place on the date given, and provided the bulk of the information."

But for many photographers assigned to work with Mr. Blair, he was often just a voice on the phone, one saying he was on his way or just around the corner.

On April 6, for example, he was supposedly reporting from Cleveland. He described a church service attended by the Rev. Tandy Sloan, whose missing son, an Army supply clerk, had been pronounced dead in Iraq the previous day. There is no evidence that Mr. Blair was either at that service or at an earlier one also described in his article.

A freelance photographer whom Mr. Blair had arranged to meet outside the Cleveland church on April 6 found it maddening that he could not seem to connect with him. The photographer, Haraz Ghanbari, was so intent on a meeting that he placed nine calls to Mr. Blair's cellphone from 9:32 a.m. to 2:07 p.m., and kept trying six more times until 10:13 p.m., when he finally gave up.

Mr. Ghanbari said he managed to reach Mr. Blair three times, and three times Mr. Blair had excuses for why they could not meet. In one instance, Mr. Ghanbari said, Mr. Blair explained that he had left the church in the middle of the service "to get his cellphone fixed"—that was why so many of his calls had gone unanswered—"and was already on his way back."

"I just thought it was weird how he never showed up," Mr. Ghanbari said.

The article that Mr. Blair eventually filed incorporated at least a half-dozen passages lifted nearly verbatim from other news sources, including four from *The Washington Post*.

Some of Mr. Blair's articles in recent months provide vivid descriptions of scenes that often occurred in the privacy of people's homes but that, travel records and interviews show, Mr. Blair could not have witnessed.

On March 24, for example, he filed an article with the dateline Hunt Valley, Md., in which he described an anxious mother and father, Martha and Michael Gardner, awaiting word on their son, Michael Gardner II, a Marine scout then in Iraq.

Mr. Blair described Mrs. Gardner "turning swiftly in her chair to listen to an anchor report of a Marine unit"; he also wrote about the red, white and blue pansies in her front yard. In an interview last week, Mrs. Gardner said Mr. Blair had spoken to her only by phone.

Some *Times* photo editors now suspect that Mr. Blair gained access to the digital photos that Doug Mills, the photographer, transmitted that night to

The Times's picture department, including photos of the Gardners watching the news, as well as the flowers in their yard.

As he often did, Mr. Blair briefed his editors by e-mail about the progress of his reporting. "I am giving them a breather for about 30 minutes," he wrote to the national editor, Jim Roberts, at one point, referring to the Gardners. "It's amazing timing. Lots of wrenching ups and downs with all the reports of casualties."

"Each time a casualty is reported," he added, "it gets tense and nervous, and then a sense of relief comes over the room that it has not been their son's group that has been attacked."

The Gardner family, who had spent considerable time on the phone with Mr. Blair, were delighted with the article. They wrote *The Times* saying so, and their letter was published.

Mr. Roberts was also pleased. He would later identify Mr. Blair's dispatch from Hunt Valley, Md., as a singular moment: this reporter was demonstrating hustle and flair. He had no reason to know that Mr. Blair was demonstrating a different sort of enterprise.

He was actually e-mailing from New York.

THE REPORTER

An Engaging Air, A Nose for Gossip

He got it.

That was the consensus about one of the college students seeking an internship at *The New York Times*. He was only 21, but this Jayson Blair, the son of a federal official and a schoolteacher from Virginia, got what it meant to be a newspaper reporter.

"I've seen some who like to abuse the power they have been entrusted with," Mr. Blair had written in seeking the internship. But, he had added, "my kindred spirits are the ones who became journalists because they wanted to help people."

Whether as a student journalist at the University of Maryland or as an intern at *The Boston Globe,* the short and ubiquitous Mr. Blair stood out. He seemed to be constantly working, whether on articles or on sources. Some, like a fellow student, Catherine Welch, admired him. "You thought, 'That's what I want to be,'" she said.

Others considered him immature, with a hungry ambition and an unsettling interest in newsroom gossip.

"He wasn't very well liked by the other interns," said Jennifer McMenamin, another Maryland student who, with Mr. Blair, was a *Globe* intern in the summer of 1997. "I think he saw the rest of the intern class as competition."

Citing a *U.S. News and World Report* researcher, *The Washington Post* reported yesterday that while reporting for *The Globe,* Mr. Blair apparently lied about having interviewed the mayor of Washington, Anthony Williams.

His interest in journalism dated at least to his years at Centreville High School, in Clifton, Va., where he asked to interview the new principal for the school paper within minutes of her introduction to the faculty. "He was always into the newspaper business, even here," the principal, Pamela Y. Latt, recalled. "He had a wonderful, positive persistence about him that we all admired."

Mr. Blair's *Times* supervisors and Maryland professors emphasize that he earned an internship at *The Times* because of glowing recommendations and a remarkable work history, not because he is black. *The Times* offered him a slot in an internship program that was then being used in large part to help the paper diversify its newsroom.

During his 10-week internship at *The Times,* in the summer of 1998, Mr. Blair wrote 19 news articles, helped other reporters and never seemed to leave the newsroom. "He did well," recalled Sheila Rule, a senior editor who oversees the internship program. "He did very well."

But Joyce Purnick, who was the metropolitan editor at the time, recalled thinking that he was better at newsroom socializing than at reporting, and told him during a candid lunch that after graduation he should work for a smaller newspaper. "I was telling him, 'Go learn the business,'" she said.

At summer's end, *The Times* offered Mr. Blair an extended internship, but he had more college course work to do before his scheduled graduation in December 1998. When he returned to the *Times* newsroom in June 1999, Ms. Rule said, everyone assumed he had graduated. He had not; college officials say he has more than a year of course work to complete.

Mr. Blair was assigned to work in *The Times's* police bureau, where he churned out article after article about the crimes of the day, impressing colleagues with his lightning-quick writing ability and his willingness to work long hours. But Jerry Gray, one of several *Times* editors to become mentors to Mr. Blair, repeatedly warned him that he was too sloppy—in his reporting and in his appearance.

"There's a theme here," Mr. Gray remembers telling the young reporter. "There are many eccentric people here, but they've earned it."

In November 1999, the paper promoted Mr. Blair to intermediate reporter, the next step toward winning a full-time staff position. While reporting on business for the metropolitan desk, editors say, he was energetic and willing to work all hours. He was also a study in carelessness, they say, with his telephone voicemail box too full to accept messages, and his writing commitments too numerous.

Charles Strum, his editor at the time, encouraged Mr. Blair to pace himself and take time off. "I told him that he needed to find a different way to nourish himself than drinking scotch, smoking cigarettes and buying Cheez Doodles from the vending machines," Mr. Strum said.

Mr. Blair persevered, although he clearly needed to cut down on mistakes and demonstrate an ability to write with greater depth, according to Jonathan Landman, who succeeded Ms. Purnick as metropolitan editor.

In the fall of 2000, Joseph Lelyveld, then executive editor, the highest-ranking editor at *The Times*, sent the strong message that too many mistakes were finding their way into the news pages; someone had even misspelled the publisher's surname, Sulzberger. That prompted Mr. Landman to appoint an editor to investigate and tally the corrections generated by the metropolitan staff.

"Accuracy is all we have," Mr. Landman wrote in a staff e-mail message. "It's what we are and what we sell."

Mr. Blair continued to make mistakes, requiring more corrections, more explanations, more lectures about the importance of accuracy. Many newsroom colleagues say he also did brazen things, including delighting in showing around copies of confidential *Times* documents, running up company expenses from a bar around the corner, and taking company cars for extended periods, racking up parking tickets.

At the same time, though, many at *The Times* grew fond of the affable Mr. Blair, who seemed especially gifted at office politics. He made a point of getting to know many of the newsroom support workers, for example. His distinctive laugh became a familiar sound.

"He had charisma, enormous charisma," David Carr, a *Times* media reporter, said. Mr. Blair, he added, often praised articles written by colleagues, and, frequently, "it was something far down in the story, so you'd know he read it."

In January 2001, Mr. Blair was promoted to full-time reporter with the consensus of a recruiting committee of roughly half a dozen people headed by Gerald M. Boyd, then a deputy managing editor, and the approval of Mr. Lelyveld.

Mr. Landman said last week that he had been against the recommendation— that he "wasn't asked so much as told" about Mr. Blair's promotion. But he also emphasized that he did not protest the move.

The publisher and the executive editor, he said, had made clear the company's commitment to diversity—"and properly so," he said. In addition, he said, Mr. Blair seemed to be making the mistakes of a beginner and was still demonstrating great promise. "I thought he was going to make it."

Mr. Boyd, who is now managing editor, the second-highest-ranking newsroom executive, said last week that the decision to advance Mr. Blair had not been based on race. Indeed, plenty of young white reporters have been swiftly promoted through the ranks.

"To say now that his promotion was about diversity in my view doesn't begin to capture what was going on," said Mr. Boyd, who is himself African-American.

"He was a young, promising reporter who had done a job that warranted promotion."

But if anything, Mr. Blair's performance after his promotion declined; he made more errors and clashed with more editors. Then came the catastrophes of Sept. 11, 2001, and things got worse.

Mr. Blair said he had lost a cousin in the terrorist attack on the Pentagon, and provided the name of his dead relative to a high-ranking editor at *The Times*. He cited his loss as a reason to be excused from writing the "Portraits of Grief" vignettes of the victims.

Reached by telephone last week, the father of his supposed cousin said Mr. Blair was not related to the family.

A few weeks after the Sept. 11 attacks, he wrote an article laden with errors. Many reporters make mistakes, and statistics about corrections are only a rough barometer of journalistic skills. When considered overall, Mr. Blair's correction rate at *The Times* was within acceptable limits. Still, this article required a correction so extensive that it attracted the attention of the new executive editor, Howell Raines.

Mr. Blair's e-mails from that time demonstrate how he expressed penitence to Mr. Landman, then vented to another editor about how he had "held my nose" while writing the apology. Meanwhile, after a disagreement with a third editor, Patrick LaForge, who tracks corrections for the metropolitan desk, he threatened to take up the issue "with the people who hired me—and they all have executive or managing editor in their titles."

A lot was going on at that time: fear of further terrorist attacks, anthrax scares, grief. Uncharacteristic behavior was not uncommon among people in the city or in the newsroom. Still, Mr. Blair's actions stood out. He made mistakes and was unavailable for long stretches.

Mr. Landman sent Mr. Blair a sharply worded evaluation in January 2002, noting that his correction rate was "extraordinarily high by the standards of the paper." Mr. Landman then forwarded copies of that evaluation to Mr. Boyd and William E. Schmidt, associate managing editor for news administration, along with a note that read, "There's big trouble I want you both to be aware of."

At that point Mr. Blair told Susan Edgerley, a deputy metropolitan editor, about his considerable personal problems, she said, and she referred him to a counseling service. When he returned to the newsroom after a two-week break, editors say, efforts were made to help him focus on accuracy rather than productivity. But the inaccuracies soon returned.

By early April, Mr. Blair's performance had prompted Mr. Landman to write that the newspaper had to "stop Jayson from writing for the *Times*." The next day, Mr. Blair received a letter of reprimand. He took another brief leave.

When he returned to the newsroom weeks later, Mr. Landman and Jeanne Pinder, the reporter's immediate supervisor, had a tough-love plan in place. Mr. Blair would start off with very short articles, again focusing on accuracy, not productivity, with Ms. Pinder brooking no nonsense about tardiness or extended unavailability.

Mr. Blair resented this short-leash approach, Mr. Landman said, but it seemed to work. The reporter's number of published corrections plummeted and, with time, he was allowed to tackle larger reporting assignments. In fact, within several weeks he was quietly agitating for jobs in other departments, away from Ms. Pinder and the metropolitan desk.

Finally, Mr. Landman reluctantly signed off on a plan to send Mr. Blair to the sports department, although he recalled warning the sports editor: "If you take Jayson, be careful." Mr. Boyd also said that the sports editor was briefed on Mr. Blair's work history and was provided with his most recent evaluation.

Mr. Blair had just moved to the sports department when he was rerouted to the national desk to help in the coverage of the sniper case developing in his hometown area. The change in assignment took Mr. Landman, Ms. Pinder and others on the metropolitan desk by surprise.

"Nobody was asking my opinion," Mr. Landman said. "What I thought was on the record abundantly."

Ms. Pinder, though, said she offered to discuss Mr. Blair's history and habits with anybody—mostly, she said, "because we wanted him to succeed."

THE BIG TIME

New Assignments For a 'Hungry Guy'

The sniper attacks in suburban Washington dominated the nation's newspapers last October. "This was a 'flood the zone' story," Mr. Roberts, the national editor, recalled, invoking the phrase that has come to embody the paper's aggressive approach to covering major news events under Mr. Raines, its executive editor.

Mr. Raines and Mr. Boyd, the managing editor, quickly increased the size of the team to eight reporters, Mr. Blair among them. "This guy's hungry," Mr. Raines said last week, recalling why he and Mr. Boyd picked Mr. Blair.

Both editors said the seeming improvement in Mr. Blair's accuracy last summer demonstrated that he was ready to help cover a complicated, high-profile assignment. But they did not tell Mr. Roberts or his deputies about the concerns that had been raised about Mr. Blair's reporting.

"That discussion did not happen," Mr. Raines said, adding that he had seen no need for such a discussion because Mr. Blair's performance had improved, and because "we do not stigmatize people for seeking help."

Instead, Mr. Boyd recommended Mr. Blair as a reporter who knew his way around Washington suburbs. "He wasn't sent down to be the first lead writer or the second or third or fourth or fifth writer," Mr. Boyd said. "He was managed and was not thrust into something over his head."

But Mr. Blair received far less supervision than he had on Mr. Landman's staff, many editors agreed. He was sent into a confusing world of feuding law enforcement agencies, a job that would have tested the skills of the most seasoned reporter. Still, Mr. Blair seemed to throw himself into the fray of reporters fiercely jockeying for leaks and scoops.

"There was a general sense he wanted to impress us," recalled Nick Fox, the editor who supervised much of Mr. Blair's sniper coverage.

Impress he did. Just six days after his arrival in Maryland, Mr. Blair landed a front-page exclusive with startling details about the arrest of John Muhammad, one of the two sniper suspects. The article, attributed entirely to the accounts of five unidentified law enforcement sources, reported that the

United States attorney for Maryland, under pressure from the White House, had forced investigators to end their interrogation of Mr. Muhammad perhaps just as he was ready to confess.

It was an important article, and plainly accurate in its central point: that local and federal authorities were feuding over custody of the sniper suspects. But in retrospect, interviews show, the article contained a serious flaw, as well as a factual error.

Two senior law enforcement officials who otherwise bitterly disagree on much of what happened that day are in agreement on this much: Mr. Muhammad was not, as Mr. Blair reported, "explaining the roots of his anger" when the interrogation was interrupted. Rather, they said, the discussion touched on minor matters, like arranging for a shower and meal.

The article drew immediate fire. Both the United States attorney, Thomas M. DiBiagio, and a senior Federal Bureau of Investigation official issued statements denying certain details. Similar concerns were raised with senior editors by several veteran reporters in *The Times*'s Washington bureau who cover law enforcement.

Mr. Roberts and Mr. Fox said in interviews last week that the statements would have raised far more serious concerns in their minds had they been aware of Mr. Blair's history of inaccuracy. Both editors also said they had never asked Mr. Blair to identify his sources in the article.

"I can't imagine accepting unnamed sources from him as the basis of a story had we known what was going on," Mr. Fox said. "If somebody had said, 'Watch out for this guy,' I would have questioned everything that he did. I can't even imagine being comfortable with going with the story at all, if I had known that the metro editors flat out didn't trust him."

Mr. Raines and Mr. Boyd, who knew more of Mr. Blair's history, also did not ask him to identify his sources. The two editors said that given what they knew then, there was no need. There was no inkling, Mr. Raines said, that the newspaper was dealing with "a pathological pattern of misrepresentation, fabricating and deceiving."

Mr. Raines said he saw no reason at that point to alert Mr. Roberts to Mr. Blair's earlier troubles. Rather, in keeping with his practice of complimenting what he considered exemplary work, Mr. Raines sent Mr. Blair a note of praise for his "great shoe-leather reporting."

Mr. Blair was further rewarded when he was given responsibility for leading the coverage of the sniper prosecution. The assignment advanced him toward potentially joining the national staff.

On Dec. 22, another article about the sniper case by Mr. Blair appeared on the front page. Citing unidentified law enforcement officials once again, his article explained why "all the evidence" pointed to Mr. Muhammad's teenage accomplice, Lee Malvo, as the triggerman. And once again his reporting drew strong criticism, this time from a prosecutor who called a news conference to denounce it.

"I don't think that anybody in the investigation is responsible for the leak, because so much of it was dead wrong," the prosecutor, Robert Horan Jr., the commonwealth attorney in Fairfax County, Va., said at the news conference.

Mr. Boyd was clearly concerned about Mr. Horan's accusations, colleagues recalled. He repeatedly pressed Mr. Roberts to reach Mr. Horan and have him specify his problems with Mr. Blair's article.

"I went to Jim and said, 'Let's check this out thoroughly because Jayson has had problems,'" Mr. Boyd said. Mr. Roberts said he did not recall being told that Mr. Blair had had problems.

Again, no editor at *The Times* pressed Mr. Blair to identify by name his sources on the article. But Mr. Roberts said he had had a more general discussion with Mr. Blair to determine whether his sources were in a position to know what he had reported.

After repeated efforts, Mr. Roberts reached Mr. Horan. "It was kind of a Mexican standoff," Mr. Horan recalled. "I was not going to tell him what was true and what was not true. I detected in him a real concern that they had published something incorrect."

"I don't know today whether Blair just had a bad source," he continued. "It was equally probable at the time that he was just sitting there writing fiction."

Mr. Roberts, meanwhile, said Mr. Horan complained about leaks, and never raised the possibility that Mr. Blair was fabricating details.

In the end, Mr. Raines said last week, the paper handled the criticisms of both articles appropriately. "I'm confident we went through the proper journalistic steps," he said.

It was not until January, Mr. Roberts recalled, that he was warned about Mr. Blair's record of inaccuracy. He said Mr. Landman quietly told him that Mr. Blair was prone to error and needed to be watched. Mr. Roberts added that he did not pass the warning on to his deputies. "It got socked in the back of my head," he said.

By then, however, those deputies had already formed their own assessments of Mr. Blair's work. They said they considered him a sloppy writer who was often difficult to track down and at times even elusive about his whereabouts. At the same time, he seemed eager and energetic.

Close scrutiny of his travel expenses would have revealed other signs that Mr. Blair was not where his editors thought he was, and, even more alarming, that he was perhaps concocting law enforcement sources. But at the time his expense records were being quickly reviewed by an administrative assistant; editors did not examine them.

On an expense report filed in January, for example, he indicated that he had bought blankets at a Marshalls department store in Washington; the receipt showed that the purchase was made at a Marshalls in Brooklyn. He also reported a purchase at a Starbucks in Washington; again, the receipt showed that it was in Brooklyn. On both days, he was supposedly writing articles from the Washington area.

Mr. Blair also reported that he dined with a law enforcement official at a Tutta Pasta restaurant in Washington on the day he wrote an article from there. As the receipt makes clear, this Tutta Pasta is in Brooklyn. Mr. Blair said he dined with the same official at Penang, another New York City restaurant that Mr. Blair placed in Washington on his expense reports.

Reached last week, the official said he had never dined with Mr. Blair, and in fact was in Florida with his wife on one of the dates.

According to cellphone records, computer logs and other records recently described by *New York Times* administrators, Mr. Blair had by this point developed a pattern of pretending to cover events in the Mid-Atlantic region when in fact he was spending most of his time in New York, where he was often at work refining a book proposal about the sniper case.

In e-mail messages to colleagues, for example, he conveyed the impression of a travel-weary national correspondent who spent far too much time in La Guardia Airport terminals. Conversely, colleagues marveled at his productivity, at his seemingly indefatigable constitution. "Man, you really get around," one fellow reporter wrote Mr. Blair in an e-mail message.

Mr. Raines took note, too, especially after Mr. Blair's tale from Hunt Valley. By April, Mr. Raines recalled, senior editors were discussing whether Mr. Blair should be considered for a permanent slot on the national reporting staff.

"My feeling was, here was a guy who had been working hard and getting into the paper on significant stories," Mr. Raines said. The plan, he said, was for Mr. Roberts to give Mr. Blair a two- or three-month tryout in the mid-Atlantic bureau to see if he could do the job.

Mr. Roberts said he resisted the idea, and told Mr. Boyd he had misgivings about Mr. Blair. "He works the way he lives—sloppily," he recalled telling Mr. Boyd, who said last week he had agreed that Mr. Blair was not the best candidate for the job.

But with his staff stretched thin to supply reporters for Iraqi war coverage and elsewhere, Mr. Roberts had little choice but to press Mr. Blair into duty on the home front.

After the Hunt Valley article in late March, Mr. Blair pulled details out of thin air in his coverage of one of the biggest stories to come from the war, the capture and rescue of Pfc. Jessica D. Lynch.

In an article on March 27 that carried a dateline from Palestine, W.Va., Mr. Blair wrote that Private Lynch's father, Gregory Lynch Sr., "choked up as he stood on his porch here overlooking the tobacco fields and cattle pastures." The porch overlooks no such thing.

He also wrote that Private Lynch's family had a long history of military service; it does not, family members said. He wrote that their home was on a hilltop; it is in a valley. And he wrote that Ms. Lynch's brother was in the West Virginia National Guard; he is in the Army.

The article astonished the Lynch family and friends, said Brandi Lynch, Jessica's sister. "We were joking about the tobacco fields and the cattle." Asked why no one in the family called to complain about the many errors, she said, "We just figured it was going to be a one-time thing."

It now appears that Mr. Blair may never have gone to West Virginia, from where he claimed to have filed five articles about the Lynch family. E-mail messages and cellphone records suggest that during much of that time he was in New York. Not a single member of the Lynch family remembers speaking to Mr. Blair.

Between the first coverage of the sniper attacks in late October and late April, Mr. Blair filed articles claiming to be from 20 cities in six states. Yet during those five months, he did not submit a single receipt for a hotel room, rental car or airplane ticket, officials at *The Times* said.

Mr. Blair did not have a company credit card—the reasons are unclear— and had been forced to rely on Mr. Roberts's credit card to pay bills from his first weeks on the sniper story. His own credit cards, he had told a *Times* administrator, were beyond their credit limit. The only expense he filed with regularity was for his cellphone, that indispensable tool of his dual existence.

"To have a national reporter who is working in a traveling capacity for the paper and not file expenses for those trips for a four-month period is certainly in hindsight something that should attract our attention," Mr. Boyd said.

On April 29, toward the end of his remarkable run of deceit, Mr. Blair was summoned to the newsroom to answer accusations of plagiarism lodged by *The San Antonio Express-News*. The concerns centered on an article that he claimed to have written from Los Fresnos, Tex., about the anguish of a missing soldier's mother.

In a series of tense meetings over two days, Mr. Roberts repeatedly pressed Mr. Blair for evidence that he had indeed interviewed the mother. Sitting in Mr. Roberts's small office, the reporter produced pages of handwritten notes to allay his editor's increasing concern.

Mr. Roberts needed more—"You've got to come clean with us," he said—and zeroed in on the mother's house in Texas. He asked Mr. Blair to describe what he had seen.

Mr. Blair did not hesitate. He told Mr. Roberts of the reddish roof on the white stucco house, of the red Jeep in the driveway, of the roses blooming in the yard. Mr. Roberts later inspected unpublished photographs of the mother's house, which matched Mr. Blair's descriptions in every detail.

It was not until Mr. Blair's deceptions were uncovered that Mr. Roberts learned how the reporter could have deceived him yet again: by consulting the newspaper's computerized photo archives.

What haunts Mr. Roberts now, he says, is one particular moment when editor and reporter were facing each other in a showdown over the core aim of their profession: truth.

"Look me in the eye and tell me you did what you say you did," Mr. Roberts demanded. Mr. Blair returned his gaze and said he had.

THE LESSONS

When Wrong, 'Get Right'

The New York Times continues as before. Every morning, stacks of *The Times* are piled at newsstands throughout the city; every morning, newspaper carriers toss plastic bags containing that day's issue onto the lawns of readers from Oregon to Maine. What remains unclear is how long those copies will carry the dust from the public collapse of a young journalist's career.

Mr. Blair is no longer welcome in the newsroom he so often seemed unable to leave. Many of his friends express anger at him for his betrayal, and at *The Times* for not heeding signs of his self-destructive nature. Others wonder what comes next for him; Thomas Kunkel, dean of the journalism program at the University of Maryland, gently suggested that the former student might return to earn that college degree.

But Mr. Blair harmed more than himself. Although the deceit of one *Times* reporter does not impugn the work of 375 others, experts and teachers of journalism say that *The Times* must repair the damage done to the public trust.

"To the best of my knowledge, there has never been anything like this at *The New York Times*," said Alex S. Jones, a former *Times* reporter and the co-author of "The Trust: The Private and Powerful Family Behind *The New York Times*" (Little Brown, 1999). He added: "There has never been a systematic effort to lie and cheat as a reporter at *The New York Times* comparable to what Jayson Blair seems to have done."

Mr. Jones suggested that the newspaper might conduct random checks of the veracity of news articles after publication. But Tom Rosenstiel, director of the Project for Excellence in Journalism, questioned how much a newspaper can guard against willful fraud by deceitful reporters.

"It's difficult to catch someone who is deliberately trying to deceive you," Mr. Rosenstiel said. "There are risks if you create a system that is so suspicious of reporters in a newsroom that it can interfere with the relationship of creativity that you need in a newsroom—of the trust between reporters and editors."

Still, in the midst of covering a succession of major news events, from serial killings and catastrophes to the outbreak of war, something clearly broke down in the *Times* newsroom. It appears to have been communication—the very purpose of the newspaper itself.

Some reporters and administrators did not tell editors about Mr. Blair's erratic behavior. Editors did not seek or heed the warnings of other editors about his reporting. Five years' worth of information about Mr. Blair was available in one building, yet no one put it together to determine whether he should be put under intense pressure and assigned to cover high-profile national events.

"Maybe this crystallizes a little that we can find better ways to build lines of communication across what is, to be fair, a massive newsroom," said Mr. Sulzberger, the publisher.

But Mr. Sulzberger emphasized that as *The New York Times* continues to examine how its employees and readers were betrayed, there will be no newsroom search for scapegoats. "The person who did this is Jayson Blair," he said. "Let's not begin to demonize our executives—either the desk editors or the executive editor or, dare I say, the publisher."

Mr. Raines, who referred to the Blair episode as a "terrible mistake," said that in addition to correcting the record so badly corrupted by Mr. Blair, he planned to assign a task force of newsroom employees to identify lessons for the newspaper. He repeatedly quoted a lesson he said he learned long ago from A. M. Rosenthal, a former executive editor.

"When you're wrong in this profession, there is only one thing to do," he said. "And that is get right as fast as you can."

For now, the atmosphere pervading the newsroom is that of an estranged relative's protracted wake. Employees accept the condolences of callers. They discuss what they might have done differently. They find comfort in gallows humor. And, of course, they talk endlessly about how Jayson could have done this.

As a reader, how do you react when you encounter a reference to something such as "the Washington sniper case"? Clearly this is a reference to a specific event occurring at the time, yet as an individual reader, you may or may not have any knowledge of it. Do you feel confused, perhaps compelled to research the issue? Or do you react in some other way entirely? Not all readers can understand every reference every writer makes to events in the world—or to literary works, historical events, or whatever. So how do you—or how do any of us—manage to read and understand texts that make connections to the world outside themselves?

The New York Times is sometimes called "the paper of record"— meaning that whatever it reports is the truth as it is known at the time. Virtually daily, the paper must print a list of corrections—an explanation of names that were misspelled in a previous edition, dates reported incorrectly, etc. Thus *The New York Times* is an official sort of record of events, yet it is, unavoidably, flawed. Even the most careful reporters, editors, and fact-checkers will, from time to time, make mistakes. So how is the situation with Jayson Blair anything but an amplified version of a situation that already exists?

Searching online or in your library, locate a copy of the Society of Professional Journalists' Code of Ethics. In a short essay, explain how the Code informs the charges against Jayson Blair that are being explained by Barry and his co-authors. Also, consider this: Can any code of professional conduct regulate the behavior of members of that profession? Or do such codes always describe an ideal to which individuals may aspire—but which no one (or few) ever reaches?

JR Moehringer is the author of numerous articles and two book-length works: his memoir The Tender Bar *and* Open *(co-authored with Andre Agassi). Raised in Manhasset, New York, Moehringer graduated from Yale University in 1986 and won a Pulitzer Prize for Feature Writing in 2000. He is currently Bureau Chief of the Los Angeles Times.*

RESURRECTING THE CHAMP

By JR Moehringer

If Bob Satterfield Packed One of the Greatest Punches of All Time, How Did He End Up on the Streets of Santa Ana? Retracing the Boxer's Path Leads One Man to Confront Many Demons—Including a Few of His Own.

I'm sitting in a hotel room in Columbus, Ohio, waiting for a call from a man who doesn't trust me, hoping he'll have answers about a man I don't trust, which may clear the name of a man no one gives a damn about. To distract myself from this uneasy vigil—and from the phone that never rings, and from the icy rain that never stops pelting the window—I light a cigar and open a 40-year-old newspaper. "Greatest puncher they ever seen," the paper says in praise of Bob Satterfield, a ferocious fighter of the 1940s and 1950s. "The man of hope—and the man who crushed hope like a cookie in his fist." Once again, I'm reminded of Satterfield's sorry luck, which dogged him throughout his life, as I'm dogging him now. I've searched high and low for Satterfield. I've searched the sour-smelling homeless shelters of Santa Ana. I've searched the ancient and venerable boxing gyms of Chicago. I've searched the eerily clear memory of one New York City fighter who touched Satterfield's push-button chin in 1946 and never forgot the panic on Satterfield's face as he fell. I've searched cemeteries, morgues, churches, museums, slums, jails, courts, libraries, police blotters, scrapbooks, phone books and record books. Now I'm searching this dreary, sleet-bound Midwestern city, where all the streets look like melting Edward Hopper paintings and the sky like a storm-whipped sea. Maybe it's fatigue, maybe it's caffeine, maybe it's the fog rolling in behind the rain, but I feel as though Satterfield has become my own 180-pound Moby Dick. Like Ahab's obsession, he casts a harsh light on his pursuer. Stalking him from town to town and decade to decade, I've learned almost everything there is to know about him, along with valuable lessons about boxing, courage and the eternal tension between fathers and sons. But I've learned more than I bargained for about myself, and for that I owe him a debt. I can't repay the debt unless the phone rings.

We met because a co-worker got the urge to clean. It was early January, 1996. The cop reporter who sits near me at the Orange County edition of *The Times* was straightening her desk when she came across an old tip, something about a once-famous boxer sleeping on park benches in Santa Ana. Passing the tip along, she deflected my thank-you with an off-the-cuff caveat, "He might be dead."

The tipster had no trouble recalling the boxer when I phoned. "Yeah, Bob Satterfield," he said. "A contender from the 1950s. I used to watch him when I watched the fights on TV." Forty years later, though, Satterfield wasn't contending anymore, except with cops. When last seen, the old boxer was wandering the streets, swilling whiskey and calling himself Champ. "Just a guy that lived too long," the tipster said, though he feared this compassion might be outdated. There was a better-than-even chance, he figured, that Satterfield was dead.

If Satterfield was alive, finding him would require a slow tour of Santa Ana's seediest precincts. I began with one of the city's largest men's shelters. Several promising candidates lingered inside the shelter and out, but none matched my sketchy notion of an elderly black man with a boxer's sturdy body. From there I drove to 1st Street, a wide boulevard of taco stands and bus stops that serves as a promenade for homeless men. Again, nothing. Next I cruised the alleys and side streets of nearby McFadden Avenue, where gutters still glistened with tinsel from discarded Christmas trees. On a particularly lively corner I parked the car and walked, stopping passersby and asking where I might find the fighter from the 1950s, the one who called himself Champ, the one who gave the cops all they could handle. No one knew, no one cared, and I was ready to knock off when I heard someone cry out, "Hiya, Champ!"

Wheeling around, I saw an elderly black man pushing a grocery cart full of junk down the middle of the street. Rancid clothes, vacant stare, sooty face, he looked like every other homeless man in America. Then I noticed his hands, the largest hands I'd ever seen, each one so heavy and unwieldy that he held it at his side like a bowling ball. Hands such as these were not just unusual, they were natural phenomena. Looking closer, however, I saw that they complemented the meaty plumpness of his shoulders and the brick-wall thickness of his chest, exceptional attributes in a man who couldn't be getting three squares a day. To maintain such a build on table scraps and handouts, he must have been immense back when.

More than his physique, what distinguished him was a faint suggestion of style. Despite the cast-off clothes, despite the caked-on dirt, there was a vague sense that he clung to some vestigial pride in his appearance. Under his grimy ski parka he wore an almost professorial houndstooth vest. Atop his crown of graying hair was a rakish brown hat with a pigeon feather tucked jauntily in its brim.

His skin was a rich cigar color and smooth for an ex-boxer's, except for one bright scar between his eyebrows that resembled a character in the Chinese alphabet. Beneath a craggy 5 o'clock shadow, his face was pleasant: Dark eyes and high cheekbones sat astride a strong, well-formed nose, and each feature followed the lead of his firm, squared-off chin. He was someone's heartthrob once. His teeth, however, were long gone, save for some stubborn spikes along the mandible.

I smiled and strolled toward him.

"Hey, Champ," I said.

"Heyyy, Champ," he said, looking up and smiling as though we were old friends. I half expected him to hug me.

"You're Bob Satterfield, aren't you?" I said.

"Battlin' Bob Satterfield!" he said, delighted at being recognized. "I'm the Champ, I fought 'em all, Ezzard Charles, Floyd Patterson—"

I told him I was a reporter from the *Los Angeles Times*, that I wanted to write a story about his life.

"How old are you?" I asked.

"I count my age as 66," he said. "But 'The Ring Record Book,' they say 72."

"Did you ever fight for the title?"

"They just didn't give me the break to fight for the title," he said woefully. "If they'd given me the break, I believe I'd be the champ."

"Why didn't they give you the break?"

"You got to be in the right clique," he said, "to get the right fight at the right time."

His voice was weak and raspy, no more than a child's whisper, his words filled with the blurred vowels and squishy consonants of someone rendered senseless any number of times by liquor and fists. He stuttered slightly, humming his "m," gargling his "l," tripping over his longer sentences. By contrast, his eyes and memories were clear. When I asked about his biggest fights, he rattled them off one by one, naming every opponent, every date, every arena. He groaned at the memory of all those beatings, but it was a proud noise, to let me know he'd held his own with giants. He'd even broken the nose of Rocky Marciano, the only undefeated heavyweight champion in history. "He was strooong, I want to tell you," Champ said, chuckling immodestly.

It happened during a sparring session, Champ said, demonstrating how he moved in close, slipping an uppercut under Marciano's left. Marciano shivered, staggered back, and Champ pressed his advantage with another uppercut. Then another. And another. Blood flowed.

"I busted his nose!" Champ shouted, staring at the sidewalk where Marciano lay, forever vanquished. "They rushed in and called off the fight and took Rock away!"

Now he was off to get some free chow at a nearby community center. "Would you care for some?" he asked, and I couldn't decide which was more touching, his largess or his mannerly diction.

* * *

"I was born Tommy Harrison," he said, twirling a chicken leg in his toothless mouth. "That's what you call my legal name. But I fought as Bob Satterfield." His handlers, he explained, didn't want him confused with another fighter,

Tommy "Hurricane" Jackson, so they gave him an alias. I asked how they chose Bob Satterfield and he shrugged.

As a boy in and around Chicago, he built his shoulders by lifting ice blocks, a job that paid pennies at first but huge dividends years later in the ring. At 15, he ran away from home, fleeing a father who routinely whipped him. For months he rode the rails as a hobo, then joined the Army. Too young to enlist, he pretended to be his older brother, George, paying a prostitute to pose as his mother at the induction center.

He learned to box in the Army as a way of eating better and avoiding strenuous duty. Faced with older and tougher opponents, he developed a slithery, punch-and-move style, which must have impressed Marciano, who was collecting talented young fighters to help him prepare for a title shot against Jersey Joe Walcott. Upon his discharge, Champ became chief sparring partner to the man who would soon become the Zeus of modern boxing. Flicking his big fists in the air, each one glimmering with chicken grease, Champ again re-created the sequence of punches that led to Marciano's broken nose, and we laughed about the blood, all that blood.

When he left Marciano's camp and struck out on his own, Champ won a few fights, and suddenly the world treated him like a spoiled prince. Women succumbed, celebrities vied to sit at his side. The mountaintop was within view. "I never really dreamed of being champ," he said, "but as I would go through life, I would think, if I ever get a chance at the title, I'm going to win that fight!"

Instead, he lost. It was February, 1953. Ezzard Charles, the formidable ex-champion, was trying to mount a comeback. Champ was trying to become the nation's top-ranked contender. They met in Detroit before a fair-sized crowd, and Champ proved himself game in the early going. But after eight rounds, his eye swollen shut and his mouth spurting blood, he crumbled under Charles' superior boxing skills. The fateful punch was a slow-motion memory four decades later. Its force was so great that Champ bit clean through his mouthpiece. At the bell, he managed to reach his corner. But when the ninth started, he couldn't stand.

Nothing would ever be the same. A procession of bums and semi-bums made him look silly. Floyd Patterson dismantled him in one round. One day he was invincible, the next he was retired.

As with so many fighters, he'd saved nothing. He got $34,000 for the Charles fight, a handsome sum for the 1950s, but he frittered it on good times and "tutti-frutti" Cadillacs. With no money and few prospects, he drifted to California, where he met a woman, raised a family and hoped for the best. The worst came instead. He broke his ankle on a construction job and didn't rest long enough for it to heal. The injury kept him from working steadily. Then, the punch he never saw coming. His son was killed.

"My son," Champ said, his voice darkening. "He was my heart."

"Little Champ" fell in with the wrong people. An angry teenager, he got on somebody's bad side, and one night he walked into an ambush. "My heart felt sad and broke," Champ said. "But I figured this happened because he was so hotheaded."

Racked with pain, Champ left the boy's mother, who still lived in the house they once shared, not far from where we sat. "Sometimes I go see her," he said. "It's kind of hard, but somehow I make it."

Park benches were his beds, though sometimes he slept at the shelter and sometimes in the backseat of a periwinkle and navy blue Cadillac he bought with his last bit of money. He missed the good life but not the riches, the fame or the women. He missed knowing that he was the boss, his body the servant. "The hard work," he whispered. "Sparring with the bags, skipping rope. Every night after a workout we'd go for a big steak and a half a can of beer. Aaah."

Finishing his lunch, Champ wrapped the leftovers in a napkin and carefully stowed them in a secret compartment of his grocery cart. We shook hands, mine like an infant's in his. When we unclasped, he looked at the five-dollar bill I'd slipped him.

"Heyyy," he said soulfully. "Thanks, amigo. All right, thank you."

My car was down the block. When I reached it, I turned to look over my shoulder. Champ was still waving his massive right hand, still groping for words. "Thank you, Champ!" he called. "All right? Thank you!"

* * *

Like Melville's ocean, or Twain's Mississippi, boxing calls to a young man. Its victims are not only those who forfeit their wits and dive into the ring. The sport seduces writers, too, dragging them down with its powerful undertow of testosterone. Many die a hideous literary death, drowning in their own hyperbole. Only a few—Ernest Hemingway, Jimmy Cannon, A.J. Liebling—cross to safety. Awash in all that blood, they become more buoyant.

For most Americans, however, boxing makes no sense. The sport that once defined the nation now seems hopelessly archaic, like jousting or pistols at six paces. The uninitiated, the cultivated, the educated don't accept that boxing has existed since pre-Hellenic Greece, and possibly since the time of the pharaohs, because it concedes one musky truth about masculinity: Hitting a man is sometimes the most satisfying response to being a man. Disturbing, maybe, but there it is.

Just the sight of two fighters belting each other around the ring triggers a soothing response, a womb-like reassurance that everything is less complicated than we've been led to believe. From brutality, clarity. As with the first taste of cold beer on a warm day, the first kiss of love in the dark, the first meaningful victory over an evenly matched foe, the brain's simplest part is appeased. Colors become brighter, shapes grow deeper, the world slides into smoother focus. And focus was what I craved the day I went searching for Champ. Focus was what made a cop reporter's moth-eaten tip look to me like the Hope diamond. Focus was what I feared I'd lost on the job.

As a newspaper writer, you spend much of your time walking up dirty steps to talk to dirty people about dirty things. Then, once in a great while, you meet an antidote to all that dirt. Champ wasn't the cleanest of men—he may have been the dirtiest man I ever met—but he was pure of heart. He wasn't the first homeless heavyweight either, not by a longshot. Another boxer lands on Skid Row every day, bug-eyed and scrambled. But none has a resume to compare with Champ's, or a memory. He offered a return to the unalloyed joy of daily journalism, not to mention the winning ticket in the Literary Lottery. He was that rarest of rare birds, a people-watcher's version of the condor: Pugilisticum luciditas. He was noble. He was innocent. He was all mine.

I phoned boxing experts throughout the nation. To my astonishment, they not only remembered Champ, they worshiped him. "Hardest hitter who ever lived." "Dynamite puncher." "One of the greatest punchers of all time." Boxing people love to exaggerate, but there was a persuasive sameness to their praise. Bob Satterfield was a beast who slouched toward every opponent with murder in his eye. He could have, should have, would have been champion, except for one tiny problem. He couldn't take a punch.

"He was a bomber," said boxing historian Burt Sugar. "But he had a chin. If he didn't take you out with the first punch, he was out with the second."

Every fighter, being human, has one glaring weakness. For some, it's a faint heart. For others, a lack of discipline. Satterfield's shortcoming was more comic, therefore more melodramatic. Nobody dished it out better, but few were less able to take it. He knocked out seven of his first 12 opponents in the first round, a terrifying boxing blitzkrieg. But over the course of his 12-year professional career he suffered many first-round knockouts himself. The skinny on Satterfield spliced together a common male fantasy with the most common male fear: Loaded with raw talent, he was doomed to fail because of one factory-installed flaw.

Rob Mainwaring, a researcher at boxing's publication of record, *The Ring* magazine, faxed me a fat Satterfield file, rife with vivid accounts of his fragility and prowess. Three times, Satterfield destroyed all comers and put himself in line for a title shot. But each time, before the big fight could be set, Satterfield fell at the feet of some nobody. In May, 1954, for instance, Satterfield tangled with an outsized Cuban fighter named Julio Mederos, banging him with five fast blows in the second round. When Mederos came to, he told a translator: "Nobody ever hit me that hard before. I didn't know any man could hit that hard." Satterfield appeared unstoppable. Six months later, however, he was stopped by an also-ran named Marty Marshall, who found Satterfield's flukish chin before some fans could find their seats.

Viewed as a literary artifact, the Satterfield file was a lovely sampler of overwrought prose. "The Chicago sleep-inducer," one fight writer called him. "Embalming fluid in either hand," said another. Then, in the next breath, came the qualifiers: "Boxing's Humpty-Dumpty." "A chin of Waterford." "Chill-or-be-chilled." It was a prankish God who connected that dainty jaw and that sledgehammer arm to one man's body, and it was the same almighty jokester who put those Hemingway wannabes in charge of chronicling his rise and fall.

Mainwaring faxed me several photos of Satterfield and one of a wife named Iona, whom he divorced in 1952. The library at *The Times*, meanwhile, unearthed still more Satterfield clippings, including a brief 1994 profile by *Orange County Register* columnist Bill Johnson. ("Bob Satterfield, one of the top six heavyweight fighters in the world from 1950 to 1956, today is homeless, living in old, abandoned houses in Santa Ana.") From Chicago newspapers, the library culled glowing mentions of Satterfield, including one describing his nightmarish blood bath with middleweight Jake LaMotta, the fighter portrayed by Robert De Niro in Martin Scorsese's 1980 "Raging Bull." Midway through the film, Satterfield's name fills the screen—then, as the name dissolves, LaMotta-De Niro smashes him in the face.

* * *

"Mr. LaMotta," I said. "I'm writing a story about an old opponent of yours, Bob Satterfield."

"Hold on," he said. "I'm eating a meatball."

I'd phoned the former champion in Manhattan, where he was busy launching his new spaghetti sauce company, LaMotta's Tomatta. His voice was De Niro's from the film—nasal, pugnacious, phlegm-filled, a cross between Don Corleone and Donald Duck. At last he swallowed and said, "Bob Satterfield was one of the hardest punchers who ever lived."

Reluctantly, I told LaMotta the bad news. Satterfield was sleeping on park benches in Santa Ana.

"You sure it's him?" he said. "I heard he was dead."

"No," I assured him, "I just talked to him yesterday."

"Awww," he said, "that's a shame. He put three bumps on my head before I knocked him out. Besides Bob Satterfield, the only ones who ever hurt me were my ex wives."

LaMotta began to reminisce about his old nemesis, a man so dangerous that no one dared spar with him. "He hit me his best punch," he said wistfully. "He hit me with plenty of lefts. But I was coming into him. He hit me with a right hand to the top of the head. I thought I'd fall down. Then he did it again. He did it three times, and when nothing happened he sort of gave up. I knocked him on his face. Flat on his face."

LaMotta asked me to say hello to Satterfield, and I promised that I would. "There but for the grace of God go I," he said. "God dealt me a different hand."

I visited Champ that day to deliver LaMotta's best wishes. I visited him many times in the days ahead, always with some specific purpose in mind. Flesh out the details of his life. Ask a few more questions. See how he was faring. Each time the drill was the same. I'd give him $5 and he'd give me a big tumble, making such a fuss over me that I'd turn red.

"A boxer, like a writer, must stand alone," Liebling wrote, inadvertently explaining the kinship between Champ and me. To my mind, anyone who flattened Rocky Marciano and put three bumps on Jake LaMotta's melon ranked between astronaut and Lakota warrior on the delicately calibrated scale of bad asses, and thus deserved at least a Sunday profile. To Champ's mind, anyone willing to listen to 40-year-old boxing stories could only be a bored writer or a benevolent Martian. Still, there was something more basic about our connection. As a man, I couldn't get enough of his hyper-virile aura. As a homeless man, he couldn't get enough of my patient silence. Between his prattling and my scribbling, we became something like fast friends.

Our mutual admiration caused me to sputter with indignation when my editors asked what hard evidence I had that Champ was Satterfield. What more hard evidence do you need, I asked, besides Champ's being the man in these old newspaper photos—allowing for 40 years of high living and several hundred quarts of cheap whiskey? Better yet, how about Champ's being able to name every opponent, and the dates on which he fought them—allowing for an old man's occasional memory lapses?

If the evidence of our senses won't suffice, I continued, let's use common sense: Champ is telling the truth because he has no reason to lie. For being Bob Satterfield, he gets no money, no glory, no extra chicken legs at senior centers and soup kitchens. Pretending to be a fighter forgotten by all but a few boxing experts? Pretending in such convincing fashion? He'd have to be crazy. Or brilliant. And I could say with some confidence that he was neither. Even so, the editors said, get something harder.

* * *

Champ's old house in Santa Ana sat along a bleak cul-de-sac, its yard bursting with cowlick-shaped weeds, its walls shedding great slices of paint. It looked like a guard shack at the border crossing of some desolate and impoverished nation.

An unhappy young woman scowled when I asked to see Champ's ex-girlfriend. "Wait here," she said.

Minutes later, she returned with a message: Go away. Champ's things have been burned, and no one has any interest in talking to you.

Next I tried the Orange County courthouse, hoping arrest records would authenticate Champ. Sure enough, plenty of data existed in the courthouse ledger. Finding various minor offenses under Thomas Harrison, alias Bob Satterfield, I rejoiced. Here was proof, stamped with the official seal of California, that Champ was Satterfield. A scoundrel, yes, but a truthful one.

Then I saw something bad. Two felony arrests, one in 1969, one in 1975. Champ had been candid about his misdemeanors, but he had never mentioned these more serious offenses. "Oh, God," I said, scanning the arrest warrant: "Thomas Harrison, also known as Bob Satterfield . . . lewd and lascivious act upon and with the body . . . child under the age of 14 years." Champ molesting his girlfriend's 10-year-old daughter. Champ punching the little girl's aunt in the mouth.

"Did you know [Champ] to be a professional prize fighter?" a prosecutor asked the aunt during a hearing.

"Yes," she said.

"Did you know that he was once a contender for the heavyweight boxing championship of the world?"

Before she could answer, Champ's lawyer raised an objection, which the judge sustained.

Champ pleaded guilty to assaulting the aunt—for which he received probation—and the molestation charge was dropped.

Then, six years later, it happened again. Same girlfriend, different daughter.

"Thomas Harrison, also known as Tommy Satterfield, also known as Bobby Satterfield . . . lewd and lascivious act."

Again, Champ avowed his innocence, but a jury found him guilty. In May 1976, Champ wrote the judge from jail, begging for a second chance. He signed the letter, "Yours truly, Thomas Harrison. Also Known as Bob Satterfield, Ex-Boxer, 5th in the World."

This is how it happens, I thought. This is how a newspaper writer learns to hate the world. I could feel the cynicism setting inside me like concrete. My reprieve from the dirtiness of everyday journalism had turned into a reaffirmation of everything I loathed and feared. My noble warrior, my male idol, my friend, was a walking, talking horror show, a homeless Humbert Humbert.

* * *

He greeted me with his typical good cheer, doffing his hat.

"Hey, Champ, whaddya say!?" he cried. "Long time no see, amigo."

"Hey, Champ," I said, glum. "Let's sit down here and have a talk."

I led him over to some bleachers in a nearby baseball field. We passed the afternoon talking about all the major characters of his life—Marciano, Charles, Little Champ. Abruptly, I mentioned the ex-girlfriend.

"Now that I'm on the outside looking in," he mumbled, "I see she wasn't 100% in my corner."

"Because she accused you of doing those awful things to her baby?"

He lifted his head, startled. He was spent, punch drunk, permanently hung over, but he knew what I was saying. "They just took her word for it," he said of the jury. "The only regret I have in life is that case she made against me with the baby." Only a monster would hurt a child, Champ said. He begged his ex-girlfriend to recant those false accusations, which he blamed on her paranoia and jealousy. And she did recant, he said, but not to the judge.

More than this he didn't want to say. He wanted to talk about Chicago, sweet home, and all the other way-off places where he knew folks. How he yearned for friendly faces, especially his sister, Lily, with whom he'd left his scrapbook and other papers for safekeeping. He told me her address in Columbus, Ohio, and her phone number. He wanted to see her before he died. See anyone. "Get me some money and head on down the road," he said, eyes lowered, half to himself.

A cold winter night was minutes off, and Champ needed to find a bed, fast. This posed a problem, since taking leave of Champ was never fast. It was hard for him to overcome the inertia that crept into his bones while he sat, harder still to break away from anyone willing to listen. Watching him get his grocery cart going was like seeing an ocean liner off at the dock. The first movement was imperceptible. "See you later, Champ," I said, hurrying him along, shaking that catcher's mitt of a hand. Then I accidentally looked into his eyes, and I couldn't help myself. I believed him.

Maybe it was faith born of guilt. Maybe it was my way of atoning. After all, I was the latest in a long line of people—managers, promoters, opponents— who wanted something from Champ. I wanted his aura, I wanted his story, I wanted his friendship. As partial restitution, the least I could give him was the benefit of the doubt.

Also, he was right. Only a monster would commit the crimes described in those court files, and I didn't see any monster before me. Just a toothless boxer with a glass chin and a pigeon feather in his hat. Shaking his hand, I heard myself say, "Go get warm, Champ," and I watched myself slip him another five-dollar bill.

* * *

LaMotta would not let up. He refused to let me write. Each time I tried, he swatted me around my subconscious. "Besides Bob Satterfield," he'd said, "the only ones who ever hurt me were my ex-wives." Men seldom speak of other men with such deference, such reverence, particularly men like LaMotta. One of the brashest fighters ever, he discussed Satterfield with all the bluster of a curtsy. "You sure it's him?" he'd asked, distressed. "I heard he was dead."

You sure it's him? The courts were sure, the cops were sure, the editors were pretty sure. But I was getting ready to tell several million people that Bob Satterfield was a homeless wreck and a convicted child molester. Was I sure?

I phoned more boxing experts and historians, promoters and managers, libraries and clubs, referees and retired fighters, and that's when I found Ernie

Terrell, former heavyweight champion. I reached him in Chicago at the South Side offices of his janitorial business.

"You remember Bob Satterfield?" I asked.

"One of the hardest punchers who ever lived," he said.

I've been hanging out with Satterfield, I said, and I need someone who can vouch for his identity. A long silence followed. A tingly silence, a harrowing silence, the kind of silence that precedes the bloodcurdling scream in a horror film. "Bob Satterfield is dead," Terrell said.

"No, he's not," I said, laughing. "I just talked to him."

"You talked to Bob Satterfield?"

"Yes. He sleeps in a park not 10 minutes from here."

"Bob Satterfield?" he said. "Bob Satterfield the fighter? Bob Satterfield's dead."

Now it was my turn to be silent. When I felt the saliva returning to my mouth, I asked Terrell what made him so sure.

"Did you go to his funeral?" I asked.

He admitted that he had not.

"Do you have a copy of his obituary?"

Again, no.

"Then how do you know he's dead?" I asked.

Suddenly, he seemed less sure.

"Hold on," he said. "We're going to get to the bottom of this."

He opened a third phone line and began conference-calling veteran corner men and trainers on the South Side. The voices that joined us on the line were disjointed and indistinct, as though recorded on scratchy vinyl records. Rather than a conference call, we were conducting a seance, summoning the spirits of boxing's past. He dialed a gym where the phone rang and rang.

When someone finally answered, Terrell asked to speak with D.D. The phone went dead for what seemed a week. In the background, I heard speed bags being thrummed and ropes being skipped, a sound like cicadas on a summer day. At last, a scruffy and querulous voice came on the line, more blues man than corner man.

"Who's this?"

"It's Ernie."

"Ernie?"

"Ernie."

"Ernie?"

"Ernie!"

"Yeah, Ernie, yeah."

"I got a guy here on the other line from the *Los Angeles Times*, in California, says he's writing a story about Bob Satterfield. You remember Bob Satterfield."

"Suuure."

"Says he just talked to Satterfield and Satterfield's sleeping in a park out there in Santa Ana."

"Bob Satterfield's dead."

"No," I said.

I told them about Champ's encyclopedic knowledge of his career. I told them about Champ's well-documented reputation among cops, judges and reporters. I told them about Champ's face matching old Satterfield photos.

"Then I will come out there and shoot that dude," D.D. said. "Because Bob Satterfield is dead."

Ten minutes later I was in Santa Ana, where I found Champ sweeping someone's sidewalk for the price of a whiskey bottle. It was a hot spring day, and he looked spent from the hard work.

"Look," I said, "a lot of people say you're dead."

"I'm the one," he said, bouncing on his feet, shadowboxing playfully with me. "Battlin' Bob Satterfield. I fought 'em all. Ezzard Charles, Rocky Marciano—"

"Don't you have any identification?" I said, exasperated. "A birth certificate? A union card? A Social Security card?"

He patted his pockets, nothing. We'd been through this.

"In that case," I said, "I'm going to have to give you a test."

Far from offended, he couldn't wait. Leaning into me, he cocked his head to one side and closed his eyes, to aid concentration.

"Who was Jack Kearns?" I asked, knowing that "Doc" Kearns, who managed Jack Dempsey in the 1920s, briefly managed Satterfield's early career.

"Jack Kearns," Champ said. "He was the first manager I ever had."

"All right," I said. "Who's this?"

I held before his nose a 45-year-old wire photo of Iona Satterfield. Champ touched her face gingerly and said, "That's Iona. That's the only woman I ever loved."

* * *

Asked to explain myself, I usually start with my father, who disappeared when I was 7 months old, walked away from his only son the way some people leave a party that's grown dull. At precisely the moment I learned to crawl, he ran. An unfair head start, I always felt.

As a boy, I could repress all stirrings of curiosity about him, because I knew what he sounded like, and this seemed sufficient. A well-known radio man in New York City, he often came floating out of my grandmother's olive-drab General Electric clock-radio, cracking jokes and doing bits, until an adult passing through the room would lunge for the dial. It was thought that The Voice upset me. No one realized that The Voice nourished me. My father was invisible, therefore mythic. He was whatever I wanted him to be, and his rumbling baritone inspired mental pictures of every male archetype, from Jesus to Joe Namath to Baloo the bear in *The Jungle Book*.

Over time, I grew impatient with the mystery surrounding him, the not knowing, particularly when he changed his name and vanished altogether. (Seeing fatherhood and child support as a maximum-security prison, he took a fugitive's pains to cover his tracks once he escaped.) As his absence came to feel more like a constant presence, I spent long hours puzzling about the potential intersections between his identity and mine. My predecessor in the generational parade, my accursed precursor, was a voice. It unnerved me. It unmanned me. One day, shortly before my 17th birthday, I made what felt like a conscious decision to find him. At least, that's what I thought until I met Champ, who forced me to see that no such conscious decision ever took place, that I'd been trying to find my father all my life, that every man is trying to find his father.

True, a love of boxing and a budding disenchantment with daily journalism sparked my original interest in Champ. Then a genuine fondness made me befriend him. But what made me study him like an insect under a microscope was my inescapable fascination with anyone who disappears, dissolves his identity, walks away from fame and family. When pushed to deconstruct my relationship with Champ, I saw that we were trading more than fivers and fellowship. Champ was using me as a surrogate for his dead son, and I was using him as a stand-in for my own deep-voiced demon, whom I met after a brief, furious search.

We sat in an airport coffee shop and talked like strangers. Strangers who had the same nose and chin. I remember random things. I remember that he was the first man I ever made nervous. I remember that he wore a black leather coat, ordered eggs Benedict and flirted relentlessly with the waitress, asking like some fussy lord if the chef made his own Hollandaise sauce. I remember that he was portly and jovial, with wild eyebrows that forked straight out from his head. I remember laughing at his stories, laughing against my will because he could be painfully funny. I remember breathing in his peppery scent, a uniquely male cocktail of rubbing alcohol, hair spray and Marlboro 100s. I remember the hug when we parted, the first time I ever hugged another man.

But what we said to each other over the hours we sat together, I don't know. The meeting was so emotionally high-watt that it shorted my memory circuits. My only other impression of that night is one of all-pervasive awe. My father, my mythic father, had boozed away his future and parlayed his considerable talents into a pile of unpaid bills. I saw none of that. If losing him was a hardship, losing my mythic idea of him would have been torture. So I chose to see him as a fallen god, an illusion he fostered with a few white lies. I loved him in the desperate way you love someone when you need to.

Now, months after meeting Champ, I asked myself if I wasn't viewing this poor homeless man through the same hopeful myopia. If so, why? The answer dawned one day while I was reading *Moby-Dick*, the bible of obsession, which provides a special sort of reading pleasure when you substitute the word "father" for "whale": "It is a thing most sorrowful, nay shocking, to expose the fall of valor in the soul. . . . That immaculate manliness we feel within ourselves . . . bleeds with keenest anguish at the undraped spectacle of a valor-ruined man."

When the valor-ruined man is your father, the anguish quadruples and the manliness hemorrhages. Sometimes the anguish reaches such a crescendo that you simply disobey your eyes. Anything to stanch the bleeding.

Because he recalled the specter of my father and his equally enigmatic cop-out, Champ might have revived that early talent I showed for self-deception. He also either benefited or suffered from the trinity of habits that constitutes my father's legacy. An obsession with questions of identity. A tendency to overestimate men. And an inability to leave the past alone.

* * *

Not every homeless man can look nonchalant speaking into a cellular phone, but Champ acclimated himself to the technology, even if he did aim the phone at that part of the heavens where he imagined Ohio to be. He told his sister he was fine, getting by, and urged her to cooperate. "Please," he said, handing me the phone, "let this man look at my scrapbook."

Establishing Champ's credibility was one thing. Establishing mine with his sister was another. Lily couldn't imagine what I wanted from her poor brother, and I couldn't blame her. I tried to explain that Champ merited a newspaper story because he'd contended for the title.

"You remember your brother fighting," I said, "as Bob Satterfield?"

"Yes," she said casually.

"And you have a scrapbook with clippings and photos?"

"I've had that scrapbook for years."

I asked her to mail me the book, but she refused. She wasn't about to ship a family heirloom to someone she'd never met. Again, I couldn't blame her.

It was then that I heard from a former boxing writer. He'd been watching TV recently when he hit on something called the Classic Sports Network, which was airing a prehistoric episode of Rocky Marciano's TV show, wherein Marciano analyzed a 1951 bout at Madison Square Garden between Rex Layne and Bob Satterfield.

When the tape arrived the next morning, I cradled it like a newborn to the nearest VCR. There was Marciano, pudgy and past his prime, a real-life version of Fred Flintstone. Beside him sat his guest, comic Jimmy Durante. After several excruciating minutes of idle chitchat, Marciano turned to Durante and said, "I want to show you the Bob Satterfield-Rex Layne fight."

Durante's eyes widened.

"Satterfield?!" he said.

"You remember him?" Marciano asked.

"So help me," Durante said, "he's my favorite. A great, great fighter. I thought he'd be a champion."

"He had the punch, Jim," Marciano said, shaking his head.

The screen went dark. A ring appeared. In the foreground stood a man in a hooded robe, his back to the camera. On either side of him stood corner men in cardigan sweaters, "SATTERFIELD" emblazoned across their backs. Doffing his robe, the fighter started forward, his torso atremble with muscles. Slowly he turned toward the camera, and I saw that he was not Champ. The resemblance was strong, as the resemblance between Champ and old photos of Satterfield had been strong. But they were different men.

My stomach tightened as the "real" Satterfield threw a walloping right. Layne dropped to one knee and shook his head, not knowing what hit him. I knew exactly how he felt.

Champ a fake. Somehow I felt less betrayed when I thought he was a child molester. It made me sick. It made no sense. He knew too much about Satterfield. He knew the record. He knew Doc Kearns. He recognized Iona. Plus, he was built like a fighter—that body, those hands. Yes, I thought, he's built like a fighter.

I phoned *The Ring* and asked Mainwaring to check his records for a heavyweight named Tommy Harrison. Minutes later, he faxed me the file. There, at long last, was Champ. This time, no allowance needed to be made for the passage of years and the corrosive effects of whiskey. That body, those hands.

Besides his name, it seemed, Champ was frequently telling the truth. Not only did he break Marciano's nose, the injury postponed a storied rematch with Walcott. Like Satterfield, he had been a highly touted contender, a guy within striking distance of the championship. Like Satterfield, he had fought Ezzard Charles. In fact, Harrison and Satterfield had fought many of the same men.

Opponents weren't the only thing they had in common. Both were Army veterans. Both were right-handers. Both were built like light-heavyweights. Both were anxious to break into the heavyweight division. Both were clobbered when they tried. Both retired in the mid-1950s. Both were born in November; their birthdays were one day apart.

"He's fast," Marciano said of Harrison in one clipping. "Has a great ring future. In a year or so, if I'm still champ, I expect trouble from him."

The file proved that Champ was a fraud, or delusional, or something in between. But it couldn't explain his motives, nor account for his corroborative sister. In fact, it raised more questions than it answered, including the most pressing question of all: If Champ wasn't Satterfield, who was?

Ernie Terrell said Satterfield was dead. But I couldn't find an obituary—not even in Chicago. How did a fighter of Satterfield's stature not rate a death notice in his native city?

Phone directories in scores of area codes listed hundreds of Satterfields, too many to dial. A search of databases throughout the Midwest found one Illinois death certificate in the name of Robert Satterfield, a truck driver buried in Restvale Cemetery, Worth, Ill. Under next of kin, a son on the South Side of Chicago.

"Robert Satterfield Junior?" I asked when the son answered the phone.

"Yes?"

"I'm writing a story about Bob Satterfield, the heavyweight of the 1950s, and I was wondering if you might be any—"

"That's my father," he said proudly.

* * *

The neighborhood was dodgy, some houses well-kept and others falling down. Few addresses were visible and some street signs were gone, so I drove in circles, getting lost twice, doubling back, and that's when I saw him. Bob Satterfield. In the flesh.

After staring at old newspaper photos and studying the tape of his fight with Rex Layne, I'd committed Satterfield's face to memory—never realizing he might have bequeathed that face to his son. Seeing Satterfield Jr. outside his house, the resemblance fooled me like a mirage, and I did what anyone in my shoes would have done: I backed straight into his neighbor's truck.

The first time I ever laid eyes on Bob Satterfield, therefore, he flinched, as though bracing for a punch.

After making sure I'd left no visible dent, we shook hands and went inside his brick house, the nicest on the block. The living room was neat and intensely bright, morning sunlight practically shattering the glass windows. He introduced me to his wife, Elaine, who took my hand somewhat timidly. Together, they waved me toward the couch, then sat far away, grimacing.

They were visibly afraid of me, but they did everything possible to make me feel welcome. She was all smiles and bottled-up energy; he was old-school polite, verging on courtly. He'd just finished a double shift at O'Hare, where he loaded cargo for a living, and he actually apologized for his exhaustion. I looked into his basset-hound eyes and cringed, knowing I'd soon add to his burdens.

I started by acknowledging their apprehension. As far as they knew, I'd come all the way from California to ask questions about a fighter few people remembered. It seemed suspicious.

"But the first time I heard the name Bob Satterfield," I said, "was when I met this man."

I dealt them several photos of Champ, like gruesome playing cards, then court papers and clippings describing Champ as Satterfield. Another profile had recently appeared in a college newspaper, and I laid this atop the pile. Lastly, I outlined Champ's criminal past. They looked at each other gravely.

"I hate this man," Elaine blurted.

Satterfield Jr. lit a cigarette and gazed at Champ. He murmured something about a resemblance, then walked to a sideboard, from which he pulled a crumbling scrapbook. Returning to his chair, he balanced the book on one knee and began assembling photos, clippings, documents, anything to help me recognize that Champ's impersonation was no victimless crime.

While I scrutinized the scrapbook, Satterfield Jr. talked about his father's life. He told me about his father's close friends, Miles Davis and Muhammad Ali, who met his first wife through Satterfield. He told me about his father's triumphs in the ring and the difficult decision to retire. (After suffering a detached retina in 1958, Satterfield fled to Paris and studied painting.) He told me about his father's ancestry, back, back, back, and I understood the desperation seeping into his voice, a desperation that made him stammer badly. He'd opened his door to a total stranger who repaid the hospitality by declaring that countless other strangers believed his beloved father was "a valor-ruined man." I'd walked up clean steps to talk to clean people and made them feel dirty.

Lastly, Satterfield Jr. produced his father's birth certificate, plus a 1977 obituary from a now-defunct Chicago newspaper. To these precious items he added a photo of his parents strolling arm in arm, kissing. When I told Satterfield Jr. about Champ pointing to Iona and calling her "the only woman I ever loved," I thought he might eat the coffee table.

"That somebody would intrude on his memory like this," Elaine said. "My father-in-law was a man. He was a man's man, nothing like the men of today. He was a prideful man. He continued to work up until his operation for cancer. If a person knows he's dying, and he still gets up to go to work, that says a lot about him as a man, and if he knew some homeless man sleeping on a park bench was impersonating him—"

She stopped herself and went to the window, struggling to keep her composure. Satterfield Jr. now began phoning family.

"I'm sitting here with a reporter from the *Los Angeles Times*," he shouted into the phone, "and he says there's a man in California who's telling everybody he's Bob Satterfield the fighter. He's homeless and he has a very bad record, and he's been molesting children and he's using Pop's name. Yeah. Uh huh. Now, now, don't cry..."

* * *

An old boxing hand once said, "You never learn anything until you're tired," and by that criterion I'm capable of learning plenty right now. After the overnight flight, after the cab ride through the rainy dawn to this downtown Columbus hotel, I'm tired enough to understand why Champ's sister doesn't trust me, and why she's turned me over to Champ's nephew, Gregory Harrison, who trusts me even less. I left word for him two hours ago saying I'd arrived, but he seems like a guy who'd rather give me a stiff beating than a straight answer, so the chance of seeing Champ's scrapbook seems remote.

Above all, I'm tired enough to understand that Champ isn't Satterfield, never was Satterfield, never will be, no matter how hard I try. But I'm also tired enough to understand why he pretended to be Satterfield. He became Satterfield because he didn't like being Tommy Harrison.

It was Satterfield Jr. who made me appreciate how ripe his father was for imitation. Fast, stylish, pretty, Satterfield was Champ's superior in every way. He was the ballyhooed one, the better one. Yes, he had the famously weak chin. But he led with it, time after time, meaning he had one hellacious heart. Champ must have studied Satterfield from afar, longingly, as I did. He must have gone to school on Satterfield, devouring facts about his life, as I did. He must have viewed Satterfield as a model, an ideal, as I also did. One day, Champ must have spied Satterfield across a musty gym, perhaps with Doc Kearns, or a smoky nightclub, where Iona was the prettiest girl in the joint, and said, "Ah, to be him." From there, it was a short, dizzy trip to "I am him."

As a man, you need someone to instruct you in the masculine verities. Your father is your first choice, but when he drops out, you search for someone else. If you're careless, the search creeps into your psyche and everyone becomes a candidate, from homeless men to dead boxers. If you're careless and unlucky, the search devours you. That doppelganger eats you up.

"One of the primary things boxing is about is lying," Joyce Carol Oates writes in *On Boxing*. "It's about systematically cultivating a double personality: the self in society, the self in the ring."

What Champ did, I think, was sprout a third self, a combination of the two, which may be what Champ has been trying to tell me all along.

After Chicago, I wanted to scold him about the people his lies were hurting. But when I found him wearing a 10-gallon cowboy hat and a polo shirt with toothbrushes stuffed in the breast pocket, my anger drained away.

"Champ," I said, "when you pretended to be Bob Satterfield, weren't you afraid the other Bob Satterfield would find out?"

Without hesitating, he put a hand to his chin and said, "I always figured the other Bob Satterfield knew about me. As long as everyone got paid, I didn't think the other Bob Satterfield would mind."

"What?"

"This is just you and me talking," he said. "But my manager, George Parnassus, he told me like this here: 'If you go to fight in Sioux City, Iowa, and you say you is Bob Satterfield, then you get a big crowd, see? But if you say you is Tommy Harrison, and like that, you only get a medium-size crowd.' "

Champ's manager had been dead 20 years. But his son, Msgr. George Parnassus, was pastor of St. Victor's Roman Catholic Church in West Hollywood. I phoned Parnassus and told him about Champ, then asked if his father might have staged bogus fights in the 1950s. Before TV came along, I ventured, most fighters were faceless names in the dark, so it might have been easy, and it might have been highly profitable, to promote look-alike fighters in out-of-the-way places. Say, Sioux City.

"Why do you say Sioux City?" he demanded.

"Because Champ said Sioux City."

"My father moved to Sioux City in the 1950s and staged fights there for a number of years."

Which is why I'm in Columbus this morning. I owed it to Champ to take one last stab at the truth. I owed it to myself. More than anyone, I owed it to Satterfield, whose absence I've come to feel like a constant presence.

"I've had a lot of disappointments," Satterfield told a reporter in 1958, sitting in a hospital with his detached retina. "I don't remember all the disappointments I've had." Maybe, 40 years later, he's still disappointed. Maybe he knows someone swiped the only shiny prize he ever had—his good name—and he can't rest until he gets it back. All this time, I've been casting Satterfield as Moby Dick, myself as Ahab. Now I'm wondering if Satterfield is the real Ahab, and Champ the whale. Which makes me the harpoon.

The phone rings.

"I'm downstairs."

* * *

Champ's nephew is sitting in the middle of the lobby, unaware or pretending to be unaware that people are staring. It's not that he looks out of place, with his floor-length black leather overcoat and gold-rimmed sunglasses. It's that he looks famous. He also looks like a younger, fitter, toothier version of Champ.

He shakes my hand tentatively and we duck into the hotel restaurant. The place is closed, but a waiter says we're welcome to have coffee. We sit by a rain-streaked window. I thank him for meeting me, but he whips off his sunglasses and stares.

"I'm not here for you," he says. "I'm here for my Uncle Tommy. And before I tell you anything you need to know, I need to know from you why you would get on a plane and fly all night, come all the way from California, to Columbus, Ohio, to write a story about my uncle?"

I try explaining my complicated relationship with his uncle, but the subject makes me more mumbly than Champ. Interrupting, he says softly: "Uncle Tommy was the father I should have had."

He tells me about the only time he met his uncle, a meeting so charged that it defined his life, and I wonder if he notices the strange look on my face.

"My Uncle Tommy was like the Last Action Hero," he says. "I wanted to be just like him."

"You were a boxer," I say.

"I was a sparring partner of Buster Douglas," he says, sitting straighter.

His nickname was Capital City Lip, but everyone nowadays calls him Lip. With the waiters watching, he throws his right, jabs his left, bobs away from an invisible opponent, taking me through several hard-won fights, and I'm reminded of the many times his uncle broke Marciano's nose for my enjoyment.

"When you hit a guy," he says dreamily, "when you hit him in the body, you demean his manner, you know? You sap his strength, you impose your will on him. I was in the tippy-top physical shape of my life! No one could beat me! I was good!"

"What happened?"

He purses his lips. His story is Champ's story, Satterfield's story, every fighter's story. One day, there was someone he just couldn't beat.

"Now I race drag bikes," he says.

"Drag bikes? Why?"

"Because someday I want to be world champion of something."

His father got him interested, he says, mentioning the man in a curious way. "My father walks down the street, people part ways," he says. "Big George, that's what everyone in Columbus calls my father. He was a boxer, too, although he didn't go as far as Uncle Tommy."

Feeling an opening, I try to tell Lip about my father. He seems confused at first, then instantly empathetic. He understands the link between boxing and growing up fatherless. Maybe only a boxer can fathom that kind of fear.

"Have you ever heard the name Bob Satterfield?" I ask.

"Yes, I have heard that name."

As a boy, Lip often heard that Uncle Tommy fought as Bob Satterfield, but he never knew why.

He promises to bring me Champ's scrapbook tomorrow, then take me to meet his father. I walk him outside to his Jeep, which is double-parked in a tow zone, hazard lights flashing, just as he left it three hours ago.

* * *

White shirt, white pants, white shoes, Lip comes for me the next morning looking like an angel of the streets. As we zoom away from the hotel, I scan the backseat, floor, dashboard. No scrapbook. The angel shakes his head.

"Aunt Lily just doesn't trust you," he says. "I was over there all morning, but she won't let that book out of her house."

I groan.

"I looked through the book myself, though," he says, lighting a cigarette, "and I don't think it has what you want. This Bob Satterfield, the book has lots of newspaper articles about his career, and there's a picture of him with my uncle—"

I wince.

"—and an article saying Satterfield and my Uncle Tommy were scheduled to fight."

Disconsolate, I stare at the bullet hole in the windshield.

We drive to Lip's father's house, where a candy-apple red Cadillac the size of a fire engine sits outside, license plate "BIG GEO." Lip takes a deep breath, then knocks. Whole minutes crawl by before the door flies open and Champ's brother appears. He looks nothing like Champ, mainly because of old burn scars across his face. But wrapped in a baby blue bathrobe and glowering hard, he does look like an old boxer. He turns and disappears inside the house. Meekly, we follow.

Off to the left is a small room crammed with trophies and boxing memorabilia. To the right seems to be the living room, though it's impossible to tell because all the lights are off. Big George keeps moving until he reaches a high-backed chair. Despite the oceanic darkness of the place, he remains clearly visible, as if lit from within by his own anger. I can see why he's such a force in Lip's life. He scares the wits out of me.

Rubbing his palms together, Lip tells his father I'm writing a story about Uncle Tommy.

"Hmph," Big George scoffs. "Tommy. He's a stranger to me. He's my brother and I love him, but he's a stranger."

"Have you ever heard the name Bob Satterfield?" I ask.

"Bob Satterfield," Big George says, "was one of the hardest punchers of all time—"

He coughs, a horrifying cough, then adds:

"—but he couldn't take a punch."

"Do you remember Tommy ever fighting as Bob Satterfield?" I ask.

"Tommy never fought as nobody else."

He stands and goes to a sideboard, where he rifles through a stack of papers and bills. "Here," he says, yanking loose a yellowed newspaper account of the night in 1953 when Champ's life began its downward spiral.

"Tommy wasn't ready for Ezzard Charles," Big George says with sudden tenderness while Lip and I read over his shoulder. "They rushed him."

The three of us stand together, silently, as though saying a prayer for Champ. Then, without warning, Lip breaks the mood, mentioning a beef he's having with Big George. They start to argue, and I see that Lip brought me here for more than an interview. He's hoping I can play referee. As with Champ, I was too busy using him to notice that he was using me.

Father and son argue for five minutes, each landing heavy verbal blows. Then Big George makes it plain that these will be the final words spoken on the subject.

"The Bible say this," he bellows. "Honor your parents! Honor your mother and father! Regardless what they say, what they do, all mothers and dads love their children! All of them!"

"He's lying to you," Lip says when we get in the car.

I look at him, startled.

"About what?"

"He knows all about Satterfield."

We drive to a beloved old gym that former champion Buster Douglas helped rebuild after knocking down Mike Tyson. Inside, we find Douglas' father, Bill, training a young featherweight. When Lip tells Douglas that I'm writing about his uncle, "a former heavyweight con-TEN-der," Douglas nods his head several times, and I feel Lip's self-worth balloon with each nod.

We watch the featherweight work the heavy bag, a black, water-filled sack that hangs from the ceiling. Each time he snaps a hard right, the bag swings like a man in a noose. His name is Andre Cray, and he's 25. Rawboned and scowling, with a flat head and rubbery limbs, he looks like an angry Gumby. When his workout ends, we ask him why he chose boxing as a trade.

"To me it's like an art," he says quietly, unwinding the padded white tape from his fists.

But this isn't the real reason, he admits. Growing up without money, without a father, boxing was the only straight path to manhood. Many of his friends chose the crooked path, a choice they didn't always live to regret. Those who prospered in the crack trade often gave Cray money and begged him not to follow their lead. Some even bought him gloves and shoes, to make sure the streets didn't claim another boxer.

He remembers those early patrons, uses their fate as inspiration. His future is bright, he figures, if he can just protect his chin and not lose heart. In 19 fights, he's scored 17 wins. When he loses, he says, the anguish is more than he can stand.

"You have family?" Lip asks.

"Yeah," Cray says. "I have a son. He'll be 1 on Tuesday."

"What's his name?"

"Andre Cray Junior."

"I imagine he inspires you a lot."

"Yeah," Cray says, looking down at his oversize hands.

Lip nods, solemn. Douglas nods. I nod.

* * *

Like a favorite movie, the one-reel "Satterfield Versus Layne" says something different every time I watch, each punch a line of multilayered dialogue. After several hundred viewings, the core theme emerges. It's about pressing forward, I think. Ignoring your pain. Standing.

"Satterfield is out of this world," Marciano says in his narrative voice-over. "He's one of the hardest hitters I've ever seen."

Satterfield lives up to his reputation in the very first minute, greeting Layne with a vicious second-clefter on the point of the chin. Kneeling, Layne takes the count, then staggers upright and hugs Satterfield until the bell.

Satterfield, in white trunks, with a pencil-thin mustache and muscles upon muscles, is a joy to look at. Decades before Nautilus, his biceps look like triple-scoop ice cream cones. By contrast, Layne looks like a soda jerk who's wandered mistakenly into the ring. Over the first three rounds he does little more than push his black trunks and flabby belly back and forth while offering his square head as a stationary target.

Still, Layne seems the luckier man. In the sixth, Satterfield puts every one of his 180 pounds behind a right hook. He brings the fist from behind his back like a bouquet of flowers, but Layne weaves, avoiding the punch by half an inch. "Just missed!" Marciano shouts. "That would have done it!"

Had that punch landed, everything would be different. Layne would be stretched out on the canvas, Satterfield would be looking forward to the title shot he craves. Instead, the eighth begins, and Satterfield's wondering what more he can do. It's LaMotta all over again. No matter what you do, the other guy keeps coming—obdurate, snarling, fresh.

Far ahead on points, Satterfield can still win a decision, as long as he protects himself, covers up, plays it safe. He does just the opposite, charging forward, chin high, the only way he knows. In the kind of punch-for-punch exchange that went out with fedoras, Satterfield and Layne stand one inch apart, winging at each other from all directions, Satterfield trying frantically to turn out Layne's dim bulb—until Layne lands a right hook on the magic chin.

"I don't think [he] can get up," Marciano says as Satterfield lies on his back, blinking at the house lights. "But look at this guy try."

Boxing's Humpty-Dumpty. The book on Satterfield proves true. Or does it? Always, this is the moment I hit the pause button and talk to Satterfield while he tries to tap some hidden wellspring of strength. Somehow, he taps it every time, a display of pure grit that never fails to make my heart beat faster.

"He's hurt bad," Marciano says, as Satterfield stands and signals the referee that he's ready for another dose. Dutifully, Layne steps forward and sends a crashing left into Satterfield's head. Then a right. And another right. Finally, the referee rushes forward and removes Satterfield's mouthpiece. Corner men leap into the ring. Photographers with flashes the size of satellite dishes shoot the covers of tomorrow's sports pages. Amid all the commotion, Layne takes a mincing step forward and does something shocking.

It's hard to believe, in an age of end-zone dances and home-run trots, that boxers in a bygone era often hugged after their meanest fights. (Some actually kissed.) But Layne gives that post-fight tenderness a new twist. As Satterfield sags against the ropes, dead-eyed, Layne reaches out to touch him ever so lightly on the cheek.

It's a haunting gesture, so intimate and unexpected that it begs imitation. Like Layne—like Champ—I want to reach out to Satterfield, to show my admiration. I want to tell him how glad I am to make his acquaintance, how grateful I am for the free instruction. More than all that, I suppose, I just want to thank him for the fight.

One day, after watching his greatest defeat, I visit his impostor.

"Heyyy," Champ says, beaming, waving hello. "What do you know about that? Hey, your picture ran through my mind many times, and then I'd say, well, my friend, he give me up."

He's wearing a white karate uniform, mismatched sneakers and a shirt from the Orange County Jail. Clouds of flies swarm around his head and grocery cart this warm November afternoon, Champ's 67th birthday. Tomorrow would have been Satterfield's 73rd.

There are many things about Champ that I don't know, things I'll probably never know. He either got money to be Satterfield, then forgot to drop the con, or wished he were Satterfield, then let the wish consume him. Not knowing doesn't bother me as I feared it would. Not getting his scrapbook doesn't torment me as I thought it might. Every man is a mystery, because manhood itself is so mysterious; that's what Champ taught me. Maturity means knowing when to solve another man's mystery, and when to respect it.

"Been traveling," I tell him. "And guess where I went?"

He cocks his head.

"Columbus. And guess who I saw? Your nephew, Gregory."

"That's my brother's son!"

"Yep. And guess who else I met. Big George."

He pulls a sour face, like his brother's, and we both laugh.

We talk about George, Lily and Lip, and Champ grows heavy with nostalgia. He recalls his childhood, particularly his stern father, who hit him so hard one day that he flayed the muscle along Champ's left bicep. Champ rolls up his sleeve to show me the mark, but I look away.

To cheer him up, to cheer us both up, I ask Champ to tell me once more about busting Marciano's nose.

"Marciano and I were putting on an exhibition that day," he says, crouching. "We were going good. But he had that long overhand right, and every time I seen it coming, I'd duck it. And I'd come up, and I'd keep hitting him on the tip of his nose."

He touches my nose with a gentle uppercut, flies trailing in the wake of his fist.

"On the tip, on the tip, I kept hitting," he says. "Finally, his nose started bleeding, and they stopped the fight."

Smiling now, more focused than I've ever seen him, Champ says he needs my advice. He's been reviewing his life lately, wondering what next. Times are hard, he says, and maybe he should head on down the road, polish up the

Cadillac and return to Columbus, though he fears the cold and what it does to an old boxer's bones.

"What do you think?" he says.

"I think you should go be with people who love you and care about you," I say.

"Yeah, that's true, that's true."

We watch the cars whizzing by, jets roaring overhead, strangers walking past.

"Well, Champ," I say, slipping him $5. "I've got to get going."

"Yeah, yeah," he says, stopping me. "Now, listen."

He rests one of his heavy hands on my shoulder, a gesture that makes me swallow hard and blink for some reason. I look into his eyes, and from his uncommonly serious expression, I know he's getting ready to say something important.

"I know you a long time," he says warmly, flashing that toothless smile, groping for the words. "Tell me your name again."

With your peers, watch the film *Resurrecting the Champ* (2007). In what ways does the film differ from Moehringer's essay? How is the character of the writer of the article portrayed differently in the film than in the actual article? Why do you think so?

"Resurrecting the Champ" is an essay about a boxer—a complex profile of Champ—but it is also about the author of the essay himself and about the profession of journalism. Who is Champ? Who is Satterfield? Can Champ be an authentic version of Satterfield...without actually being Satterfield? What role does the author play in this construction and reconstruction of the identities of both Champ and Satterfield? In an essay, explain how effectively Moehringer blends all three of these topics. How well does he profile Champ, tell his own story, and raise questions about his chosen profession?

Watch the film *Resurrecting the Champ* (2007) and find three reviews by critics (one published in a newspaper or magazine, one [by a professional movie critic] published online, and one provided on a site such as Amazon.com or Netflix.com by a viewer). How do these reviews differ from one another—in length, style, tone, etc.? How do the responses of these critics differ from your own feelings about or responses to the film? What criteria does each review seem to be applying in its analysis of the film? Are they the same criteria you would apply if you were to review the film?

James Frey is the author of three books: A Million Little Pieces, My Friend Leonard, *and* Bright Shiny Morning. *All three were national bestsellers. Frey writes, in* A Million Little Pieces, *excerpted here, of his struggles with addiction and his ultimate recovery. This memoir achieved its fame almost entirely because of its selection by Oprah Winfrey to be one of the books featured on her popular television program. It achieved its infamy with the aid of the journalists at the online publication* The Smoking Gun.

excerpt from
A MILLION LITTLE PIECES

By James Frey

CHAPTER 1

I wake to the drone of an airplane engine and the feeling of something warm dripping down my chin. I lift my hand to feel my face. My front four teeth are gone, I have a hole in my cheek, my nose is broken and my eyes are swollen nearly shut. I open them and I look around and I'm in the back of a plane and there's no one near me. I look at my clothes and my clothes are covered with a colorful mixture of spit, snot, urine, vomit and blood. I reach for the call button and I find it and I push it and I wait and thirty seconds later an Attendant arrives.

How can I help you?

Where am I going?

You don't know?

No.

You're going to Chicago, Sir.

How did I get here?

A Doctor and two men brought you on.

They say anything?

They talked to the Captain, Sir. We were told to let you sleep.

How long till we land?

About twenty minutes.

Thank you.

Although I never look up, I know she smiles and feels sorry for me. She shouldn't.

A short while later we touch down. I look around for anything I might have with me, but there's nothing. No ticket, no bags, no clothes, no wallet. I sit and I wait and I try to figure out what happened. Nothing comes.

Once the rest of the Passengers are gone I stand and start to make my way to the door. After about five steps I sit back down. Walking is out of the question. I see my Attendant friend and I raise a hand.

Are you okay?

No.

What's wrong?

I can't really walk.

If you make it to the door I can get you a chair.

How far is the door?

Not far.

I stand. I wobble. I sit back down. I stare at the floor and take a deep breath.

You'll be all right.

I look up and she's smiling.

Here.

She holds out her hand and I take it. I stand and I lean against her and she helps me down the Aisle. We get to the door.

I'll be right back.

I let go of her hand and I sit down on the steel bridge of the Jetway that connects the Plane to the Gate.

I'm not going anywhere.

She laughs and I watch her walk away and I close my eyes. My head hurts, my mouth hurts, my eyes hurt, my hands hurt. Things without names hurt.

I rub my stomach. I can feel it coming. Fast and strong and burning. No way to stop it, just close your eyes and let it ride. It comes and I recoil from the stench and the pain. There's nothing I can do.

Oh my God.

I open my eyes.

I'm all right.

Let me find a Doctor.

I'll be fine. Just get me out of here.

Can you stand?

Yeah, I can stand.

I stand and I brush myself off and wipe my hands on the floor and I sit down in the wheelchair she has brought me. She goes around to the back of the chair and she starts pushing.

Is someone here for you?

I hope so.

You don't know.

No.

What if no one's there?

It's happened before, I'll find my way.

We come off the Jetway and into the Gate. Before I have a chance to look around, my Mother and Father are standing in front of me.

Oh Jesus.

Please, Mom.

Oh my God, what happened?

I don't want to talk about it, Mom.

Jesus Christ, Jimmy. What in Hell happened?

She leans over and she tries to hug me. I push her away.

Let's just get out of here, Mom.

My Dad goes around to the back of the chair. I look for the Attendant but she has disappeared. Bless her.

You okay, James?

I stare straight ahead.

No, Dad, I'm not okay.

He starts pushing the chair.

Do you have any bags?

My Mother continues crying.

No.

People are staring.

Do you need anything?

I need to get out of here, Dad. Just get me the fuck out of here.

They wheel me to their car. I climb in the backseat and I take off my shirt and I lie down. My Dad starts driving, my Mom keeps crying, I fall asleep.

About four hours later I wake up. My head is clear but everything throbs. I sit forward and I look out the window. We've pulled into a Filling Station somewhere in Wisconsin. There is no snow on the ground, but I can feel the cold. My Dad opens the Driver's door and he sits down and he closes the door. I shiver.

You're awake.

Yeah.

How are you feeling?

Shitty.

Your Mom's inside cleaning up and getting supplies. You need anything?

A bottle of water and a couple bottles of wine and a pack of cigarettes.

Seriously?

Yeah.

This is bad, James.

I need it.

You can't wait.

No.

This will upset your Mother.

I don't care. I need it.

He opens the door and he goes into the Filling Station. I lie back down and I stare at the ceiling. I can feel my heart quickening and I hold out my hand and I try to keep it straight. I hope they hurry.

Twenty minutes later the bottles are gone. I sit up and I light a smoke and I take a slug of water. Mom turns around.

Better?

If you want to put it that way.

We're going up to the Cabin.

I figured.

We're going to decide what to do when we get there.

All right.

What do you think?

I don't want to think right now.

You're gonna have to soon.

Then I'll wait till soon comes.

We head north to the Cabin. Along the way I learn that my Parents, who live in Tokyo, have been in the States for the last two weeks on business. At four A.M. they received a call from a friend of mine who was with me at a Hospital and had tracked them down in a hotel in Michigan. He told them that I had fallen face first down a Fire Escape and that he thought they should find me some help. He didn't know what I was on, but he knew there was a lot of it and he knew it was bad. They had driven to Chicago during the night.

So what was it?

What was what?

What were you taking?

I'm not sure.

How can you not be sure?

I don't remember.

What do you remember?

Bits and pieces.

Like what?

I don't remember.

We drive on and after a few hard silent minutes, we arrive. We get out of the car and we go into the House and I take a shower because I need it. When I get out there are some fresh clothes sitting on my bed. I put them on and I go to my Parents' room. They are up drinking coffee and talking but when I come in they stop.

Hi.

Mom starts crying again and she looks away. Dad looks at me.

Feeling better?

No.

You should get some sleep.

I'm gonna.

Good.

I look at my Mom. She can't look back. I breathe.

I just.

I look away.

I just, you know.

I look away. I can't look at them.

I just wanted to say thanks. For picking me up.

Dad smiles. He takes my Mother by the hand and they stand and they come over to me and they give me a hug. I don't like it when they touch me so I pull away.

Good night.

Good night, James. We love you.

I turn and I leave their Room and I close their door and I go to the Kitchen. I look through the cabinets and I find an unopened half-gallon bottle of whiskey. The first sip brings my stomach back up, but after that it's all right. I go to my Room and I drink and I smoke some cigarettes and I think about her. I drink and I smoke and I think about her and at a certain point blackness comes and my memory fails me.

CHAPTER 2

Back in the car with a headache and bad breath. We're heading north and west to Minnesota. My Father made some calls and got me into a Clinic and I don't have any other options, so I agree to spend some time there and for now I'm fine with it. It's getting colder.

My face has gotten worse and it is hideously swollen. I have trouble speaking, eating, drinking, smoking. I have yet to look in a mirror.

We stop in Minneapolis to see my older Brother. He moved there after getting divorced and he knows how to get to the Clinic. He sits with me in the backseat and he holds my hand and it helps because I'm scared.

We pull into the Parking Lot and park the car and I finish a bottle and we get out and we start walking toward the Entrance of the Clinic. Me and my Brother and my Mother and my Father. My entire Family. Going to the Clinic. I stop and they stop with me. I stare at the Buildings. Low and long and connected. Functional. Simple. Menacing.

I want to run or die or get fucked up. I want to be blind and dumb and have no heart. I want to crawl in a hole and never come out. I want to wipe my existence straight off the map. Straight off the fucking map. I take a deep breath.

Let's go.

We enter a small Waiting Room. A woman sits behind a desk reading a fashion magazine. She looks up.

May I help you?

My Father steps forward and speaks with her as my Mother and Brother and I find chairs and sit in them.

I'm shaking. My hands and my feet and my lips and my chest. Shaking. For any number of reasons.

My Mother and Brother move next to me and they take my hands and they hold them and they can feel what is happening to me. We look at the floor and we don't speak. We wait and we hold hands and we breathe and we think.

My Father finishes with the woman and he turns around and he stands in front of us. He looks happy and the woman is on the phone. He kneels down.

They're gonna check you in now.

All right.

You're gonna be fine. This is a good place. The best place.

That's what I hear.

You ready?

I guess so.

We stand and we move toward a small Room where a man sits behind a desk with a computer. He meets us at the door.

I'm sorry, but you have to leave him here.

My Father nods.

We'll check him in and you can call later to make sure he's all right.

My Mother breaks down.

He's in the right place. Don't worry.

My Brother looks away.

He's in the right place.

I turn and they hug me. One at a time and hold tight. Squeezing and holding, I show them what I can. I turn and without a word I walk into the Room and the man shuts the door and they're gone.

The man shows me a chair and returns to his desk. He smiles.

Hi.

Hello.

How are you?

How do I look?

Not good.

I feel worse.

Your name is James. You're twenty-three. You live in North Carolina.

Yeah.

You're going to stay with us for a while. You okay with that?

For now.

Do you know anything about this Facility?

No.

Do you want to know anything?

I don't care.

He smiles, stares at me for a moment. He speaks.

We are the oldest Residential Drug and Alcohol Treatment Facility in the World. We were founded in 1949 in an old house that sat on the land where these Buildings, and there are thirty-two interconnected Buildings here, sit now. We have treated over twenty thousand Patients. We have the highest success rate of any Facility in the World. At any given time, there are between two hundred and two hundred and fifty Patients spread through six Units, three of which house men and three of which house women. We believe that Patients should stay here for as long a term as they need, not something as specific as a twenty-eight-day Program. Although it is expensive to come here, many of our Patients are here on scholarships that we fund and through subsidies that we support. We have an endowment of several hundred million dollars. We not only treat Patients, we are also one of the leading Research and Educational Institutions in the field of Addiction Studies. You should consider yourself fortunate to be here and you should be excited to start a new chapter in your life.

I stare at the man. I don't speak. He stares back at me, waiting for me to say something. There is an awkward moment. He smiles.

You ready to get started?

I don't smile.

Sure.

He gets up and I get up and we walk down a hall. He talks and I don't.

The doors are always open here, so if you want to leave, you can. Substance use is not allowed and if you're caught using or possessing, you will be sent Home. You are not allowed to say anything more than hello to any women aside from Doctors, Nurses or Staff Members. If you violate this rule, you will be sent Home. There are other rules, but those are the only ones you need to know right now.

We walk through a door into the Medical Wing. There are small Rooms and Doctors and Nurses and a Pharmacy. The cabinets have large steel locks. He shows me to a Room. It has a bed and a desk and a chair and a closet and a window. Everything is white.

He stands at the door and I sit on the bed.

A Nurse will be here in a few minutes to talk with you.

Fine.

You feel okay?

No, I feel like shit.

It'll get better.

Yeah.

Trust me.

Yeah.

The man leaves and he shuts the door and I'm alone. My feet bounce, I touch my face, I run my tongue along my gums. I'm cold and getting colder. I hear someone scream.

The door opens and a Nurse walks into the Room. She wears white, all white, and she is carrying a clipboard. She sits in the chair by the desk.

Hi, James.

Hi.

I need to ask you some questions.

All right.

I also need to check your blood pressure and your pulse.

All right.

What type of substances do you normally use?

Alcohol.

Every day?

Yes.

What time do you start drinking?

When I wake up.

She marks it down.

How much per day?

As much as I can.

How much is that?

Enough to make myself look like I do.

She looks at me. She marks it down.

Do you use anything else?

Cocaine.

How often?

Every day.

She marks it down.

How much?

As much as I can.

She marks it down.

In what form?

Lately crack, but over the years, in every form that it exists.

She marks it down.

Anything else?

Pills, acid, mushrooms, meth, PCP and glue.

Marks it down.

How often?

When I have it.

How often?

A few times a week.

Marks it down.

She moves forward and draws out a stethoscope.

How are you feeling?

Terrible.

In what way?

In every way.

She reaches for my shirt.

Do you mind?

No.

She lifts my shirt and she puts the stethoscope to my chest. She listens.

Breathe deeply.

She listens.

Good. Do it again.

She lowers my shirt and she pulls away and she marks it down.

Thank you.

I smile.

Are you cold?

Yes.

She has a blood pressure gauge.

Do you feel nauseous?

Yes.

She straps it on my arm and it hurts.

When was the last time you used?

She pumps it up.

A little while ago.

What and how much?

I drank a bottle of vodka.

How does that compare to your normal daily dosage?

It doesn't.

She watches the gauge and the dials move and she marks it down and she removes the gauge.

I'm gonna leave for a little while, but I'll be back.

I stare at the wall.

We need to monitor you carefully and we will probably need to give you some detoxification drugs.

I see a shadow and I think it moves but I'm not sure.

You're fine right now, but I think you'll start to feel some things.

I see another one. I hate it.

If you need me, just call.

I hate it.

She stands up and she smiles and she puts the chair back and she leaves.

I take off my shoes and I lie under the blankets and I close my eyes and I fall asleep.

I wake and I start to shiver and I curl up and I clench my fists. Sweat runs down my chest, my arms, the backs of my legs. It stings my face.

I sit up and I hear someone moan. I see a bug in the corner, but I know it's not there. The walls close in and expand they close in and expand and I can hear them. I cover my ears but it's not enough.

I stand. I look around me. I don't know anything. Where I am, why, what happened, how to escape. My name, my life.

I curl up on the floor and I am crushed by images and sounds. Things I have never seen or heard or ever knew existed. They come from the ceiling, the door, the window, the desk, the chair, the bed, the closet. They're coming from the fucking closet. Dark shadows and bright lights and flashes of blue and yellow and red as deep as the red of my blood. They move toward me and they scream at me and I don't know what they are but I know they're helping the bugs. They're screaming at me.

I start shaking. Shaking shaking shaking. My entire body is shaking and my heart is racing and I can see it pounding through my chest and I'm sweating and it stings. The bugs crawl onto my skin and they start biting me and I try to kill them. I claw at my skin, tear at my hair, start biting myself. I don't have any teeth and I'm biting myself and there are shadows and bright lights and flashes and screams and bugs bugs bugs. I am lost. I am completely fucking lost.

I scream.

I piss on myself.

I shit my pants.

The Nurse returns and she calls for help and Men in White come in and they put me on the bed and they hold me there. I try to kill the bugs but I can't move so they live. In me. On me. I feel the stethoscope and the gauge and they stick a needle in my arm and they hold me down.

I am blinded by blackness.

I am gone.

A NOTE TO THE READER

A Million Little Pieces is about my memories of my time in a drug and alcohol treatment center. As has been accurately revealed by two journalists at an Internet Web site, and subsequently acknowledged by me, during the process of writing the book, I embellished many details about my past experiences, and altered others in order to serve what I felt was the greater purpose of the book. I sincerely apologize to those readers who have been disappointed by my actions.

I first sat down to write the book in the spring of 1997. I wrote what is now the first forty pages of it. I stopped because I didn't feel ready to continue to do it, didn't think I was ready to express some of the trauma I had experienced. I started again in the fall of 2000. I had been working in the film industry and was deeply unsatisfied with what I was doing. I had wanted to write books and was writing films. I saved enough money to give myself eighteen months to write the book.

I didn't initially think of what I was writing as nonfiction or fiction, memoir or autobiography. I wanted to use my experiences to tell my story about addiction and alcoholism, about recovery, about family and friends and faith and love, about redemption and hope. I wanted to write, in the best-case scenario, a book that would change lives, would help people who were struggling, would inspire them in some way. I wanted to write a book that would detail the fight addicts and alcoholics experience in their minds and in their bodies, and detail why that fight is difficult to win. I wanted to write a book that would help the friends and family members of addicts and alcoholics understand that fight.

As I wrote, I worked primarily from memory. I also used supporting documents, such as medical records, therapists' notes, and personal journals, when I had them, and when they were relevant. I wanted the stories in the book to ebb and flow, to have dramatic arcs, to have the tension that all great stories require. I altered events and details all the way through the book. Some of those include my role in a train accident that killed a girl from my school. While I was not, in real-life, directly involved in the accident, I was profoundly affected by it. Others involved jail time I served, which in the book is three months, but which in reality was only several hours, and certain criminal events, including an arrest in Ohio, which was embellished. There has been much discussion, and dispute, about a scene in the book involving a root-canal procedure that takes place without anesthesia. I wrote that passage from memory, and have medical records that seem to support it. My account has been questioned by the treatment facility, and they believe my memory may be flawed.

In addition, names and identifying characteristics of all the treatment patients in the book and all of the facility's employees, characteristics including occupations, ages, places of residence, and places and means of death, were changed to protect the anonymity of those involved in this period in my life. This was done in the spirit of respecting every individual's anonymity, which is something we were urged to do while in treatment, and to continue to do after we left.

I made other alterations in my portrayal of myself, most of which portrayed me in ways that made me tougher and more daring and more aggressive than in reality I was, or I am. People cope with adversity in many different ways, ways that are deeply personal. I think one way people cope is by developing a skewed perception of themselves that allows them to overcome and do things they thought they couldn't do before. My mistake, and it is one I deeply regret, is writing about the person I created in my mind to help me cope, and not the person who went through the experience.

There is much debate now about the respective natures of works of memoir, nonfiction, and fiction. That debate will likely continue for some time, I believe, and I understand others strongly disagree, that memoir allows the writer to work from memory instead of from a strict journalistic or historical standard. It is about impression and feeling, about individual recollection. This memoir is a combination of facts about my life and certain embellishments. It is subjective truth, altered by the mind of a recovering drug addict and alcoholic. Ultimately, it's a story, and one that I could not have written without having lived the life I've lived.

I never expected the book to become as successful as it has, to sell anywhere close to the number of copies it has sold. The experience has been shocking for me, incredibly humbling, and at times terrifying. Throughout this process, I have met thousands of readers, and heard from many thousands more, who were deeply affected by the book, and whose lives were changed by it. I am deeply sorry to any readers who I have disappointed and I hope these revelations will not alter their faith in the book's central message—that drug addiction and alcoholism can be overcome, and there is always a path to redemption if you fight to find one. Thirteen years after I left treatment, I'm still on the path, and I hope, ultimately, I'll get there.

James Frey
New York
January 2006

As he writes his story, Frey is creative in his approach. Rather than following grammatical conventions, even with matters like capitalization and the use of quotation marks around spoken dialogue, Frey follows his own textual path. How does Frey's approach to the surface-level conventions of writing affect you as a reader? Are there places where you see writing like his, so that this seems completely acceptable? Or is this style so outside the norm that you find it difficult to interpret? Grammatical conventions change across time and in different situations, as you know: Both "ax" and "axe" are acceptable spellings. Any sentence that ends with a period could, depending on the author's intent, end with a question mark or exclamation point. The text message or email you send to a friend likely follows different (unwritten) rules than a text message or email to an older member of your family. So what's to stop any and every writer from taking Frey's approach to the situation—making up their own style and leaving readers to react as they will?

In an essay, explain how reading Frey's note to his readers influences your own reading of his memoir. If the writer admits to exaggerating some details in order to force the story to follow the conventions of dramatic storytelling, then how does the reader react to that story... which is supposed to be the "true" story of the writer's life? Ultimately, can any story that is dramatically narrated be entirely true—or does the very act of narration "turn life into literature" (to paraphrase Norman Maclean)? Can a story be fiction, even though it happened? Can a story be true, even if it never happened?

Is dramatic invention a natural part of the human drive to tell stories? Is there something almost natural or unavoidable about making a story better in the telling? If so, then isn't it natural for a writer of memoir—a genre focused on the personal experience of the past—to sometimes slip into the sort of exaggeration Frey has indulged?

AUTHENTICITY

According to the biography published in The Journal of American Culture, Geoff Hamilton was "a Killiam Postdoc-toral Fellow, affiliated with the Department of English, at the University of British Columbia." He now teaches at St. Olaf College, where his areas of specialization include modern literature and contemporary American culture. In this scholarly article, he considers the swirling chaos that occurs where authorship, identity, authenticity, and publishing cross paths.

MIXING MEMOIR AND DESIRE:
James Frey, Wound Culture, and the "Essential American Soul"

By Geoff Hamilton

I made other alterations in my portrayal of myself, most of which pictured me in ways that made me tougher and more daring and more aggressive than in reality I was, or I am. People cope with adversity in many different ways, ways that are deeply personal. I think one way people cope is by developing a skewed perception of themselves that allows them to overcome and do things they thought they couldn't do before. My mistake, and it is one I deeply regret, is writing about the person I created in my mind to help me cope, and not the person who went through the experience.

—James Frey's "a note to the reader," *A Million Little Pieces*

The imagined person we encounter in James Frey's blockbuster "memoir," *A Million Little Pieces* (*AMLP*) (2003), proved alluring not just to the author and supposed addict himself, but to an American public deeply interested in stories of recovery, personal transformation, and heroic self-reliance. The "James" of *AMLP*—troubled, swaggering, prone to violence, intimate with death, in hot pursuit of a radically autonomous selfhood—is close kin to a prominent type in the national literary canon, as well as a familiar protagonist in what Mark Seltzer calls contemporary "wound culture," where versions of that type and their relationship to "torn and opened private bodies and torn and opened psyches" (Seltzer 109) command extraordinary attention.

The popularity of "James," up until the public debunking of his authenticity, had much to do with his status as a contemporary permutation (if a rather pathetic one) of D.H. Lawrence's "essential American soul," the mythical New World man who is "hard, isolate, stoic, and a killer" (Lawrence 68). Fantasies of "regeneration through violence," as Richard Slotkin has so compellingly demonstrated in his studies of frontier mythology, still linger long after the closing of geographic frontiers (Slotkin, *Regeneration*; *Gunfighter*). Commenting from across the Atlantic on "the brash explicitness of American capitalism," Terry Eagleton puts the point bluntly: "The pioneer spirit [of the nation] was displaced rather than dissolved. The epic rapacity which subdued the land in the first place carried on as regular business. Probably no other people on earth use the word 'aggressive' in such a positive fashion, and no group outside psychoanalytic circles is so fond of the word 'dream'" (Eagleton 66). We find in *AMLP* an evocation—profound, timely, and disturbing—of the enduring magic of these words in the popular imagination.

Teasing out the literary and cultural affinities of Frey's imagined person or personified coping strategy helps us understand better, I suggest, the abiding attraction of radical autonomy as a personal ideal, along with the inevitable implication of violent action in such autonomy.

Frey's "non-fiction" book explores a young addict's time at a rehabilitation clinic, and it presents to us a pop-cultural protagonist we know well: the injured soul who overcomes daunting challenges, manages to heal, grow strong, and flourish, and who brings his pain and redemption to the public as abject confession and spiritual guide. The initial success of *AMLP* depended heavily on its claims to gritty realism in its public probing of private wounds, its supposed "honesty" in relaying the harrowing details of personal redemption, and of course also its visual legitimization in the form of the photogenic and brash young author himself, alive to tell the tale, who claimed in early interviews that he wanted to be "the f—ing best" writer of his generation (qtd. in Valby 64).[1] This was a story, above all, about success in self-creation.

When Frey's claims to have written a true story were revealed as largely fraudulent by journalists at thesmokinggun.com and by Oprah Winfrey, a former patron, his authority as an honest evangelist was sabotaged.[2]

teaching

That the book strains credulity (or should) on nearly every page—from its preternaturally stoic and arrogant narrator, to its preposterously stereotyped supporting cast, to its relentless maudlin plot twists—is a curious and rather overlooked element of this saga. Every con artist relies on some susceptibility in his audience, and for Frey part of this was his readers' desire for a protagonist with an exceptional command of the spectacle of the wound.[3] Frey's imaginary self, the narrator I will call "James," secures this authority in a number of ways. Most important among these, perhaps, is his ferocious dispatch of rivals as he stakes his narrative claim on his own torn body and psyche. Though damaged by addiction, James insists that he "just won't let [him]self be a victim," and adds that "People in here, People everywhere, they all want to take their own problems, usually created by themselves, and try to pass them off on someone or something else" (Frey 272). Such an assertion reduces other wounded souls to the status of mere whiners or weak-willed impostors, while James constructs himself as a paragon of independence—honest, tough and clear-eyed, blaming no one, a rugged individualist. He may *formerly* have been dependent on drugs, but now, *rara avis*, he is dependent on nothing.

Pity is another password in James's strategizing, for he suggests, amid all this radical independence and contempt for other wounded aspirants, his openness to the world and its suffering. As John Dolan notes acerbically in his review of *AMLP*,[4] the book's conclusion is full of "bizarrely detailed descriptions of every single hug and tearful farewell between [James] and his new pals," and "[James] and his tough-guy friends spend more time weeping and hugging than the runners-up in a Miss America competition" (Dolan). While complicating the construction of James' archaic manliness, the narrative's emphasis on empathic displays further consolidates its exemplary position in wound culture. The rhetorical move from passion to *com*passion reminds the audience that, in spite of the aloofness of this distinctively wounded man, it may still imagine itself as "a public that meets in pathology" (Seltzer 138). James may be contemptuous of the cult of victimology, but he holds open the imaginative possibility of gathering round his wounds for mutual consolation.

Even more intriguingly, James is not merely more courageous and knowing than others about his suffering—though he always reminds us that he is both— but also, in an ominous and enigmatic turn, a man with the potential *to inflict wounds*. *AMLP*, in telling its story of contemporary self-reliance, presents a dangerous self whose autonomy is claimed through a privileged intimacy with violence. What James calls "The Fury," a sort of seething will-to-destruction within him, is identified as the source of his troubled life and drug abuse. The frightening reality, he claims, is that "I want to kill kill kill" (Frey 285), an inclination that, whether directed within or without, is an essential condition of his existence. It is only by continually struggling against this dark force that James can fashion his individuality.

AMLP relies on the most macerated cultural clichés in order to tell its story of redemption, but it does so cunningly, with enough ferocity and indefatigable insistence to satisfy the contemporary hunger for true tales of wounding. Frey proffers, as Lawrence says of James Fenimore Cooper, that older mythographer of the half-savage, "a wish-fulfilment vision, a kind of yearning myth," full of spurious assumptions that are yet "real in their way, and almost prophetic" (Lawrence 56). An important element of the success of Frey's book, I suggest, is the way it uses the strategies outlined above to conjure two broad fantasies, however paradoxical: on the one hand, of a paradise of limitless empathy exchanged over mutual woundedness, a fusion of the individual with the genial Other in which all barriers between persons deliquesce in a sort of lachrymal *jouissance*; on the other, of a heroic resistance to every mode of inclusion, in which the sneering isolato, after enduring a trip through the underworld defined by the mythology of the American frontier, emerges self-reliant and contemptuous of all organization. The former is the official fantasy embraced by Oprah Winfrey in her initial endorsement of *AMLP*, and it is summed up by Frey in his apology and apologia to readers as "there is always a path to redemption if you fight to find one" (*AMLP*). The latter is its antisocial but alluring shadow, a sadistic fantasy of the individual's eternal "fight" that is made socially acceptable by the balm of its virtuous counterpart.

Examining the public embrace of these fantasies, particularly in light of Lawrence's *Studies in Classic American Literature*, reveals some of the important features of a "national malady of trauma and violence" (Seltzer 6), for James Frey's work and its reception are uncannily symptomatic—real in their way and almost prophetic—of the "abnormal normalcy" (6) of America's wound culture.

> And Natty, what sort of a white man is he? Why, he is a man with a gun. He is a killer, a slayer. Patient and gentle as he is, he is a slayer. Self-effacing, self-forgetting, still he is a killer.
>
> —D.H. Lawrence, *Studies in Classic American Literature*

AMLP opens *in cruentus media res*, its wounded narrator hurtling along through a mile-high existential void: "I wake to the drone of an airplane engine and the feeling of something warm dripping down my chin. I lift my hand to feel my face. My front four teeth are gone, I have a hole in my cheek, my nose is broken and my eyes are swollen nearly shut. I open them and I look around and I'm in the back of a plane and there's no one near me" (Frey 1). Lost in the wildernesses of addiction and scarred by battle, James has been summoned to a rehabilitation facility, or outpost, in Minnesota, where he will have the chance to overcome his chemical dependence. The stakes, of course, are high. As a counselor named Joanne tells him: "James, you are an incredibly Addicted Person. You have been told by qualified Doctors that any drug or alcohol use is going to kill you" (Frey 196).[5]

James may have escaped death by making it to the facility, but *killing* will remain essential to what he experiences there. His drug abuse, he repeatedly tells us, is intimately linked with an urge both suicidal and homicidal. Describing the after effects of a drug binge, he recalls feeling "fear, dread and a murderous rage" (44). His aggression is often directed inwards—"[I] need to kill. Kill my heart, kill my mind, kill myself" (44)—but it also manifests itself in conflicts with other dangerous men. The most impressive of these is an older addict at the facility named Leonard—familiar as the cliché of a hardened mobster with a tender inner core—who authenticates James' lethality: "I'm not scared of anyone and you scare the shit out of me. Ed and Ted won't eat with me anymore 'cause they're worried that you might snap on them, and all day all anybody talked about was how you stared Lincoln down and laughed in his face when he tried to get rough with you" (97). The narrator's macho posturing in such scenes suggests a burlesque distillation of Hemingway, with an occasional stiff nod towards Norman Mailer's theoretical ballast. Watching a boxing match, James is moved to expound on the fundamentally violent nature of all men: "[Fighting] ignites in us our true selves, the selves that have been diluted by thousands of years of culture and refinement, the selves that we are constantly told to deny for the greater good" (335).[6] The world of addicts, criminals, and the down-and-out that James confronts while in rehab is positioned much closer to this "true self," and he becomes, like Cooper's Bumppo and other frontier heroes, the rare man who will mediate between the savage and the civilized, surviving the former and invigorating the latter. Some *individual* good, based on a physical dynamism usually tamed by cultural inhibitions, is part of what he learns to cultivate. In doing so he will seek to ratify Mailer's provocative assertion, made at the beginning of the 1960s, that "the message locked within the labyrinth of the genes would insist that violence was locked with creativity, and adventure was the secret of love" (Mailer, "Superman" 39–40).

In a discussion with Leonard, James explains some of the history of his violent impulses:

> I've always felt these things. I don't think there are any words that describe them exactly, but they are a combination of rage, anger, extreme pain. They mix together into what I call the Fury. I have known the Fury for as long as I can remember. It is the one thing that has been with me throughout my entire life. I am starting to learn how to deal with it, but until recently, the only way I knew was through drinking and drugs. I took something, whatever it was, and if I took enough of it, the Fury would subside. The problem was that it would always come back, usually stronger, and that would require more and stronger substances to kill it, and that was always the goal, to kill it. From the first time I drank, I knew drinking would kill it. From the first time I took drugs, I knew drugs would kill it. I took them willingly, not because of some genetic link or some function of some disease, but because I knew they would kill the goddamn Fury. Even though I knew I was killing myself, killing the Fury was more important. (268)

James' repetition of "kill" is a crucial hyperbole, as the description is of a metaphorical opponent who "always come[s] back," who *will not die*. The agony of addiction thus involves an immortal foe who endlessly returns to enrage and be slain, with the narrator becoming a sort of serial killer of the divided mind or wounded will.[7] Dismissing the biological determinism of any "genetic link or some function of some disease" (268), James positions this violent drama as entirely within the ambit of that will. He ultimately resists the temptations of drug abuse *and* the notion of addiction as disease, even winning over Joanne, the chief wise woman of the outpost. She confirms the young man's distinction by dubbing him "the single most stubborn Person that I've ever met," while also admitting that "Despite the fact that I can't really endorse or condone your philosophy, I am gradually becoming a Believer" (272).

James' dark adventures as an addict, in which he "Drank smoked got arrested doled out a beating or two took a beating or two cheated lied deceived used women slept with prostitutes took more money [...]" (351), are indispensable to his authenticity as a survivor. He is the protagonist in a kind of contemporary captivity narrative, and his struggles to escape are what define his heroism, his forging of an exceptional self-reliance. James amplifies this heroism, putting his aggression to good use, by rescuing Lilly, the love interest he finds in rehab, from a captivity within a captivity when she relapses into addiction. Tracking her down at a crackhouse, he must first negotiate with one of its gatekeepers, a kind of native warrior wearing "expensive basketball shoes" and possessing a voice "Deep and thick like a sledgehammer with Ghetto inflections" (311). James, of course, knows what to do: "I hold his stare, but not in an aggressive way. I hold it passively and in a relaxed manner, without fear and with patience" (312). Entering the house, James receives the curses of one of its denizens: "There ain't nothing here, Motherfucker, there ain't nothing for you, you dirty white Devil you dirty white Pig" (314). Discovering Lilly in sexual congress with an "old man," James takes action: "He reaches for a bottle I see it out of the corner of my eye and I stop and I turn around and I take one step toward him. He's within striking distance and he has a bottle in his hand. I strike. A quick hard backhand across one of his cheeks. It stuns him and I take another step forward. He shrinks against the wall and I stare at him" (315).

This rescue—melodramatic, decisive, more than faintly ridiculous—nevertheless conforms to Richard Slotkin's definition of the function of the early American captivity narrative as "archetypal drama":

> In it a single individual, usually a woman, stands passively under the strokes of evil, awaiting rescue by the grace of God. The sufferer represents the whole, chastened body of Puritan society; and the temporary bondage of the captive to the Indian is dual paradigm—of the bondage of the soul to the flesh and to the temptations arising from original sin, and of the self-exile of the English Israel from England. In the Indian's devilish clutches, the captive had to meet and reject the temptation of Indian marriage and/or the Indian's "cannibal" Eucharist. To partake of the Indian's love or of his equivalent of bread and wine was to debase, to un-English the very soul. The captive's ultimate redemption by the grace of Christ and the efforts of the Puritan magistrates is likened to the regeneration of the soul

in conversion. The ordeal is at once threatful of pain and evil and promising of ultimate salvation. Through the captive's proxy, the promise of a similar salvation could be offered to the faithful among the reading public, while the captive's torments remained to harrow the hearts of those not yet awakened to their fallen nature. (Slotkin, *Regeneration* 94-95)

Lilly is ultimately lost, but James resists being contaminated by the "savagery" he confronts, and it is in confronting it that his exceptional character is made. When a fellow patient tries to provoke him by revealing that Lilly has traded sex for drugs and been gang-raped, he must channel his aggression—"The Fury is at full strength. I want to kill kill kill" (Frey 285)—in order to ward off a fear of contamination, here literalized by his antagonist: "If I were you, I'd be careful. That Girl's got some dangerous shit floating around inside of her, and if she hasn't already, she'll probably give you something that'll make your dick fall off" (285). James' encounters with racialized others exhibit, as Philip L. Simpson notes in his discussion of Joyce Carol Oates' serial-killer novel *Zombie* (1995), "the bipolar degree to which American individualism both privileges itself as a hermetic construction and fears/covets the Other for what untapped depths it may harbor" (Simpson 171). In challenging the "savage Other" who threatens a permanent estrangement from civilization, in battling that foe and not succumbing, James is able to empower himself and realize what Slotkin calls the "'moral truth' of the frontier [...] that violence and savage war [are] the necessary instruments of American progress" (Slotkin, *Gunfighter* 77).

What is being created in James' struggles, as he constructs them, is a paragon of self-reliance able to channel the reservoir of aggression represented by "the Fury" into hyper-masculine action. Whatever this self is, its radical solitude is definitive in establishing its authenticity as an alienated soul, and the *self-completeness* of its triumph over addiction. James says of the pain he finds at the dentist: "I have always dealt with pain alone. I will deal with it alone now" (65). Later, even more grandly, he insists that "Belonging is not something I have ever concerned myself with and is not something I give two shits about. I have lived alone. I am about to die alone" (94). In discovering a reason to live, James' aloneness has not been abandoned but simply redirected. Exiting rehab and its institutional methods of deliverance, he tests his resolve by immediately going to a bar. Demanding a "pint glass" full of hard liquor from a quizzical bartender, he adopts an aggressive posture, "[letting the man] know that I'm not leaving until I have it" (379). As James debates whether to give in to temptation, he once again confronts his unruly opponent: "The Fury rises from its silent state it screams bloody fucking murder it is stronger than it has ever been before. It screams you are mine, Motherfucker. You are mine and you will always be mine" (380).[8] Having rejected the idea of addiction as a "disease," or something beyond the control of the will, James makes possible a complete triumph of willpower: "Addiction is a decision. [...] Each and every time" (258). That decision is, finally, to be out of control—"an Addict"—or in control—"a human" (258), while any other explanation is simply "an excuse" (258). The main part of the book ends with James' victory, which he claims is entirely his own: "I have a decision to make. It is a simple decision. It has nothing to do with God or Twelve of anything other than twelve beats of my heart. Yes or no. It is [sic] simple decision. Yes or no" (381).[9]

Making oneself on one's own is intimately linked to violence, as James suggests in his definition of the ultimate male *telos*: "To stand alone in front of another man and to either hurt him or be hurt is what men were built to do. Boxing allows us to live with the most base of those instincts, and to still feel a sense of what it is like to fight" (335). As Seltzer notes in relation to acts of serial murder, such a dynamic of self-creation typically emerges as "a male violence that is anti-female and anti-homosexual, or more exactly a male violence that is directed at the antimale or '*unmale*'" (Seltzer 67). Efforts to generate the independent self rely on maintaining gendered differences, while "failures of self-distinction—the dissolution of the man in the flood/crowd—are instantly referred to the terms of sexual difference and the terms of sexual difference to spectacular public violence" (n. 230). In order to define and defend his manhood, James fights off homosexual advances (Frey 76), and even tells of brutally attacking a French priest who sexually propositions him, an act for which, he says, "I don't feel regret or remorse" (360).[10] Self-dissolution is continually countered by such brazen declarations, which reinforce the will's potent autonomy, its telling separation.

James strives to assert this separation in publicizing his wounds, and fittingly, many of his most rage-filled moments occur when he is made to sit in an audience and hear other addicts publicizing *their* stories. Hearing, as he puts it, "a man about my own age [...] telling his life story," James distances himself from this potential *doppelgänger* by belittling his claims to genuine woundedness: "I suspect that this man would have joined a Twelve Step Group had he felt he had been watching too much television or eating too many hot dogs or playing too much Space Invaders picking his goddamn nose too many times a day" (94). James sums up another rival's "life story" as a failure at self-distinction: "He was bad and he joined AA and now he's good. I have heard it too many times" (Frey 190). On another occasion, after watching a television drama in which a young woman overcomes her addiction to heroin, he proffers a revenge fantasy in which he exposes the show's authors as false messengers:

> If I could, I would hunt down the Creators of this utter bullshit fantasy fairy-tale piece of crap and I would lock them in a room and feed them drugs until they were profoundly and chronically Addicted to them. Then I would overdose them, drive them to the nearest inner-city ER, and I would drop them off at the door, right next to the homeless Guys with knives, the Addicts with AIDS and the Cops and the Ambulance Drivers smoking cigarettes. I'd leave them there for a couple of days, and then I'd come back and check on them. If they were still alive or still around, which would be highly unlikely, I'd ask them if their experience has in any way whatsoever resembled the experience they presented to the Public. (112-13)

In the competition for an audience, the authenticity of one's knowledge is the guarantee of self-distinction, and James repeatedly imagines himself as a righteously violent truth-monger slaying his fraudulent rivals. After listening to a "Rock Star" who makes extravagant claims about his drug consumption, James remarks that if he had more energy, he would "chase this Chump Motherfucker down and give him a beating," make him apologize to his audience, and finally warn him about further fabrications: "After the apology, I tell him that if I ever heard of him spewing his bullshit fantasies in Public again, I would cut off his precious hair, scar his precious lips, and take all of his goddamn gold records and shove them straight up his ass" (159).

"Public," one of the nouns James chooses to capitalize, is the key term in these passages, for it is in public that James exposes his wounds, and in public that he will or will not achieve self-distinction. These scenes thus expose, in Seltzer's formulation, the "radical entanglement between serial violence and the problem of the crowd or the mass," and they are terrifying for James because in "the merging of the individual into the crowd" (Seltzer 237), the masculine, reliant self is lost—dissolved—in space. James' imperative for self-creation is to be *in command* of a public (a self worth listening to by the mass), but not in any way *of it* (a self radically set apart from the mass). As he puts it, "I am not going to be dependent on anything but myself" (363)—an implicit revision of the first epigraph to Emerson's "Self Reliance," "Ne te quaesiveris extra" ("Do not seek yourself outside [yourself]").

James' failure at this autogenetic enterprise is betrayed not just by the appalling triteness of his rhetoric, but also by the vindictiveness of his stance, a revenge against self-dissolution characterized by Nietzsche as *ressentiment*. Seltzer notes the relation of this concept to contemporary wound culture:

> *Ressentiment*, in short, seeks to deaden the pain of relentless self-exposure and failed self-accountability in two directions: by externalizing it (locating a site, or another, on which to revenge one's wound) and by generalizing it (remaking the world in the image of the wound, an injury landscape and a wound culture). The "sovereign subordinated subject" thus achieves its revenge through the imposition of suffering and through the predication of a culture of suffering. (Seltzer 117)

A paragon of *ressentiment*, James is patently self-deceived when he insists that he "just won't let [him]self be a victim" (Frey 272). *Always* feeling himself a victim, he pursues a radical independence that calls out for serial, public displays of violence: "This is the subject who finds that he is not himself, who discovers that his proper being is over there, in that double who enrages him; and who thus expels this exteriority or extimacy within, converting stranger intimacy into stranger violence" (Seltzer 146). Here we might think of James as aspiring to brotherhood with Natty Bumppo but finding himself instead a blood(y) relation of Edgar Allan Poe's William Wilson, fearing the proximity, inside and out, of his double: "[In] spite of the bravado with which in public I made a point of treating him and his pretensions, I secretly felt that I feared him, and could not help thinking the equality which he maintained so easily with myself, a proof of his true superiority" (Poe 630). Such a figure fails at what matters most to him—*being himself alone*—and the apocalyptic endpoint of his failure is a suicidal assault on some mirrored image.

The last words of the main part of *AMLP* are James' "Yes, I'm ready" (382), followed by an epilogue giving a brief summary of what is alleged to have happened to the narrative's other characters. Many of these are dead or presumed so, furnishing a final touch of ostensibly brutal reality. Belying the tragic outcomes, however, is what has been glimpsed by the narrator during his trip through the wilderness. The book's goodbye scenes, so beautifully parodied by Dolan in his review, are indeed crucial to the appeal of James' message, for they suggest, however implausibly, the ultimate benignity of the "savage world" that has been endured. James' last meeting with Lincoln, a counsellor and recovering addict, in which the men "hold strong and firm [...] stare in each other's eyes and there is a bond of respect" (312), and his discussions with Leonard, the career criminal who strangely asks to "adopt" him as his "son" (345), reinforce the enormous potential of violent adventure and manly endurance for fostering comradeship as well as the autonomous self. Lethal aggression is neatly converted to compassion in the men's bonding, an alchemy exposed tropologically in James' comforting of an older man named Miles:

> He looks down and he shakes his head. I stand up and I walk over to him and I lean over and I put my arms around him and I hug him. He hugs me back and he starts crying. I don't know what to say, so I say nothing. I hug him and I let him hug me and I hope that somehow and in whatever way, I am helping him. [...] His crying becomes sobbing becomes violent sobbing. He squeezes me tight. I have my arms around him they are my only weapon against his grief. We sit and he cries and I hold him. Whatever has happened has happened he'll talk about it if he wants to talk my arms are my only weapon. We sit and Miles cries.
>
> Violent sobs become sobs becomes crying. (329)

The dark imperative of "kill kill kill" has been sublimated here into fraternal displays, as weapons are turned over, in a kind of spiritual amnesty, for hugs and tears. By the end of *AMLP* James has become what Lawrence says of Natty Bumppo, "a saint with a gun" (Lawrence 55). The fellow addicts and down-and-outs he has encountered are revealed, moreover, as versions of what Lawrence said of Cooper's Indians, "gentlemen through and through, though they may take an occasional scalp" (55).

Lawrence's discussion of Michel de Crèvecoeur offers further incisive commentary on the kind of fantasy at work here. The French-American's *Letters from an American Farmer* (1782), which defined for many Europeans the lineaments of the American Dream, reads like a proleptic exposé of *AMLP*.[11] Both Crèvecoeur and Frey subordinate the inveterately antipathetic qualities of their worlds to a sentimental image of the "natural man"—in Frey the abject wounded—as "an object of undefiled brotherliness" (35):

> [Crèvecoeur] wanted, of course, to imagine the dark, savage way of life, to get it all off pat in his head. He wanted to know as the Indians and savages know, darkly, and in terms of otherness. He was simply crazy, as the Americans say, for this. Crazy enough! For at the same time he was absolutely determined that Nature is sweet and pure, that all men are brothers, and equal, and that they love one another like so many cooing doves. He was determined to have life according to his own prescription. Therefore, he wisely kept away from any too close contact with Nature, and took refuge in commerce and the material world. But yet, he was determined to know the savage way of life, to his own *mind's* satisfaction. So he just faked us the last *Letters*. A sort of wish-fulfillment. (35–36)

James' wish, for a "dark, savage way of life" that assembles a public in redemptive commiseration, dramatically exposes the basic duplicity sustaining contemporary wound culture: an insistence on the explicit display of real wounds (or what passes for them), coupled with an unreal deliverance from them.

A half century ago, Mailer diagnosed totalitarian cultural tendencies and conformism as major evils threatening American selfhood, while prescribing a hearty dose of hipsterism as some kind of partial cure. "One is Hip or one is Square," he wrote provocatively in "The White Negro" (1955) of the nation's essential either/or, "[...] one is a rebel or one conforms, one is a frontiersman in the Wild West of American night life, or else a Square cell, trapped in the totalitarian tissues of American society, doomed willy-nilly to conform if one is to succeed" (313). James' neo-hipster tale of radical, hard-fought autonomy plumps wholeheartedly for a night out in the wilds, its hero donning the rugged accoutrements of individualism in order to avoid conformist doom, while proffering an invitation to the masses to join him, so long as no one encroaches on the frontiersman's prickly need for space. The implausibility of this course of treatment, at least in its popular conception, was made clear by the exposure of Frey as a rather creepy fantasist (or, in the frank term employed by Oprah Winfrey in her eventual pillorying of him, a liar). Assaults on the truth proliferate so wildly and maddeningly in today's media that this author's fabrications may seem venial, or merely an example of postmodern convention. The public's receptivity to Frey's frontier fantasy, however, deserves special scrutiny, for it suggests, darkly, the enduring imaginative resonance among Americans of Lawrence's "essential soul" and his forbidding mythos.

NOTES

1. Daniel Nester, writing in the summer of 2005, summarizes the early success of Frey's work:

> *A Million Little Pieces* garnered critical praise across the board—the *New Yorker* called it "frenzied, electrifying"—and it received blurbs from film director Gus Van Sant and novelist Bret Easton Ellis. It was a *New York Times* best-seller and Amazon's No. 1 title of 2003. There were nationwide book tours for the hardcover *and* paperback releases, and movie rights were sold. Frey wrote the screenplay. The movie is now in production, slated for a 2006 release. (Nester 32)

The proposed movie has been shelved.

2. *AMLP* reached superbook status in the fall of 2005 when Oprah Winfrey selected it for her book club. It had sold 3.5 million copies by the end of that year, making it the second best-selling book of the year behind *Harry Potter and the Half-Blood Prince* (Grossman 58). In January of 2006, journalists from the online site thesmokinggun.com exposed some of the many fabrications and exaggerations in Frey's memoir, and the author was ultimately subjected to a humiliating confrontation with an outraged Winfrey on her talk show.

3. Frey, in this regard, is both commander and commanded, as his unreserved mixing of truth and fiction, memory and desire, suggests his kinship with Seltzer's serial killers, "pathological subjects" in whom there is a "direct, traumatic communication between inside and outside, private and public spheres," and in which the "passage from fantasy to act (the literalization of word in thing, fantasy in act)" reveals "the opening of a passage between private desire and public acts" (Seltzer 146).

4. Dolan, a book reviewer for the online magazine *eXile*, was one of the first to note the gross implausibility of many of the events depicted in *AMLP*, as well as the book's egregious reliance on sentimental and masculinist clichés

(he titled his review "A Million Pieces of Shit," and opens it by declaring that "This is the worst thing I've ever read" (Dolan "AMPS")).

5. James' idiosyncratic punctuation—an element, of course, of his fierce individualism—includes the capitalization of some nouns.

6. Also palpable here, though without the satire, is Chuck Palahniuk's satirical novel *Fight Club* (1996):

> You aren't alive anywhere like you're alive at fight club. When it's you and one other guy under that one light in the middle of all those watching. Fight club isn't about winning or losing fights. Fight club isn't about words. You see a guy come to fight club for the first time, and his ass is a loaf of white bread. You see this same guy here six months later, and he looks carved out of wood. This guy trusts himself to handle anything. There's grunting and noise at fight club like at the gym, but fight club isn't about looking good. There's hysterical shouting in tongues like at church, and when you wake up Sunday afternoon you feel saved. (Palahniuk 51)

7. It is unclear whether James has in mind the Greek Furies, avengers from the underworld, but the suggestion of some kind of otherworldly influence in the creation of his character is certainly palpable. Whatever it is that James encounters in becoming himself, it transcends the merely social.

8. Looking into the pint glass, James confronts his own reflection: "I look into myself. Into the pale green of my own eyes. I like what I see. I am comfortable with it. It is fixed and focused. It will not blink. For the first time in my life, as I look into my own eyes, I like what I see" (381). This passage is oddly redolent of Emerson's famous moment of transcendence in "Nature": "Standing on the bare ground,—my head bathed by the blithe air, and uplifted into infinite space,—all mean egotism vanishes. I become a transparent eye-ball; I am nothing; I see all; the currents of the Universal Being circulate through me; I am part or particle of God" (Emerson 24).

9. James' narrative has, of course, a lot to do with God. St. Augustine's *Confessions*—to which, like other works in the rehab genre, this text owes a great debt—is the ancestral voice being mimicked here (knowingly or not) in the text's structural patterning of the lost soul's movement towards redemption. As Charles Guignon says of Augustine's story,

It finds inner correlates for the biblical notions of beginning, fall, world-defining moment of transformation and salvation, and presents an individual's life as having a narrative structure organized around the idea of salvation. This Christian *soteriological* storyline, in which all events are organized and given meaning in relation to the concern with salvation, provides the narrative schema that continues to shape almost all our self-narratives to this day. (Guignon 15)

10. Dolan remarks of this anachronistic confession: "It's odd that a novel in which a gay-bashing [attempted] murder is treated so casually should be so esteemed in the U.S. I thought y'all had decided that it was no longer OK to beat gay men to death for casual come-ons. But then the US is moving back in time so quickly that perhaps I'm thinking of a moment now far in the future" (Dolan).

11. Crèvecoeur, in a lovely coincidence, employed a fictional narrator in his epistles named James.

WORKS CITED

Dolan, John. "A Million Pieces of Shit." *the eXile*. 167. 29 May 2003. 26 Sept. 2006 (http://www.exile.ru/2003-May-29/book_review.html)

Eagleton, Terry. *Holy Terror*. Oxford: Oxford UP, 2005.

Emerson, Ralph Waldo. "Nature." *Selections from Ralph Waldo Emerson*. Ed. Stephen E. Whicher. Boston: Houghton Mifflin, 1960. 21–56.

————. "Self Reliance." *Selections from Ralph Waldo Emerson*. Ed. Stephen E. Whicher. Boston: Houghton Mifflin, 1960. 147–68.

Frey, James. *A Million Little Pieces*. New York: Doubleday, 2003.

Grossman, Lev. "The Trouble with Memoirs." *Time* 23 Jan. 2006, 167–4: 58.

Guignon, Charles. *On Being Authentic*. London: Routledge, 2004.

Lawrence, D.H. *Studies in Classic American Literature*. London: Penguin, 1977.

Mailer, Norman. "Superman Comes to the Supermarket." *The Presidential Papers*. New York: G.P. Putnam's Sons, 1963.

Nester, Daniel. "The Transformation of James Frey." *Poets & Writers* (July/August 2005) 33.4: 30–34.

The Oprah Winfrey Show. 26 Jan. 2006. King World Productions.

Poe, Edgar Allan. "William Wilson." *Complete Tales and Poems of Edgar Allan Poe*. New York: Vintage, 1975. 626–41.

Seltzer, Mark. *Serial Killers: Death and Life in America's Wound Culture*. New York: Routledge, 1998.

Simpson, Philip L. *Psycho Paths: Tracking the Serial Killer Through Contemporary American Film and Fiction*. Carbondale: Southern Illinois UP, 2000.

Slotkin, Richard. *Regeneration Through Violence: The Mythology of the American Frontier, 1600–1860*. Norman: U of Oklahoma P, 1973.

———. *Gunfighter Nation: The Myth of the Frontier in Twentieth-Century America*. Norman: U of Oklahoma P, 1998.

Valby, Karen. "James Frey Does Not Care What You Think About Him (Please Love Him)." *Entertainment Weekly* No. 703, 4 Apr. 2003: 60–64.

Explore

How do you define the following genres of nonfiction writing, both on their own and in relation to each other: history, biography, autobiography, journalism, personal essay, and memoir? Is each of these types of writing held to a different standard of "truth"? Why?

Compose

In his note to his readers, James Frey explains the flaws in the absolute accuracy of his memoir in personal and publishing-related ways. His drive to exaggerate, he writes, was driven by his larger-than-life version of himself that he created as a coping mechanism, and the changes in events (or in his involvement in those events) occurred because of his desire to see his life fit more neatly into a narrative pattern, with rising action, a climax, and resolution. Hamilton places the matter in a much larger cultural context, however—one that goes well beyond exaggeration and the demands of narrative structure. In an essay, consider both Frey's note and Hamilton's argument about American mythology. In what ways do the two texts make similar arguments about the facts and fictions in *A Million Little Pieces*?

Collaborate

In a discussion with your peers, consider this: When Oprah Winfrey selected James Frey's memoir as a part of her book club, she made him a very famous writer, a household name in America and beyond (no small feat in a nation where as many as 60,000 new books appear each year). When the Web site The Smoking Gun exposed James Frey as a liar and fraud (to use the most extreme words applied to him), Oprah Winfrey did her best to destroy Frey. In your reading of the situation—and you may want to consult the expose in The Smoking Gun for an elaboration on Frey's failings in relation to truth, along with video from the *Oprah Winfrey Show* (both when the book was popular and after the scandal broke)—how fair is this to Frey? He told a story that, true or not, affected millions of readers. True or not, the story had power to move its readers. Does its baseline reality matter?

According to her biographical note at Bark, Amaris Ketcham "is an honorary Kentucky Colonel and the former Managing Editor of Willow Springs." Her work has appeared most recently in Rio Grande Review and Utne Reader. In the blog entry that follows, Ketcham considers, in a humorous way, just how complicated the matter is when readers attempt to establish the truthfulness of a given piece of nonfiction.

HOW TO DETERMINE TRUTH

By Amaris Ketcham

Perhaps you've already seen the scale over at Nieman Storyboard for determining the "truth" (read: facts) of a memoir. If not, here it is:

Every memoir starts with 100 points.

A. Demonstrated inaccuracies. Subtract 0-40 points.

B. Does the book reflect negatively on identifiable people (dead or alive), or is it clearly in service of proving political or moral positions? Subtract 0-25 points.

C. Did the author try to corroborate facts with outside sources? Add 0-5 points.

D. Some word-for-word dialogue is necessary but it is factually problematic. Subtract 1 point for each percent of text composed of dialogue.

E. Cliches, flat writing and poor word choices suggest a lack of mature and considered reflection on the past. Subtract 0-15 points for bad writing.

F. Statements in text laying out clear ground rules vis a vis truth. Add 0-10 points.

G. Self-deprecation or self-criticism. Add 0-5 points.

They've even created a PDF that you can print out to compare your own memoir to a range of famous ones, to work determining how your facts stack up. St. Augustine's *Confessions* ends up with 101 points; Nabokov's *Speak, Memory*, 106—supertruths, if you will. James Frey comes out only a little better than Margaret Jones (remember her? she wrote that memoir about growing up in the "LA gangland" when in reality she grew up in a nice house furnished by Pottery Barn catalogues), with 29 and 20 points, respectively.

I've always disliked the debate over whether a memoir has to be 100% factual. Sure, I understand that no one wants to read a memoir that's completely fabricated and only sold as a memoir for marketing. But applying any kind of coherent structure or narrative to the past is fictionalizing it. Truth and fact aren't the same things—Truth is more important than Fact. Well, you know both sides of the debate. I decided to put my writing to the test with their scale. Here's what my graph looked like:

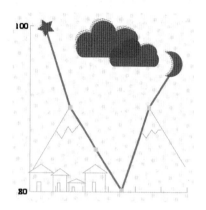

As you can see, something screwy happened when I plotted out my writing according to its factuality. After deducting some points for all the fake names that people had given themselves and I had recorded as their names (look, if you call yourself Rookie Foolery, I'm not going to write you as "Kevin") some more points for not fact-checking details (was is sunny that day in New Mexico? who knows? can I make an educated guess?), and some points for dialogue, I added some points for establishing a contract with the reader up front and making fun of the character that was Younger Me without deprecating other characters. Then I plotted out some clouds and a star and a moon, connected it all to some mountains and town in the foothills. Dammit. I couldn't help adding a scene. Subtract a hundred points for constructing nonfiction in the same way that people construct fiction. I decided to take a closer look at what's going on with my memoir:

So I made a pie chart to show the percentages of falsehoods within my writing. On the small scale of lies, I have hyperboles. Maybe the temperature didn't feel so hot that a mercury thermometer could have shattered. I don't even think that you could feel that heat. There are characters with obviously fake names. For some of them, I didn't even know their real names. And there's dialogue. My bigger lies are what will really get me into trouble with Nonfiction Police Chief

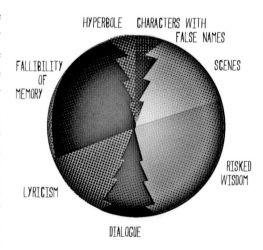

Oprah and cohorts. There are scenes because scenes are fun to read and write and understand. We're wired for sensory detail. Scenes are nothing but big lies in memoir, because they are related to another big lie: that memory is somehow accurate. You'll see that fallibility of memory takes up a large portion of the pie chart. To balance out those lies, I've tried to construe meaning from them, i.e. reflection and risked wisdom. Attributing meaning to existence, even if there you are lucky and consequences seem to logically arise from actions, is a kind of falsehood. But we like meaning and reflection, so it's staying in the work. Finally, lyrical writing takes a chunk of the deceit because it focuses more on emotional truths than factual ones.

After this exercise, I still wasn't satisfied with my self-analysis, so I thought that I would throw the big scheme of writing into a scatter plot:

Wow, now we're getting somewhere. As you can see from the diagram, the most problematic area, the Deceit-Tricks quadrant should be blank, whereas the Deceit-Craft quadrant holds many of the elements of good fiction. Belief-Tricks should probably only contain a few problematic areas, while Belief-Craft should be well-weighted with elements of fiction and elements of nonfiction.

This graph somehow ended up looking like Orion, which is probably not a coincidence. He was a hunter (and what are writers but hunters of truth!) and totally made up (and what are good memoirists but personas?). That, and I spend a lot of time looking at the sky.

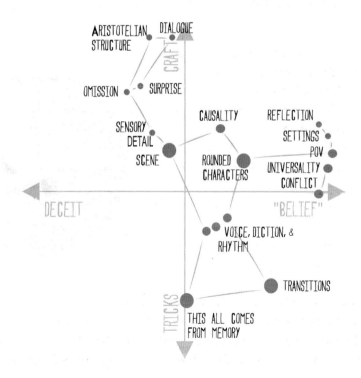

Watch at least two different news programs (on two different networks) on the same day. In theory, both programs should report at least some of the same stories, given that they're focused upon reporting the news of the day. But do they? List the stories covered by each program—and consider how each story is discussed. Do both programs cover the same events in the same basic way? Or do they emphasize different points, reveal different details, use different tones, etc.?

Consider these types of nonfiction: history, biography, autobiography, journalism, personal essay, and memoir. How do the "rules" discussed by Amaris apply to each? Does a historian, for example, have license to invent dialogue? Do journalists use false names for the same purposes as writers of memoir?

Searching online and/or in the library, locate Edmund Morris' biography of Ronald Reagan, titled *Dutch*. As a group, consider the approach Morris took to writing this book, particularly his use of fictional characters and scenes. Is a biography or memoir such as this simply a text that stretches the boundaries of the nonfiction genre? Or is it an unacceptable breach of the sorts of conventions that Amaris discusses?

In a short essay, consider this question: How does a writer tell any story without inventing some details? No one can remember every word of dialogue ever spoken in his or her presence, and no memoir can include every event that takes place. Writers must pick and choose what events to discuss and how to narrate them...yet they must also remain true to the baseline reality. Maybe. What do you think?

Ed Dante is the pseudonym of a professional essay writer who specializes in ghost writing everything from essays for English composition to doctoral dissertations. As he describes the work, the hours are long, but the pay makes the work worthwhile.

THE SHADOW SCHOLAR
The man who writes your students' papers tells his story

BY ED DANTE

Editor's note: Ed Dante is a pseudonym for a writer who lives on the East Coast. Through a literary agent, he approached The Chronicle wanting to tell the story of how he makes a living writing papers for a custom-essay company and to describe the extent of student cheating he has observed. In the course of editing his article, The Chronicle reviewed correspondence Dante had with clients and some of the papers he had been paid to write. In the article published here, some details of the assignment he describes have been altered to protect the identity of the student.

The request came in by e-mail around 2 in the afternoon. It was from a previous customer, and she had urgent business. I quote her message here verbatim (if I had to put up with it, so should you): "You did me business ethics propsal for me I need propsal got approved pls can you will write me paper?"

I've gotten pretty good at interpreting this kind of correspondence. The client had attached a document from her professor with details about the paper. She needed the first section in a week. Seventy-five pages.

I told her no problem.

It truly was no problem. In the past year, I've written roughly 5,000 pages of scholarly literature, most on very tight deadlines. But you won't find my name on a single paper.

I've written toward a master's degree in cognitive psychology, a Ph.D. in sociology, and a handful of postgraduate credits in international diplomacy. I've worked on bachelor's degrees in hospitality, business administration, and accounting. I've written for courses in history, cinema, labor relations, pharmacology, theology, sports management, maritime security, airline services, sustainability, municipal budgeting, marketing, philosophy, ethics, Eastern religion, postmodern architecture, anthropology, literature, and public administration. I've attended three dozen online universities. I've completed 12 graduate theses of 50 pages or more. All for someone else.

You've never heard of me, but there's a good chance that you've read some of my work. I'm a hired gun, a doctor of everything, an academic mercenary. My customers are your students. I promise you that. Somebody in your classroom uses a service that you can't detect, that you can't defend against, that you may not even know exists.

I work at an online company that generates tens of thousands of dollars a month by creating original essays based on specific instructions provided by cheating students. I've worked there full time since 2004. On any day of the academic year, I am working on upward of 20 assignments.

In the midst of this great recession, business is booming. At busy times, during midterms and finals, my company's staff of roughly 50 writers is not large enough to satisfy the demands of students who will pay for our work and claim it as their own.

You would be amazed by the incompetence of your students' writing. I have seen the word "desperate" misspelled every way you can imagine. And these students truly are desperate. They couldn't write a convincing grocery list, yet they are in graduate school. They really need help. They need help learning and, separately, they need help passing their courses. But they aren't getting it.

For those of you who have ever mentored a student through the writing of a dissertation, served on a thesis-review committee, or guided a graduate student through a formal research process, I have a question: Do you ever wonder how a student who struggles to formulate complete sentences in conversation manages to produce marginally competent research? How does that student get by you?

I live well on the desperation, misery, and incompetence that your educational system has created. Granted, as a writer, I could earn more; certainly there are ways to earn less. But I never struggle to find work. And as my peers trudge through thankless office jobs that seem more intolerable with every passing month of our sustained recession, I am on pace for my best year yet. I will make roughly $66,000 this year. Not a king's ransom, but higher than what many actual educators are paid.

Of course, I know you are aware that cheating occurs. But you have no idea how deeply this kind of cheating penetrates the academic system, much less how to stop it. Last summer *The New York Times* reported that 61 percent of undergraduates have admitted to some form of cheating on assignments and exams. Yet there is little discussion about custom papers and how they differ from more-detectable forms of plagiarism, or about why students cheat in the first place.

It is my hope that this essay will initiate such a conversation. As for me, I'm planning to retire. I'm tired of helping you make your students look competent.

It is late in the semester when the business student contacts me, a time when I typically juggle deadlines and push out 20 to 40 pages a day. I had written a short research proposal for her a few weeks before, suggesting a project that connected a surge of unethical business practices to the patterns of trade liberalization. The proposal was approved, and now I had six days to complete the assignment. This was not quite a rush order, which we get top dollar to write. This assignment would be priced at a standard $2,000, half of which goes in my pocket.

A few hours after I had agreed to write the paper, I received the following e-mail: "sending sorces for ur to use thanx."

I did not reply immediately. One hour later, I received another message:

"did u get the sorce I send

please where you are now?

Desprit to pass spring projict"

Not only was this student going to be a constant thorn in my side, but she also communicated in haiku, each less decipherable than the one before it. I let her know that I was giving her work the utmost attention, that I had received her sources, and that I would be in touch if I had any questions. Then I put it aside.

From my experience, three demographic groups seek out my services: the English-as-second-language student; the hopelessly deficient student; and the lazy rich kid.

For the last, colleges are a perfect launching ground—they are built to reward the rich and to forgive them their laziness. Let's be honest: The successful among us are not always the best and the brightest, and certainly not the most ethical. My favorite customers are those with an unlimited supply of money and no shortage of instructions on how they would like to see their work executed. While the deficient student will generally not know how to ask for what he wants until he doesn't get it, the lazy rich student will know exactly what he wants. He is poised for a life of paying others and telling them what to do. Indeed, he is acquiring all the skills he needs to stay on top.

As for the first two types of students—the ESL and the hopelessly deficient— colleges are utterly failing them. Students who come to American universities from other countries find that their efforts to learn a new language are confounded not only by cultural difficulties but also by the pressures of grading. The focus on evaluation rather than education means that those who haven't mastered English must do so quickly or suffer the consequences. My service provides a particularly quick way to "master" English. And those who are hopelessly deficient—a euphemism, I admit—struggle with communication in general.

Two days had passed since I last heard from the business student. Overnight I had received 14 e-mails from her. She had additional instructions for the assignment, such as "but more again please make sure they are a good link betwee the letictiure review and all the chapter and the benfet of my paper. finally do you think the level of this work? how match i can get it?"

I'll admit, I didn't fully understand that one.

It was followed by some clarification: "where u are can you get my messages? Please I pay a lot and dont have ao to faile I strated to get very worry."

Her messages had arrived between 2 a.m. and 6 a.m. Again I assured her I had the matter under control.

It was true. At this point, there are few academic challenges that I find intimidating. You name it, I've been paid to write about it.

Customers' orders are endlessly different yet strangely all the same. No matter what the subject, clients want to be assured that their assignment is in capable hands. It would be terrible to think that your Ivy League graduate thesis was riding on the work ethic and perspicacity of a public-university slacker. So part of my job is to be whatever my clients want me to be. I say yes when I am asked if I have a Ph.D. in sociology. I say yes when I am asked if I have professional training in industrial/organizational psychology. I say yes when asked if I have ever designed a perpetual-motion-powered time machine and documented my efforts in a peer-reviewed journal.

The subject matter, the grade level, the college, the course—these things are irrelevant to me. Prices are determined per page and are based on how long I have to complete the assignment. As long as it doesn't require me to do any math or video-documented animal husbandry, I will write anything.

I have completed countless online courses. Students provide me with passwords and user names so I can access key documents and online exams. In some instances, I have even contributed to weekly online discussions with other students in the class.

I have become a master of the admissions essay. I have written these for undergraduate, master's, and doctoral programs, some at elite universities. I can explain exactly why you're Brown material, why the Wharton M.B.A. program would benefit from your presence, how certain life experiences have prepared you for the rigors of your chosen course of study. I do not mean to be insensitive, but I can't tell you how many times I've been paid to write about somebody helping a loved one battle cancer. I've written essays that could be adapted into Meryl Streep movies.

I do a lot of work for seminary students. I like seminary students. They seem so blissfully unaware of the inherent contradiction in paying somebody to help them cheat in courses that are largely about walking in the light of God and providing an ethical model for others to follow. I have been commissioned to write many a passionate condemnation of America's moral decay as exemplified by abortion, gay marriage, or the teaching of evolution. All in all, we may presume that clerical authorities see these as a greater threat than the plagiarism committed by the future frocked.

With respect to America's nurses, fear not. Our lives are in capable hands— just hands that can't write a lick. Nursing students account for one of my company's biggest customer bases. I've written case-management plans, reports on nursing ethics, and essays on why nurse practitioners are lighting the way to the future of medicine. I've even written pharmaceutical-treatment courses, for patients who I hope were hypothetical.

I, who have no name, no opinions, and no style, have written so many papers at this point, including legal briefs, military-strategy assessments, poems, lab reports, and, yes, even papers on academic integrity, that it's hard to determine which course of study is most infested with cheating. But I'd say education is the worst. I've written papers for students in elementary-education programs, special-education majors, and ESL-training courses. I've written lesson plans for aspiring high-school teachers, and I've synthesized reports from notes that customers have taken during classroom observations. I've written essays for those studying to become school administrators, and I've completed theses for those on course to become principals. In the enormous conspiracy that is student cheating, the frontline intelligence community is infiltrated by double agents. (Future educators of America, I know who you are.)

As the deadline for the business-ethics paper approaches, I think about what's ahead of me. Whenever I take on an assignment this large, I get a certain physical sensation. My body says: Are you sure you want to do this again? You know how much it hurt the last time. You know this student will be with you for a long time. You know you will become her emergency contact, her guidance counselor and life raft. You know that for the 48 hours that you dedicate to writing this paper, you will cease all human functions but typing, you will Google until the term has lost all meaning, and you will drink enough coffee to fuel a revolution in a small Central American country.

But then there's the money, the sense that I must capitalize on opportunity, and even a bit of a thrill in seeing whether I can do it.

And I can. It's not implausible to write a 75-page paper in two days. It's just miserable. I don't need much sleep, and when I get cranking, I can churn out four or five pages an hour. First I lay out the sections of an assignment—introduction, problem statement, methodology, literature review, findings, conclusion—whatever the instructions call for. Then I start Googling.

I haven't been to a library once since I started doing this job. Amazon is quite generous about free samples. If I can find a single page from a particular text, I can cobble that into a report, deducing what I don't know from customer reviews and publisher blurbs. Google Scholar is a great source for material, providing the abstract of nearly any journal article. And of course, there's Wikipedia, which is often my first stop when dealing with unfamiliar subjects. Naturally one must verify such material elsewhere, but I've taken hundreds of crash courses this way.

After I've gathered my sources, I pull out usable quotes, cite them, and distribute them among the sections of the assignment. Over the years, I've refined ways of stretching papers. I can write a four-word sentence in 40 words. Just give me one phrase of quotable text, and I'll produce two pages of ponderous explanation. I can say in 10 pages what most normal people could say in a paragraph.

I've also got a mental library of stock academic phrases: "A close consideration of the events which occurred in _____ during the _____ demonstrate that _____ had entered into a phase of widespread cultural, social, and economic change that would define _____ for decades to come." Fill in the blanks using words provided by the professor in the assignment's instructions.

How good is the product created by this process? That depends—on the day, my mood, how many other assignments I am working on. It also depends on the customer, his or her expectations, and the degree to which the completed work exceeds his or her abilities. I don't ever edit my assignments. That way I get fewer customer requests to "dumb it down." So some of my work is great. Some of it is not so great. Most of my clients do not have the wherewithal to tell the difference, which probably means that in most cases the work is better than what the student would have produced on his or her own. I've actually had customers thank me for being clever enough to insert typos. "Nice touch," they'll say.

I've read enough academic material to know that I'm not the only bullshit artist out there. I think about how Dickens got paid per word and how, as a result, *Bleak House* is ... well, let's be diplomatic and say exhaustive. Dickens is a role model for me.

So how does someone become a custom-paper writer? The story of how I got into this job may be instructive. It is mostly about the tremendous disappointment that awaited me in college.

My distaste for the early hours and regimented nature of high school was tempered by the promise of the educational community ahead, with its free exchange of ideas and access to great minds. How dispiriting to find out that college was just another place where grades were grubbed, competition overshadowed personal growth, and the threat of failure was used to encourage learning.

Although my university experience did not live up to its vaunted reputation, it did lead me to where I am today. I was raised in an upper-middle-class family, but I went to college in a poor neighborhood. I fit in really well: After paying my tuition, I didn't have a cent to my name. I had nothing but a meal plan and my roommate's computer. But I was determined to write for a living, and, moreover, to spend these extremely expensive years learning how to do so. When I completed my first novel, in the summer between sophomore and junior years, I contacted the English department about creating an independent study around editing and publishing it. I was received like a mental patient. I was told, "There's nothing like that here." I was told that I could go back to my classes, sit in my lectures, and fill out Scantron tests until I graduated.

I didn't much care for my classes, though. I slept late and spent the afternoons working on my own material. Then a funny thing happened. Here I was, begging anybody in authority to take my work seriously. But my classmates did. They saw my abilities and my abundance of free time. They saw a value that the university did not.

It turned out that my lazy, Xanax-snorting, Miller-swilling classmates were thrilled to pay me to write their papers. And I was thrilled to take their money. Imagine you are crumbling under the weight of university-issued parking tickets and self-doubt when a frat boy offers you cash to write about Plato. Doing that job was a no-brainer. Word of my services spread quickly, especially through the fraternities. Soon I was receiving calls from strangers who wanted to commission my work. I was a writer!

Nearly a decade later, students, not publishers, still come from everywhere to find me.

I work hard for a living. I'm nice to people. But I understand that in simple terms, I'm the bad guy. I see where I'm vulnerable to ethical scrutiny.

But pointing the finger at me is too easy. Why does my business thrive? Why do so many students prefer to cheat rather than do their own work?

Say what you want about me, but I am not the reason your students cheat.

You know what's never happened? I've never had a client complain that he'd been expelled from school, that the originality of his work had been questioned, that some disciplinary action had been taken. As far as I know, not one of my customers has ever been caught.

With just two days to go, I was finally ready to throw myself into the business assignment. I turned off my phone, caged myself in my office, and went through the purgatory of cramming the summation of a student's alleged education into a weekend. Try it sometime. After the 20th hour on a single subject, you have an almost-out-of-body experience.

My client was thrilled with my work. She told me that she would present the chapter to her mentor and get back to me with our next steps. Two weeks passed, by which time the assignment was but a distant memory, obscured by the several hundred pages I had written since. On a Wednesday evening, I received the following e-mail:

"Thanx u so much for the chapter is going very good the porfesser likes it but wants the folliing suggestions please what do you thing?:

"'The hypothesis is interesting but I'd like to see it a bit more focused. Choose a specific connection and try to prove it.'

"What shoudwe say?"

This happens a lot. I get paid per assignment. But with longer papers, the student starts to think of me as a personal educational counselor. She paid me to write a one-page response to her professor, and then she paid me to revise her paper. I completed each of these assignments, sustaining the voice that the student had established and maintaining the front of competence from some invisible location far beneath the ivory tower.

The 75-page paper on business ethics ultimately expanded into a 160-page graduate thesis, every word of which was written by me. I can't remember the name of my client, but it's her name on my work. We collaborated for months. As with so many other topics I tackle, the connection between unethical business practices and trade liberalization became a subtext to my everyday life.

So, of course, you can imagine my excitement when I received the good news:

"thanx so much for uhelp ican going to graduate to now".

Dante is writing this article for a specific audience: teachers. With that in mind, consider these questions: How does Dante describe himself in this article? How does he explain what he does and why he does it? How does he describe his customers? As a reader, how do you react? How do you think Dante's intended audience members would react?

As a group, consider Dante's work and the students for whom he does it. Many books and articles that are published are not actually written by the person who claims to be the author of the text; there is a long tradition of hiring a ghostwriter to produce a political memoir, an article for a major newspaper by a presidential candidate, a how-to book by a successful businessperson, etc. Is the work Dante does different from this, however? Why or why not?

In a short essay, consider this: Are there circumstances under which you can imagine a student hiring another person to do school work for them? What might these circumstances be? Are there legitimate circumstances under which you can imagine a student hiring another person to do school work for them? How might the teacher be responsible for creating such an environment of "cheating" (to use a seriously loaded term)?

AUTHENTICITY

Jef Akst is a frequent contributor to The Scientist. *In the blog entry published here, Akst considers the question of self-plagiarism among scientists, asking when this occurs or if it's even possible, given that plagiarism, by definition, involves stealing the work of another individual. The matter is, naturally, not confined to the sciences alone, for in the humanities it is a natural part of the research and writing process to build new work on the shoulders of previous projects.*

WHEN IS SELF-PLAGIARISM OK?

BY JEF AKST

When Robert Barbato of the E. Philip Saunders College of Business at Rochester Institute of Technology (RIT) heard he was being accused of plagiarizing his own work, he was a bit surprised. "I can't plagiarize myself—those are my own words," he said.

And he is not alone in his views. Some scientists and publishers argue that it's "unavoidable" for scientists to re-use portions of their own text (not images or data, of course) from previous papers, and doing so may even be good practice. But others disagree, including many journals—who have retracted papers in response.

"There are many ways you can say the same thing even when it comes to very technical language," said Miguel Roig of St. John's University, who has written extensively about plagiarism in academic literature. "It's a matter of what some have labeled poor scholarly etiquette."

In Barbato's case, the institutional committee formed to review the case unanimously decided to dismiss it. While the authors had reused some text in the introduction and methodology sections in two papers they had submitted simultaneously on gender differences in entrepreneurial business endeavors, the data were different and the papers reached vastly different conclusions. "Nobody saw anything wrong with this really," recalled Patrick Scanlon of RIT's department of communication, who served on the committee.

"Sometimes [text reuse] is just unavoidable," agreed Catriona Fennell, director of journal services at Elsevier. "Really, how many different ways can you say the same thing?" Because scientists tend to study the same topic over many years or even their entire careers, some aspects of their research papers, particularly the literature review and methodology, will be repeated. Once they've figured out how to word it succinctly and accurately, some argue, it's best left unchanged. "You're laying the groundwork for an ongoing discussion [so] making changes might actually be a bad idea," Scanlon said. "It would muddy the waters."

Indeed, even editors that tend to be on the strict side when it comes to text recycling make exceptions. *Anesthesia & Analgesia* recently pulled a paper due to the offense, as reported on the Retraction Watch blog, but the journal's Editor-in-Chief Steven Shafer said that the publication does not retract papers that only reuse text in the methodology section. "This is a very difficult area," admitted Shafer. While the recently retracted paper contained "multiple areas of duplicated verbatim or nearly verbatim text throughout," he said, not all cases are so straightforward, and each one "must be a judgment call."

With evidence that duplicate publications are on the rise, and estimates of more than 200,000 duplicates already archived in Medline, the scientific community is in dire need of better guidelines as to where to draw the line with respect to self-plagiarism—and a better way of catching those that cross it.

"It's unfortunately a very gray area," said Jonathan Bailey, a copyright and plagiarism consultant and a writer for the website Plagiarism Today. "[When people] come to me asking what the lines are, I always have to say the same thing: 'You're going to have to talk to the publication you're submitting to.'"

The problem is that most publications don't have "hard and fast rules," Fennell said of Elsevier's journals. The most comprehensive guidelines with respect to self-plagiarism come from the Committee on Publication Ethics (COPE), but these guidelines refer only to truly "redundant publication," in which authors are attempting to pawn off old research as fresh and new. They contain no advice about scientists re-using their own text.

"There's nothing that says you can't have over 30 percent of your introduction being highly similar," said Harold "Skip" Garner, executive director of the Virginia Bioinformatics Institute, who has published several articles on plagiarism in scientific publishing. "There's nothing like that because it's impossible to calculate."

The good news is that with the bulk of publishing now done electronically and the advent of text similarity software to recognize possible cases of redundant publishing, identifying copied text is becoming a much less onerous task than it used to be. eTBLAST, for example, is a free text comparison program that searches the millions of abstracts archived in Medline, as well as a few other publically available databases. Once the publication spots a possible duplication, it's added to the Déjà vu database of highly similar citations, where scientists can evaluate and comment on the entries.

Probably the most widely used program to spot plagiarism in scientific publishing is Crosscheck, launched in June 2008 by CrossRef. A total of 119 publishers (nearly 50,000 journals) subscribe to the plagiarism detection program, including Elsevier, Wiley-Blackwell, and Springer, who donate their full text content to the database, which currently holds some 25 million pieces of scientific literature, and is "growing steadily," according to CrossRef Product Manager Kirsty Meddings. Crosscheck's subscribers can scan the database with the same iThenticate software used by Turnitin to check for possible duplications.

So far, the journals that have put the technology to use say it's working. Of the 60 papers flagged as having a high percentage of overlap with other publications in the first three months that the Society for Industrial and Applied Mathematics used Crosscheck (starting last March), "about 60 percent were self-plagiarism," said David Marshall, the publisher at SIAM. "That is the majority of what we're uncovering."

"In my view, [having these programs] is one of the best things that ever happened because it puts scientists on notice," Roig said. Indeed, some journals have taken to explicitly announcing that they use Crosscheck in their instructions to authors, and/or post the Crosscheck logo on their website, hoping that just the threat of getting caught will act as a deterrent.

Even with these programs, however, editors must be careful, Bailey warned— even high degree of text similarity can sometimes be legit. "It really is about context," Fennell agreed. "It's good software, but it doesn't replace human judgment."

The problem now is how to weed through the hundreds of thousands of suspected cases of duplicated publications currently in the scientific literature. "It's one thing to be a deterrent and preventative in the future," said Garner, but "who's going to clean up the mess that's already there?"

According to Akst, how is "self-plagiarism" defined? By whom is it defined? In a short essay, explain your understanding of Akst's argument and detail whether or not, in your view, it is even possible for a writer to plagiarize him- or herself.

Working in groups, locate at least three different policies on plagiarism—including, perhaps, the policy of your own school or even your own class. To whom do the policies apply? Are there different rules about plagiarism for different writers—students and professors, for example? Why?

Draft your own policy against plagiarism—a policy that will apply to all writers in your academic setting. How do you account for the different conventions practiced in different types of writing—between research papers in a literature class and lab reports in a biology class, for example? How do you account for students who may have the opportunity in their major to write on the same topic again and again? How is this different—or is it?—from professors writing on the same subject multiple times?

Catherine Rampell reports on economic issues for The New York Times. *Her recent publications focus on the economic power emerging in China and on the downward trend in employment possibilities for graduates of law school. In the article that follows, she turns her interest in economics to the ever-more-profit-driven world of higher education.*

A HISTORY OF COLLEGE GRADE INFLATION

By Catherine Rampell

We've written before about some of the work of Stuart Rojstaczer and Christopher Healy, grade inflation chroniclers extraordinaire. They have put together a new, comprehensive study of college grading over the decades, and let me tell you, it is a doozy.

The researchers collected historical data on letter grades awarded by more than 200 four-year colleges and universities. Their analysis (published in the *Teachers College Record*) confirms that the share of A grades awarded has skyrocketed over the years. Take a look at the red line (squares) in the chart on the next page, which refers to the share of grades given that are A's:

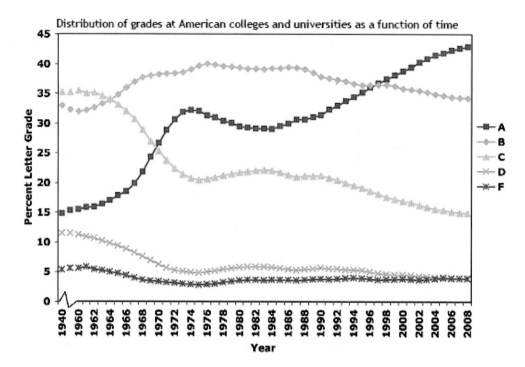

Distribution of grades at American colleges and universities as a function of time

Note: 1940 and 1950 (nonconnected data points in figure) represent averages from 1935 to 1944 and 1945 to 1954, respectively. Data from 1960 onward represent annual averages in their database, smoothed with a three-year centered moving average.

Most recently, about 43 percent of all letter grades given were A's, an increase of 28 percentage points since 1960 and 12 percentage points since 1988. The distribution of B's has stayed relatively constant; the growing share of A's instead comes at the expense of a shrinking share of C's, D's and F's. In fact, only about 10 percent of grades awarded are D's and F's.

As we have written before, private colleges and universities are by far the biggest offenders on grade inflation, even when you compare private schools to equally selective public schools. Here's another chart showing the grading curves for public versus private schools in the years 1960, 1980 and 2007:

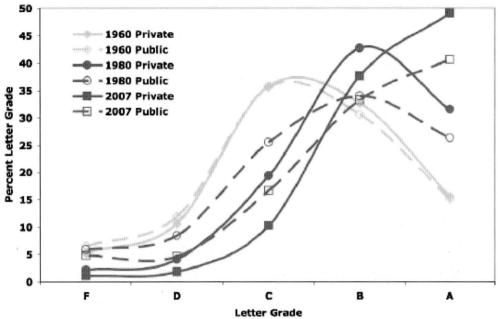

National average grading curves as a function of time, 1960, 1980, and 2007 for public and private schools

Note: 1960 and 1980 data represent averages from 1959–1961 and 1979–1981, respectively.

As you can see, public and private school grading curves started out as relatively similar, and gradually pulled further apart. Both types of institutions made their curves easier over time, but private schools made their grades *much* easier.

By the end of the last decade, A's and B's represented 73 percent of all grades awarded at public schools, and 86 percent of all grades awarded at private schools, according to the database compiled by Mr. Rojstaczer and Mr. Healy. (Mr. Rojstaczer is a former Duke geophysics professor, and Mr. Healy is a computer science professor at Furman University.)

Southern schools have also been less generous with their grading than institutions in other geographic regions, and schools that focus on science and engineering tend to be stingier with their A's than liberal arts schools of equal selectivity.

What accounts for the higher G.P.A.'s over the last few decades?

The authors don't attribute steep grade inflation to higher-quality or harder-working students. In fact, one recent study found that students spend significantly less time studying today than they did in the past.

Rather, the researchers argue that grade inflation began picking up in the 1960s and 1970s probably because professors were reluctant to give students D's and F's. After all, poor grades could land young men in Vietnam.

They then attribute the rapid rise in grade inflation in the last couple of decades to a more "consumer-based approach" to education, which they say "has created both external and internal incentives for the faculty to grade more generously." More generous grading can produce better instructor reviews, for example, and can help students be more competitive candidates for graduate schools and the job market.

The authors argue that grading standards may become even looser in the coming years, making it increasingly more difficult for graduate schools and employers to distinguish between excellent, good and mediocre students.

More disturbing, they argue, are the potential effects on educational outcomes.

"When college students perceive that the average grade in a class will be an A, they do not try to excel," they write. "It is likely that the decline in student study hours, student engagement, and literacy are partly the result of diminished academic expectations."

At one point, Rampell notes that in a consumer-based model of education, where students are treated like customers, good grades become payment for good teaching evaluations. In your experience, is this true? Do good teachers give more high grades than bad teachers? And what defines a "good" or "bad" teacher? (As you work through these questions, keep in mind that arguments about "good" and "bad" teaching are not usually just academic: Good teachers are often rewarded with merit pay, better classes, etc. Bad teachers are often fired.)

As a group, discuss your experiences with grading (without revealing more than you're comfortable sharing publicly, of course). What were your experiences of grading in high school? Was the highest possible GPA a 4.0 or something higher? How often did students fail—not just on individual tests or in certain classes but overall (to the point that they did not advance from one grade to the next)? Should grades always fall along a bell curve, with a few students failing, a few students receiving the highest grades, and the bulk of the students clustered in the middle of the scale? Should grades do something else? What precisely do grades measure?

In an essay, explain why you think grade inflation is or is not a problem at your school. What evidence do you have for your position (keeping in mind the fact that official data is one type of evidence, while lived experience is another entirely)?

Working with your peers, research the number of students who have attended college annually since 1940. How might changes in population size, in culture, and in demographic makeup account for the "inflation" in grades that Rampell charts?

Alfie Kohn, a one-time teacher, is a controversial figure in the world of education—where he frequently bucks prevailing views on controversial issues. His books include Unconditional Parenting: Moving from Rewards and Punishments to Love and Reason, Feel-Bad Education: And Other Essays on Children and Schooling, *and* The Homework Myth: Why Our Kids Get Too Much of a Bad Thing.

THE DANGEROUS MYTH OF GRADE INFLATION

By Alfie Kohn

Grade inflation got started ... in the late '60s and early '70s.... The grades that faculty members now give ... deserve to be a scandal.

—Professor Harvey Mansfield, Harvard University, 2001

Grades A and B are sometimes given too readily—Grade A for work of no very high merit, and Grade B for work not far above mediocrity. ... One of the chief obstacles to raising the standards of the degree is the readiness with which insincere students gain passable grades by sham work.

—Report of the Committee on Raising the Standard,
Harvard University, 1894

Complaints about grade inflation have been around for a very long time. Every so often a fresh flurry of publicity pushes the issue to the foreground again, the latest example being a series of articles in *The Boston Globe* last year that disclosed—in a tone normally reserved for the discovery of entrenched corruption in state government—that a lot of students at Harvard were receiving A's and being graduated with honors.

The fact that people were offering the same complaints more than a century ago puts the latest bout of harrumphing in perspective, not unlike those quotations about the disgraceful values of the younger generation that turn out to be hundreds of years old. The long history of indignation also pretty well derails any attempts to place the blame for higher grades on a residue of bleeding-heart liberal professors hired in the '60s. (Unless, of course, there was a similar countercultural phenomenon in the 1860s.)

Yet on campuses across America today, academe's usual requirements for supporting data and reasoned analysis have been suspended for some reason where this issue is concerned. It is largely accepted on faith that grade inflation—an upward shift in students' grade-point averages without a similar rise in achievement—exists, and that it is a bad thing. Meanwhile, the truly substantive issues surrounding grades and motivation have been obscured or ignored.

The fact is that it is hard to substantiate even the simple claim that grades have been rising. Depending on the time period we're talking about, that claim may well be false. In their book *When Hope and Fear Collide* (Jossey-Bass, 1998), Arthur Levine and Jeanette Cureton tell us that more undergraduates in 1993 reported receiving A's (and fewer reported receiving grades of C or below) compared with their counterparts in 1969 and 1976 surveys. Unfortunately, self-reports are notoriously unreliable, and the numbers become even more dubious when only a self-selected, and possibly unrepresentative, segment bothers to return the questionnaires. (One out of three failed to do so in 1993; no information is offered about the return rates in the earlier surveys.)

To get a more accurate picture of whether grades have changed over the years, one needs to look at official student transcripts. Clifford Adelman, a senior research analyst with the U.S. Department of Education, did just that, reviewing transcripts from more than 3,000 institutions and reporting his results in 1995. His finding: "Contrary to the widespread lamentations, grades actually declined slightly in the last two decades." Moreover, a report released just this year by the National Center for Education Statistics revealed that fully 33.5 percent of American undergraduates had a grade-point average of C or below in 1999-2000, a number that ought to quiet "all the furor over grade inflation," according to a spokesperson for the Association of American Colleges and Universities. (A review of other research suggests a comparable lack of support for claims of grade inflation at the high-school level.)

[*Addendum 2004*: A subsequent analysis by Adelman, which reviewed college transcripts from students who were graduated from high school in 1972, 1982, and 1992, confirmed that there was no significant or linear increase in average grades over that period. The average GPA for those three cohorts was 2.70, 2.66, and 2.74, respectively. The proportion of A's and B's received by students: 58.5 percent in the '70s, 58.9 percent in the '80s, and 58.0 percent in the '90s. Even when Adelman looked at "highly selective" institutions, he again found very little change in average GPA over the decades.]

However, even where grades *are* higher now as compared with then, that does not constitute proof that they are inflated. The burden rests with critics to demonstrate that those higher grades are undeserved, and one can cite any number of alternative explanations. Maybe students are turning in better assignments. Maybe instructors used to be too stingy with their marks and have become more reasonable. Maybe the concept of assessment itself has evolved, so that today it is more a means for allowing students to demonstrate what they know rather than for sorting them or "catching them out." (The real question, then, is why we spent so many years trying to make good students look bad.) Maybe students aren't forced to take as many courses outside their primary areas of interest in which they didn't fare as well. Maybe struggling students are now able to withdraw from a course before a poor grade appears on their transcripts. (Say what you will about that practice, it challenges the hypothesis that the grades students receive in the courses they complete are inflated.)

The bottom line: No one has ever demonstrated that students today get A's for the same work that used to receive B's or C's. We simply do not have the data to support such a claim.

Consider the most recent, determined effort by a serious source to prove that grades are inflated: "Evaluation and the Academy: Are We Doing the Right Thing?" a report released this year by the American Academy of Arts and Sciences. Its senior author is Henry Rosovsky, formerly Harvard's dean of the faculty. The first argument offered in support of the proposition that students couldn't possibly deserve higher grades is that SAT scores have dropped during the same period that grades are supposed to have risen. But this is a patently inapt comparison, if only because the SAT is deeply flawed. It has never been much good even at predicting grades during the freshman year in college, to say nothing of more important academic outcomes. A four-year analysis of almost 78,000 University of California students, published last year by the UC president's office, found that the test predicted only 13.3 percent of variation in freshman grades, a figure roughly consistent with hundreds of previous studies. (I outlined numerous other problems with the test in "Two Cheers for an End to the SAT," *The Chronicle*, March 9, 2001.)

Even if one believes that the SAT is a valid and valuable exam, however, the claim that scores are dropping is a poor basis for the assertion that grades are too high. First, it is difficult to argue that a standardized test taken in high school and grades for college course work are measuring the same thing. Second, changes in aggregate SAT scores mostly reflect the proportion of the eligible population that has chosen to take the test. The American Academy's report states that average SAT scores dropped slightly from 1969 to 1993. But over that period, the pool of test takers grew from about one-third to more than two-fifths of high-school graduates—an addition of more than 200,000 students.

Third, a decline in overall SAT scores is hardly the right benchmark against which to measure the grades earned at Harvard or other elite institutions. Every bit of evidence I could find—including a review of the SAT scores of entering students at Harvard over the past two decades, at the nation's most selective colleges over three and even four decades, and at all private colleges since 1985—uniformly confirms a virtually linear rise in both verbal and math scores, even after correcting for the renorming of the test in the mid-1990s. To cite just one example, the latest edition of "Trends in College Admissions"reports that the average verbal-SAT score of students enrolled in all private colleges rose from 543 in 1985 to 558 in 1999. Thus, those who regard SAT results as a basis for comparison should *expect* to see higher grades now rather than assume that they are inflated.

The other two arguments made by the authors of the American Academy's report rely on a similar sleight of hand. They note that more college students are now forced to take remedial courses, but offer no reason to think that this is especially true of the relevant student population—namely, those at the most selective colleges who are now receiving A's instead of B's. [*Addendum 2004*: Adelman's newer data challenge the premise that there has been *any* increase. In fact, "the proportion of all students who took at least one remedial course (in college) dropped from 51 percent in the (high school) class of 1982 to 42 percent in the class of 1992."]

Finally, they report that more states are adding high-school graduation tests and even standardized exams for admission to public universities. Yet that trend can be explained by political factors and offers no evidence of an objective decline in students' proficiency. For instance, scores on the National Assessment of Educational Progress, known as "the nation's report card" on elementary and secondary schooling, have shown very little change over the past couple of decades, and most of the change that has occurred has been for the better. As David Berliner and Bruce Biddle put it in their tellingly titled book *The Manufactured Crisis* (Addison-Wesley, 1995), the data demonstrate that "today's students are at least as well informed as students in previous generations." The latest round of public-school bashing—and concomitant reliance on high-stakes testing—began with the Reagan administration's "Nation at Risk" report, featuring claims now widely viewed by researchers as exaggerated and misleading.

* * *

Beyond the absence of good evidence, the debate over grade inflation brings up knotty epistemological problems. To say that grades are not merely rising but inflated—and that they are consequently "less accurate" now, as the American Academy's report puts it—is to postulate the existence of an objectively correct evaluation of what a student (or an essay) deserves, the true grade that ought to be uncovered and honestly reported. It would be an understatement to say that this reflects a simplistic and outdated view of knowledge and of learning.

In fact, what is most remarkable is how rarely learning even figures into the discussion. The dominant disciplinary sensibility in commentaries on this topic is not that of education—an exploration of pedagogy or assessment—but rather of economics. That is clear from the very term "grade inflation," which is, of course, just a metaphor. Our understanding is necessarily limited if we confine ourselves to the vocabulary of inputs and outputs, incentives, resource distribution, and compensation.

Suppose, for the sake of the argument, we assumed the very worst—not only that students are getting better grades than did their counterparts of an earlier generation, but that the grades are too high. What does that mean, and why does it upset some people so?

To understand grade inflation in its proper context, we must acknowledge a truth that is rarely named: The crusade against it is led by conservative individuals and organizations who regard it as analogous—or even related—to such favorite whipping boys as multicultural education, the alleged radicalism of academe, "political correctness"(a label that permits the denigration of anything one doesn't like without having to offer a reasoned objection), and too much concern about students' self-esteem. Mainstream media outlets and college administrators have allowed themselves to be put on the defensive by accusations about grade inflation, as can be witnessed when deans at Harvard plead nolo contendere and dutifully tighten their grading policies.

What are the critics assuming about the nature of students' motivation to learn, about the purpose of evaluation and of education itself? (It is surely revealing when someone reserves time and energy to complain bitterly about how many students are getting A's—as opposed to expressing concern about, say, how many students have been trained to think that the point of going to school is to get A's.)

"In a healthy university, it would not be necessary to say what is wrong with grade inflation,"Harvey Mansfield asserted in an opinion article last year (*The Chronicle*, April 6, 2001). That, to put it gently, is a novel view of health. It seems reasonable to expect those making an argument to be prepared to defend it, and also valuable to bring their hidden premises to light. Here are the assumptions that seem to underlie the grave warnings about grade inflation:

The professor's job is to sort students for employers or graduate schools. Some are disturbed by grade inflation—or, more accurately, grade compression—because it then becomes harder to spread out students on a continuum, ranking them against one another for the benefit of post-college constituencies. One professor asks, by way of analogy, "Why would anyone subscribe to *Consumers Digest* if every blender were rated a 'best buy'?"

But how appropriate is such a marketplace analogy? Is the professor's job to rate students like blenders for the convenience of corporations, or is it to offer feedback that will help students learn more skillfully and enthusiastically? (Notice, moreover, that even consumer magazines don't grade on a curve. They report the happy news if it turns out that every blender meets a reasonable set of performance criteria.)

Furthermore, the student-as-appliance approach assumes that grades provide useful information to those post-college constituencies. Yet growing evidence—most recently in the fields of medicine and law, as cited in publications like *The Journal of the American Medical Association* and the *American Educational Research Journal*—suggests that grades and test scores do not in fact predict career success, or much of anything beyond subsequent grades and test scores.

Students should be set against one another in a race for artificially scarce rewards. "The essence of grading is exclusiveness," Mansfield said in one interview. Students "should have to compete with each other," he said in another.

In other words, even when no graduate-school admissions committee pushes for students to be sorted, they ought to be sorted anyway, with grades reflecting relative standing rather than absolute accomplishment. In effect, this means that the game should be rigged so that no matter how well students do, only a few can get A's. The question guiding evaluation in such a classroom is not "How well are they learning?"but "Who's beating whom?"The ultimate purpose of good colleges, this view holds, is not to maximize success, but to ensure that there will always be losers.

A bell curve may sometimes—but only sometimes—describe the range of knowledge in a roomful of students at the beginning of a course. When it's over, though, any responsible educator hopes that the results would skew drastically to the right, meaning that most students learned what they hadn't known before. Thus, in their important study, *Making Sense of College Grades* (Jossey-Bass, 1986), Ohmer Milton, Howard Pollio, and James Eison write, "It is not a symbol of rigor to have grades fall into a 'normal' distribution; rather, it is a symbol of failure—failure to teach well, failure to test well, and failure to have any influence at all on the intellectual lives of students."Making sure that students are continually re-sorted, with excellence turned into an artificially scarce commodity, is almost perverse.

What does relative success signal about student performance in any case? The number of peers that a student has bested tells us little about how much she knows and is able to do. Moreover, such grading policies may create a competitive climate that is counterproductive for winners and losers alike, to the extent that it discourages a free exchange of ideas and a sense of community that's conducive to exploration.

Harder is better (or Higher grades mean lower standards). Compounding the tendency to confuse excellence with victory is a tendency to confuse quality with difficulty—as evidenced in the accountability fad that has elementary and secondary education in its grip just now, with relentless talk of "rigor" and "raising the bar." The same confusion shows up in higher education when professors pride themselves not on the intellectual depth and value of their classes but merely on how much reading they assign, how hard their tests are, how rarely they award good grades, and so on. "You're going to have to *work* in here!" they announce, with more than a hint of machismo and self-congratulation.

Some people might defend that posture on the grounds that students will perform better if A's are harder to come by. In fact, the evidence on this question is decidedly mixed. Stringent grading sometimes has been shown to boost short-term retention as measured by multiple-choice exams—never to improve understanding or promote interest in learning. The most recent analysis, released in 2000 by Julian R. Betts and Jeff Grogger, professors of economics at the University of California at San Diego and at Los Angeles, respectively, found that tougher grading was initially correlated with higher test scores. But the long-term effects were negligible—with the exception of minority students, for whom the effects were negative.

It appears that something more than an empirical hypothesis is behind the "harder is better"credo, particularly when it is set up as a painfully false dichotomy: Those easy-grading professors are too lazy to care, or too worried about how students will evaluate them, or overly concerned about their students' self-esteem, whereas *we* are the last defenders of what used to matter in the good old days. High standards! Intellectual honesty! No free lunch!

The American Academy's report laments an absence of "candor"about this issue. Let us be candid, then. Those who grumble about undeserved grades sometimes exude a cranky impatience with—or even contempt for—the late adolescents and young adults who sit in their classrooms. Many people teaching in higher education, after all, see themselves primarily as researchers and regard teaching as an occupational hazard, something they're not very good at, were never trained for, and would rather avoid. It would be interesting to examine the correlation between one's view of teaching (or of students) and the intensity of one's feelings about grade inflation. Someone also might want to examine the personality profiles of those who become infuriated over the possibility that someone, somewhere, got an A without having earned it.

Grades motivate. With the exception of orthodox behaviorists, psychologists have come to realize that people can exhibit qualitatively different kinds of motivation: intrinsic, in which the task itself is seen as valuable, and extrinsic, in which the task is just a means to the end of gaining a reward or escaping a punishment. The two are not only distinct but often inversely related. Scores of studies have demonstrated, for example, that the more people are rewarded, the more they come to lose interest in whatever had to be done in order to get the reward. (That conclusion is essentially reaffirmed by the latest major meta-analysis on the topic: a review of 128 studies, published in 1999 by Edward L. Deci, Richard Koestner, and Richard Ryan.)

Those unfamiliar with that basic distinction, let alone the supporting research, may be forgiven for pondering how to "motivate"students, then concluding that grades are often a good way of doing so, and consequently worrying about the impact of inflated grades. But the reality is that it doesn't matter how motivated students are; what matters is *how* students are motivated. A focus on grades creates, or at least perpetuates, an extrinsic orientation that is likely to undermine the love of learning we are presumably seeking to promote.

Three robust findings emerge from the empirical literature on the subject: Students who are given grades, or for whom grades are made particularly salient, tend to display less interest in what they are doing, fare worse on meaningful measures of learning, and avoid more challenging tasks when given the opportunity—as compared with those in a non-graded comparison group. College instructors cannot help noticing, and presumably being disturbed by, such consequences, but they may lapse into blaming students ("grade grubbers") rather than understanding the systemic sources of the problem. A focus on whether too many students are getting A's suggests a tacit endorsement of grades that predictably produces just such a mind-set in students.

These fundamental questions are almost completely absent from discussions of grade inflation. The American Academy's report takes exactly one sentence— with no citations—to dismiss the argument that "lowering the anxiety over grades leads to better learning," ignoring the fact that much more is involved than anxiety. It is a matter of why a student learns, not only how much stress he feels. Nor is the point just that low grades hurt some students' feelings, but that grades, per se, hurt all students' engagement with learning. The meaningful contrast is not between an A and a B or C, but between an extrinsic and an intrinsic focus.

Precisely because that is true, a reconsideration of grade inflation leads us to explore alternatives to our (often unreflective) use of grades. Narrative comments and other ways by which faculty members can communicate their evaluations can be far more informative than letter or number grades, and much less destructive. Indeed, some colleges—for example, Hampshire, Evergreen State, Alverno, and New College of Florida—have eliminated grades entirely, as a critical step toward *raising* intellectual standards. Even the American Academy's report acknowledges that "relatively undifferentiated course grading has been a traditional practice in many graduate schools for a very long time." Has that policy produced lower quality teaching and learning? Quite the contrary: Many people say they didn't begin to explore ideas deeply and passionately until graduate school began and the importance of grades diminished significantly.

If the continued use of grades rests on nothing more than tradition ("We've always done it that way"), a faulty understanding of motivation, or excessive deference to graduate-school admissions committees, then it may be time to balance those factors against the demonstrated harms of getting students to chase A's. Ohmer Milton and his colleagues discovered—and others have confirmed—that a "grade orientation"and a "learning orientation" on the part of students tend to be inversely related. That raises the disturbing possibility that some colleges are institutions of higher learning in name only, because the paramount question for students is not "What does this mean?" but "Do we have to know this?"

A grade-oriented student body is an invitation for the administration and faculty to ask hard questions: What unexamined assumptions keep traditional grading in place? What forms of assessment might be less destructive? How can professors minimize the salience of grades in their classrooms, so long as grades must still be given? And: If the artificial inducement of grades disappeared, what sort of teaching strategies might elicit authentic interest in a course?

To engage in this sort of inquiry, to observe real classrooms, and to review the relevant research is to arrive at one overriding conclusion: The real threat to excellence isn't grade inflation at all; it's grades.

REFERENCES

Adelman, Clifford. "A's Aren't That Easy," *New York Times*, May 17, 1995.

Betts, Julian R. and Jeff Grogger, "The Impact of Grading Standards on Student Achievement, Educational Attainment, and Entry-Level Earnings," *National Bureau of Economic Research*, September 2000, Working Paper 7875.

Kohn, Alfie. "Two Cheers for an End to the SAT," *Chronicle of Higher Education* March 9, 2001, pp. B12-13.

Levine, Arthur and Jeanette S. Cureton, *When Hope and Fear Collide* [San Francisco: Jossey-Bass, 1998], pp. 124-27.)

Mansfield, Harvey C. "Grade Inflation: It's Time to Face the Facts," *Chronicle of Higher Education*, April 6, 2001, p. B24

Ohmer Milton, Howard R. Pollio, and James A. Eison. *Making Sense of College Grades* (San Francisco: Jossey-Bass, 1986).

Rosovsky, Henry and Matthew Hartley, *Evaluation and the Academy: Are We Doing the Right Thing?: Grade Inflation and Letters of Recommendation* (American Academy of Arts and Sciences, February 2002)

Searching online—and drawing upon your own previous educational experiences—consider what grades actually mean. What is an A? How is it different from an A-, and how is an A- different from a B+? While such questions sound like mere sophistry, they matter: Grades determine many things, from placement in a particular class to scholarship eligibility. Good grades do open doors, just as bad grades close them. But what do "good" and "bad" grades actually mean?

As a group, consider this: If there have always been complaints about grade inflation, as Kohn argues, then why does the issue keep coming up again and again, year after year? Who complains about grade inflation? Why?

In an essay, explain what constitutes a true educational experience. If a student attends a university where grades are never given in any courses, is his/her education more or less authentic than the education of a student who attends a traditional university? Why?

Jeffrey A. Erickson is Assistant Principal at Minnetonka High School in Minnesota. According to his school's web site, "Minnetonka High School serves as the flagship of the Minnetonka School District, which has been recognized as a school district of excellence by the United States Department of Education." As part of that excellence, Erickson has worked to change not only grading policies but the entire ethos of grading itself in his school.

HOW GRADING REFORM CHANGED OUR SCHOOL

By Jeffrey A. Erickson

At a suburban high school in Minnesota, grading reform has resulted in a fundamentally new way to approach learning.

Last summer, I took great joy in watching my daughter take swimming lessons. One of the most difficult tasks for her was swimming the front crawl 50 feet to the other side of the pool. During the three-week course, with ongoing guidance and feedback from her teacher, she relentlessly practiced this task every day. Only during the last class did she finally reach her goal and swim across the pool. Her final report for the class recommended that she move to the next level.

How shocked I would have been if her teacher had informed me that my daughter's final mark in the swimming course would be determined by the average of her performance over the entire course—that even though she had mastered the front crawl at the end of the class, she failed because the teacher had included all her unsuccessful attempts in calculating the grade.

Perhaps this scenario seems outlandish. But in the world of schooling, averaging is just one of many common but questionable practices that can significantly distort the accuracy of grades.

THE GUIDING QUESTION

At Minnetonka High School, a suburban school serving nearly 2,900 students in Minnetonka, Minnesota, the need for grading reform became evident in the early 2000s. Parents were calling for more transparency and consistency. Teacher surveys revealed that the purpose for grading varied from classroom to classroom and that teachers were using a wide range of factors to determine grades. Attendance, behavior, effort, extra credit, and participation were all in the mix along with actual achievement of curriculum standards. We needed to articulate a clear focus for grading.

Changing our school's grading practices required that we take a fundamental look at one guiding question: What should go into a grade? Our answer: Grades should reflect only what a student knows and is able to do. This principle became the impetus for our work. As we analyzed our policies and procedures, we discovered many practices that were either inflating or deflating grades.

Inflating Grades

Is there a connection between a strong bladder and grades? Amazingly, in some cases there is. A substitute teacher was covering a colleague's classes for the day. The regular teacher instructed him that if a student asked to go to the bathroom, he should ask that student for his or her pink pass because the student might decide to keep the pass and remain in the room. Why? At the end of the quarter, students could submit their unused pink passes for extra points to be added to their final grade.

This may seem like an extreme example, but it's common practice for teachers to award extra points for bringing in tissue boxes, completing extra-credit assignments, returning permission slips, contributing canned food to the food drive, and so on. Such practices inflate grades and distort their meaning. The whole grading process becomes a game rather than a reflection of learning.

Another source of grade inflation is grading "on the curve." When scores on a particular test are initially low, the teacher applies a curving process, and everyone's score is magically inflated. Typically, the top student score in a class becomes the "perfect" score, and the rest are sorted from that point.

Deflating Grades

Factors unrelated to student achievement of standards—such as behavioral infractions, unexcused absences, cheating, late or missing work, or averaging— can also deflate grades.

An example of the effects of averaging occurred when Pam decided to take a risk and register for an advanced placement course in the fall of her junior year. Unfortunately, she soon became overwhelmed by the course's content and demands. After trying hard but receiving a first-quarter grade of *F*, she decided to change to a general-level class, where she achieved great success. During the second quarter, she earned an *A* on her classwork and a *B+* on the final exam. Two weeks later, the final grades for the semester were issued. Before I reveal the grade Pam received, what grade do *you* think would demonstrate what she knew and was able to do for this course?

Pam was surprised and confused when she saw that her final grade was a *D+*. Following common practice with course transfers, her first-quarter *F* had been carried over into the new course. Needless to say, her parents called the school. Fortunately, Minnetonka district policy allows a teacher to conduct additional assessments if he or she agrees that a report card grade does not fairly represent the student's performance. In this case, the teacher gave Pam two additional summative exams that she had missed from the first quarter, and her grade was converted to an *A-*.

Student behavior can also complicate grades. For example, in our school, many students used their cell phones to text or send e-mails during class. Some teachers attempted to use grades to control this behavior. One teacher would reduce a student's percentage grade by two points every time the student inappropriately took out a cell phone. In some cases, this practice reduced students' grades by two letters.

Schools also frequently consider student attendance when calculating grades. Students with unexcused absences and tardies may find their grades reduced at the end of the quarter—a consequence issued up to nine weeks after the offense.

PRACTICALITY + BEST PRACTICE

Establishing a common purpose for grades enabled Minnetonka High School to reexamine and change many of the practices that were inflating or deflating grades. On the basis of our belief that grades should show what a student knows and is able to do, we developed a policy for consistently and objectively reporting student academic achievement.

Teachers are now required to use two assessment categories—formative (not more than 15 percent of the grade) and summative (not less than 85 percent). Grades in these two categories determine the quarter and semester grade. Within the summative category, teachers of the same course must conduct at least four common assessments, one of which must be a performance task. Throughout the learning process, the formative assessments inform the students of their progress in mastering material that will appear in the upcoming summative exam. Teachers are responsible for articulating clear learning targets that students understand and can attain.

Of course, few people would argue that participation, effort, and positive attitude are unimportant. However, including these elements in a grade would distort our purpose of communicating achievement. Instead, we report students' performance on these factors to students and parents during conferences.

We also developed a system to replace the old practice of applying the "curve" to adjust test scores. Now, after every assessment, the teacher conducts an item analysis. If a significant number of students miss certain questions, the teacher reflects on whether he or she provided enough instruction on those topics. In terms of scoring, the teacher omits these test questions from students' grades, reteaches the lesson, and reassesses the topic.

We determined that behavioral infractions are legitimate concerns and should be addressed—just not with grades. When grades cannot be used to control students, we must replace them with sound classroom management and student engagement strategies.

For instance, we replaced the system of reducing grades for unexcused absences with a highly responsive and immediate intervention and consequence system. When a student skips a class, a phone call goes home that same day. A staff member meets with the student within 36 hours to find out why the student was absent and issues a detention for an unexcused class absence.

Initially, some educators and parents expressed fear about what would happen: Would students skip class when grades were no longer connected to attendance? This proved not to be the case. Instead, we experienced a 55 percent reduction in unexcused absences, a 66 percent decline in disciplinary referrals, and a 37 percent reduction in suspensions. We did not eliminate consequences for misbehavior; we simply developed more effective and appropriate consequences.

Homework practices were another fruitful area for change. Homework had typically been graded based on completion. Parents were often confused when they saw that their child's mark on the final chapter or unit summative test was a *D* or *F* after the child had received a series of perfect homework scores. Over time, homework practices have evolved. Instead of giving students homework scores that reflect completion, teachers now frequently give a quiz on the previous day's homework, thus providing real-time progress updates. As a result, students and parents see a higher level of consistency between the homework grades and final assessments.

SECOND CHANCE FOR LEARNING

Of all the grading dilemmas, retakes and redos surge to the top as one of the most highly disputed. Those who argue against retakes claim that this practice coddles students and doesn't reflect the real world.

Imagine that you've just taken a major test for your high school Spanish class, and in spite of your preparation you bombed it. You ask the teacher for a chance to take a retest to improve your learning and score. Your teacher tells you that he doesn't offer retakes and that you just need to try harder next time. You leave defeated, muttering, "Well, I just can't get Spanish." If this pattern continues, it won't take much time for you to doubt your potential for growth and success.

Students need multiple chances to grow and show what they know. If the goal is for all students to master essential learning, the philosophy *teach, test, and move on* should be replaced with *teach, test, and now what?* The essential question that each teacher should ask after every assessment is, Now what do I do for the students who didn't get it? In Minnetonka, the only unacceptable answer is "move on."

When the answer is to provide a retake, the most important step is what happens between the first and second test. The purpose of retakes is never for the student to simply show up and hope for the best. Corrective instruction must occur between the test and retest.

For example, Polly, a social studies teacher, requires students to review all incorrect answers on the original assessment and find the correct answers. Next, the student must come in and work with her to complete review pages. Only when it's evident that the student is ready to be reassessed does Polly offer a retake. The new score replaces the old one—there's no averaging or limit to what the student can earn. This is not letting students off the hook; it's holding them accountable for mastering the information.

Each year, we have refined and more deeply implemented our new grading philosophy. At the end of the 2009–10 school year, we posed the question to staff, "What if no student failed at Minnetonka?" In analyzing the data, we discovered that the primary reason for course failure was not lack of understanding of the material, but missing work. We decided that the consequence for not doing the work should be—doing the work. Students are now required to complete missing work during their lunch periods or before school. We also stepped up communication; teachers phone parents of struggling students every three weeks to report on progress.

This combination of increased student accountability and improved home-school communication has produced dramatic results. The number of Fs in grades 9–12 has dropped 63 percent, and the number of Ds has dropped 32 percent from 2009 to the current term. When an entire faculty implements this consequence and moves away from practices that deflate grades—and hope—an entire culture can be transformed.

PROFESSIONAL DEVELOPMENT

To sustain the fundamental kind of grading reform undertaken by Minnetonka, educators need meaningful professional development. They not only need to study grading research, but they also need new learning opportunities around effective classroom management, assessment, and instruction.

Minnetonka created the High School Instructional Leadership Team to redesign professional development in the school. The team works to set the agenda and professional development for all monthly staff meetings and other teacher work days. During each meeting, teachers share research as well as their own experiences.

For example, in a recent meeting, Sarah described an experience concerning her 9th grade English students. During the second semester, the students read two

Greek tragedies, *Oedipus the King* and *Antigone*. When they took their summative assessment for the first play, some students demonstrated a sound understanding of the play itself but performed poorly on a specific section dealing with passage analysis. The students requested a retake. Sarah's dilemma was how to balance the need to start the next play with the fact that students had not mastered the skill of passage analysis. Knowing her students well, she was concerned that they would spend much of their time working on the old material and fall behind with *Antigone*.

Sarah's solution? During study of the second play, she continued to have her students practice passage analysis through intensive formative assessments. When they took the *Antigone* summative assessment, students who had previously struggled with passage analysis had the option to complete an extra section in which they applied this skill to the new play. Sarah replaced the students' previous results with their new scores.

As a result of this strategy, more than 65 percent of her students increased their scores and demonstrated a higher level of mastery of passage analysis. Sarah said that her students felt empowered by this experience.

For the reluctant teacher, the argument that "retakes are great, but they won't work in my classroom" is diminished when colleagues like Sarah show how they've used retests with good results. This timely professional development has transformed our school and sustained our grading work.

A CULTURE TRANSFORMED

Parents, students, and teachers had been comfortable with the old system, with its cushion of "free" points from extra credit and homework completion. We spent much time during the first year educating parents and students about the new policy. During parent-teacher conferences, we held breakout sessions that helped parents understand the need for grading reform and the research supporting it.

Initially, some parents and students feared that Minnetonka's new grading policies would mean that grades would be lower. After the first-semester grades that first year were calculated, it was clear that these fears would not come true. Although there were slightly fewer *A*s, the combined percentage of *A*s and *B*s was the same. In addition, we have seen a significant increase in overall student achievement. Between 2006 and 2010,

- ACT composite scores rose from an average of 24.1 to an average of 25.7.
- The number of students taking advanced placement (AP) exams rose from 505 to 661.
- The number of students participating in the AP Scholars program rose from 160 to 258.
- The Minnesota Comprehensive Reading Exam (grade 10) passing rate increased from 85.5 percent to 92.3 percent.

The school climate has changed, too. No longer do teachers receive panicked calls at the end of the quarter seeking extra-credit opportunities to boost a grade. Regardless of the teacher, the protocols for late work, retests, and evaluating nonacademic factors—to name a few—are the same. Teachers, principals, students, and parents share a common understanding of the school's grading and assessment policies.

Ever since we began the process years ago, teachers have been highly involved in the conversation. They routinely ask themselves, Do my grades reflect students' academic achievement? Are there nonacademic factors influencing the grades?

More broadly, the questions Why are we doing this? and What research supports it? have become central to our ongoing conversations about school improvement. Our relentless focus on grading and assessment practices has helped create a culture of learning at all levels.

According to Erickson, there are many factors that can "deflate" a student's grade—factors that have nothing (or little) to do with actual student ability and achievement. What are these factors? Should they be part of a student's grade, even if they cause the grade to then give an inaccurate account of what a student is capable of doing?

Erickson argues, "Of all the grading dilemmas, retakes and redos surge to the top as one of the most highly disputed." Ultimately, does Erickson favor allowing students multiple chances to succeed on assignments? Why? In your experiences, should students—some or all—be allowed to redo assignments that they fail? Why? Does taking a test over and over, until they succeed, make students' grades in a class more accurate? Or less?

According to The Chronicle of Higher Education, Kelly E. Field joined their staff in 2004 and is now Chief Washington Reporter. Her areas of expertise include Federal aid to students, student loans, Congressional appropriations, and Veterans educational benefits. Her undergraduate degree focused upon Spanish and psychology, while her MA is in journalism.

FACULTY AT FOR-PROFITS ALLEGE CONSTANT PRESSURE TO KEEP STUDENTS ENROLLED
Instructors say they have been encouraged to dumb down courses and change failing grades

BY KELLY FIELD

Three times during the past decade, the Pittsburgh campus of Kaplan Career Institute was named "school of the year" by Kaplan Higher Education, a for-profit higher-education company with more than 70 campuses nationwide. The award recognized the college for its rapid growth and high graduation and job-placement rates.

But some former faculty members say the honor came at a steep price: To keep those numbers high, administrators would pressure employees to falsify attendance records, raise grades, and manipulate job-placement numbers. If a professor refused to change a student's grade, the professor's supervisor would do it, the faculty members say.

"We were constantly told to lower the bar, that we were helping poor people," says Dolores A. Howland-Justice, a former instructor who has filed a lawsuit that accuses Kaplan of fraudulently obtaining millions of dollars in federal student aid by inflating its graduation and job-placement rates. "We were 'do gooders'—that was really played upon."

Kaplan is fighting the lawsuit in the U.S. District Court for Southern Florida, where the case has been consolidated with a lawsuit that makes similar claims against the related Kaplan University. A Florida judge tossed out part of the Pittsburgh suit in December but granted the plaintiffs the right to file an amended claim.

Kaplan declined to respond to questions for this article, citing the pending litigation.

Faculty complaints about the quality and rigor of for-profit education are hardly limited to Kaplan, a subsidiary of the *Washington Post Company*, with about 112,000 students in campus-based and online programs. In interviews with *The Chronicle* and lawsuits filed around the country, more than a dozen current and former professors from six of the seven largest publicly traded education companies say they were leaned on to dumb down courses, offer lengthy extensions, and change failing grades. They describe a system in which expectations are low, cheating is tolerated, and faculty are under tremendous pressure to keep students enrolled.

"We were supposed to keep students in the classroom by any means necessary," says Luccia Rogers, a former professor at Career Education Corporation's Collins College, who says the college fudged grades and forgave repeated plagiarism—claims that the college denies. "It was all about keeping people in the seats to keep the federal money coming in."

Federal student aid is the lifeblood of for-profit colleges, many of which get close to 90 percent of their revenue from Pell Grants, student loans, and other government programs. But the money comes with a key condition: To receive the aid, students must show that they are making "satisfactory academic progress" toward a degree or credential. If they drop or fail too many classes, the government cuts them off.

'ENTERTAIN THEM AND RETAIN THEM'

Ms. Howland-Justice, who resigned in 2006, said the pressure to pass students began shortly after she joined Kaplan as an instructor in the business program, in 2000. A program director approached her in the hall, she says, and told her that a certain student needed to pass. Ms. Howland-Justice responded, "Well, they failed," and the program director repeated herself: "They need to pass." When she failed the student anyway, her supervisor called her in for questioning.

"I pushed it away, but it was definitely a sign, a red flag," she said in an interview last month.

She also quickly discovered that she was expected to do more than just teach; she was supposed to track down absent students, too. Each week, she said, faculty held a "retention meeting" to swap notes on where they'd seen students last. Professors were given lists of absent students to call during their office hours and were required to record why the student had missed class. Students spotted meeting with their advisers, or even glimpsed on the street, would be marked present, she said.

Sometimes supervisors would suggest creative ways to persuade students to return, such as offering to pay for their transportation or reminding them that their student-loan refund check was ready for pickup, she said.

James Watson, who taught at the college for 17 years before he was laid off in 2006, said faculty were encouraged to tell students they could make up all of the work they had missed, even if they had been absent for weeks. If students were at risk of failing, professors would give them extra-credit assignments to bring their grades up. Twice a semester, the campus would hold "make up days." Faculty members would roll out carts piled high with folders containing all the work students had missed that term.

"We were expected to bend over backwards to make sure every student passed," said Mr. Watson, who is not part of the lawsuit. "The pressure was solely and completely on us. It was not on the students' shoulders."

When students failed, it was because "we had not done enough to motivate them," he said.

Ms. Howland-Justice said administrators would tell faculty members that they weren't "fun" enough, that they should engage students through games like Bingo and Jeopardy. To encourage students to show up for class, the college would throw pizza parties and ice-cream socials, and hold raffles for iPods and gift cards.

"I once had a professor say to me, 'You know what your problem is? You think you're here to teach,'" Ms. Howland-Justice said. "Entertain them and retain them, that was our job."

Victoria G. Gatsiopoulos, a former director of career services at Kaplan's Pittsburgh campus and a plaintiff in the lawsuit, saw what became of the college's students when they graduated. She said many students struggled to find work in their fields and sometimes remained in the jobs they'd held before they enrolled.

In 2006, she and Ms. Howland-Justice bonded during a cigarette break and began sharing information. Ms. Gatsiopoulos brought their concerns to the company's compliance manager, confident, she said, that the problems would be fixed. When she was told that investigators found no major problems, she was devastated, she said.

"I was 'Ms. Kaplan,'" she said. "I really believed I could fix things."

Ms. Howland-Justice resigned, and the two women filed a lawsuit against Kaplan in November 2006. Ms. Gatsiopoulos was fired just over a year later, in what was described as a reduction in force. She believes the firing was retaliatory.

Their suit, which seeks the return of millions in federal student aid and Ms. Gatsiopoulos's job back, was filed under the federal False Claims Act, which allows whistle-blowers to sue on behalf of the federal government and receive a share of any money collected. If Kaplan is found liable, it will be required to pay up to three times the amount of fraudulently obtained student aid plus a civil penalty of $5,000 to $10,000 per infraction. As whistle-blowers, Ms. Gatsiopoulos and Ms. Howland-Justice would be entitled to up to 30 percent of the damages.

The lawsuit accuses the college of changing grades and stretching its job-placement statistics to comply with a federal rule that requires short-term programs to graduate and place at least 70 percent of their students in designated, or related, fields of employment. The suit claims that a graduate employed as a telemarketer was counted as working in "business administrative fashion merchandising," and that a fast-food restaurant manager was counted as working in "criminal justice."

Kaplan has moved to dismiss the lawsuit, arguing, among other things, that Ms. Justice and Ms. Gatsiopoulos have failed to prove that its programs are subject to the so-called 70-percent rule. In December the court dismissed that portion of the case on those grounds but granted the former employees the right to amend their claims. They filed an amended complaint in January and are awaiting a ruling.

The Pittsburgh case is one of three false-claims lawsuits against Kaplan that were consolidated in the Florida court in 2009. The broadest of the complaints, filed by three former academic officers at Kaplan University, accuses the company of coercing professors into inflating grades by tying their employment to student-satisfaction surveys administered at the end of the term. The plaintiffs argue that professors who give D's and F's are more likely to get negative student reviews and not be invited back.

"The bottom line is that if students rate you high, you will remain employed," said Carlos Urquilla-Diaz, a plaintiff and former professor, who was fired in 2006.

REWARDING RETENTION

At some for-profit companies, the link between faculty compensation and retention is explicit. The American Public University System pays adjunct faculty members by the student rather than the course, offering $130 per student in undergraduate courses and $150 per student in graduate courses. But students must complete 60 percent of the class for the faculty member to receive the full amount; if a student drops the course before then, the professor gets only 45 percent of the fee, or $58.50 for an undergraduate. Full-time faculty, which make up a quarter of the total, receive a salary.

At Everest College Phoenix online, 15 percent of a professor's evaluation is based on his or her efforts to track down absent and at-risk students to offer "assistance and encouragement."

Some campuses of Heald College base 20 percent of each faculty evaluation on "student outcomes," a category that takes into account student surveys as well as retention and pass rates. The target rate for each is 85 percent, according to Ayn Embar-Seddon O'Reilly, an instructor who has taught online courses for both Everest College Phoenix and Heald. She says professors with high retention and pass rates are rewarded with pay raises and additional classes.

Both colleges are owned by Corinthian Colleges Inc, which enrolls 102,000 students at 120 campuses in the United States and Canada.

Kent Jenkins, a spokesman for the company, says completion and success rates are only "one factor among many" in faculty reviews, and are not used to determine bonuses. "They are an indication of the quality of teaching," he says. "If a disproportionate number of students are not completing, or dropping, it suggests there is a problem with the instruction."

Kaplan University, which tracks new professors by their courses' enrollments, drops, and grades using elaborate color-coded spreadsheets, assigns instructors a "U Rate" based on the percentage of students who withdraw or fail, according to former administrators involved in the lawsuit against the university. They say deans and department chairs were told to speak with faculty members with retention or pass rates below a high cutoff, and were pressured not to renew contracts for faculty members with high U Rates.

In a letter sent to the *Chronicle* shortly before publication of this article, a Kaplan spokesman said U Rates are used to evaluate course delivery methods, "to determine what works best for our students and where we can do better."

"Institutions across all sectors use metrics, such as Kaplan's U Rate, as one of many means to establish standards for assessing learning outcomes," wrote Ron Iori, senior vice president for communications.

At ITT Technical Institute's more than 125 campuses, professors receive printouts every week showing the percentage of students attending each class. Professors whose classes maintain an 80-percent attendance rate and who score high on student-satisfaction surveys are awarded bonuses at the end of the term, a former instructor says. She requested anonymity to protect her business's reputation from damage.

Lauren Littlefield, a spokeswoman for ITT Educational Services Inc., the parent company, says the bonus is consistent with "best practices" in the industry. "We hold our faculty accountable for the success of their students, and we use various incentives to motivate our faculty in this regard," she says, adding that the arrangement includes controls "to mitigate the risk of grade inflation."

Though nonprofit colleges also evaluate professors based on student satisfaction, "they don't monitor failure the same way for-profits do," on an instructor-by-instructor basis, says Guilbert C. Hentschke, a professor of education at the University of Southern California who is an expert on faculty governance. For-profits, he said, tend to "assign more accountability down to the department chair or the professor themself."

"The power is much closer to the classroom," he says.

Tying faculty pay to student satisfaction and student success encourages professors at for-profit colleges to reach out to absent and struggling students. That extra support can be crucial to the sector's students, many of whom are low-income, working adults, or the first in the family to attend college. But critics say the practice shifts the burden of responsibility from students to professors and creates incentives for instructors to relax their academic standards.

In interviews with *The Chronicle*, current and former professors from a wide range of for-profit colleges said they were pressured—and in some cases ordered—to offer extensions, forgive plagiarism, and inflate grades to keep students enrolled and the federal aid flowing.

Kate M. Burkes, who has taught online courses for the University of Phoenix, said plagiarism is widespread at the college. She said she reported one student for plagiarism seven times.

Chad Christian, a spokesman for the Apollo Group Inc., Phoenix's parent company and the largest for-profit-education company by far, says plagiarism is "strictly forbidden" under the student code of conduct and can lead to suspension or expulsion. He said the company responded within a week and a half of Ms. Burkes's initial report, sending a letter to the student to inform him that he was under investigation. The student didn't respond to the letter and was eventually placed on academic suspension.

Faculty complaints about grade changes are widespread in the for-profit sector. In recent years, faculty members from several for-profit colleges have filed lawsuits alleging that they had been fired after reporting altered grades or refusing to raise grades. Two such lawsuits are pending against ITT Educational Services, which paid $725,000 to California in 2005 to reimburse the state for Cal Grants awarded to academically ineligible students. The payment settled the state's portion of a lawsuit filed by two former employees that accused the company of falsifying grades to qualify the students for the grants, a claim the company denied.

But Mr. Hentschke, the faculty-governance expert, says it would be a mistake to conclude that there are more problems among for-profits than in the nonprofit sector simply because more lawsuits have been filed against them.

"Lawsuits happen where the money is," he says.

NO CONSEQUENCES

Instructors from several colleges said administrators often sided with students in disputes over grades, undermining the faculty's authority. One former professor at the Art Institutes chain of colleges, who asked not to be named because she was looking for another job, said students knew that if they complained loudly enough or threatened to sue, their grades would be raised. Department chairmen would sometimes order professors to change grades so students could meet the B average required for a state scholarship, she said.

"My job was to make money for the company—it wasn't to be an educator," she said.

Instructors on the Art Institute's Seattle campus cited similar practices in their failed bid to unionize last year. One of the organizers, who asked not to be named for fear of retaliation, said his students' grades had been changed at least a half-dozen times. He said he was trying to leave the institution, "but it's like a scarlet letter, coming from a for-profit."

Another organizer said faculty were encouraged to give high grades "to keep the students happy." Annual reviews amounted to a "popularity contest," as he put it, in which lenient graders were rewarded for high scores on student-satisfaction surveys.

Jacki Muller, a spokeswoman for Education Management Corporation, parent company of the Art Institutes (and the second-largest for-profit by enrollment), says it is "difficult, if not impossible, to respond to or defend against anonymous allegations that imply an inherent disregard for the principles contained within our code of conduct." She says students' course evaluations are one of five factors considered in annual reviews.

Ms. Rogers, the former Collins College instructor, said some admissions representatives would routinely call professors and question their grades. When she tried to create what she considered "minimal" admissions standards for an online program she was developing, an admissions consultant accused her of being elitist.

A professor at Sanford-Brown College, in Vienna, Va., has filed a complaint alleging that instructors are forbidden to give midterm exams because doing so "discourages" students. The instructor provided *The Chronicle* with a 2010 e-mail from a dean that said the college was continuing its no-midterm policy because it "seemed to work last mod[ule] in keeping up our retention numbers around midterm."

The instructor's complaint, which was sent to the college's accreditor and the U.S. Department of Education, also claims that the campus "culture" does not allow for failing grades.

"Those of us who have worked here for several years feel our honor has been soiled," the instructor wrote in an e-mail to the accreditor.

During the most recent term, 215 of Sanford-Brown's roughly 1,000 students had a 4.0 grade-point average, and 114 had a GPA of 3.5 to 3.75, according to an announcement posted on a campus bulletin board.

Mark D. Spencer, a spokesman for the college's parent company, Career Education Corporation, says it interviewed eight faculty members as part of an internal investigation into the complaint and found nothing to corroborate the instructor's claims. He said the current average GPA on the Vienna campus is 3.1, with 7 percent of students failing. He says the college conducts weekly assessments of student learning, even though it no longer offers midterms.

Allegations of grade inflation in higher education are not new and hardly unique to the for-profit sector, which enrolls about 10 percent of all students. For years, professors and administrators have complained about grade inflation in the nonprofit sector and sought to remedy it.

Still, recent data from the Education Department show that A's are significantly more common at for-profit colleges than at nonprofits. According to the National Postsecondary Student Aid Study, a national survey of students who enrolled in 2007 and 2008, a quarter of students attending for-profits reported receiving "mostly A's," twice as many as at public colleges. At public two-year colleges, 17.5 percent of students said they got mostly A's.

Mr. Watson, the former professor at Kaplan, said administrators would regularly remind faculty members that they were providing opportunities to students who hadn't had many, and that "you have to give them breaks." But what the college was really offering, he said, was the opportunity to pass with little effort.

"When you enable students to do nothing to earn a grade," Mr. Watson said, "they're going to do nothing, and that's a simple fact."

OPPORTUNITY KNOCKS

The Pittsburgh campus of Kaplan Career Institute sits in a nondescript building downtown, on a corner overlooking the double-helix trusses of the Smithfield Street Bridge. From the other side of the Monongahela River, the blue torch of the Kaplan logo stands out among the blank facades of nearby buildings.

A security guard at the entrance directs visitors to the admissions office, where a sign on the door reads, "We build futures, one success story at a time." Inside the reception area, a TV monitor plays images of smiling professors and triumphant graduates, punctuated by the musical refrain, "Wait 'til you see my smile."

An inspirational poster on one recruiter's wall sums up the pitch to prospective students with a photograph of a basketball hoop and the caption: "Opportunity: You always miss 100 percent of the shots you don't take."

Today, Ms. Justice works as a psychiatric counselor at the University of Pittsburgh Medical Center. Ms. Gatsiopoulos is unemployed, and Mr. Watson, who has a master's degree in IT education, works the night shift stocking shelves at a grocery store. About 1,200 students on Kaplan's Pittsburgh campus are now enrolled in certificate and associate-degree programs. The most popular program, criminal justice, costs roughly $31,000, including books and supplies. In 2008, three-quarters of the college's students received Pell Grants or loans. The graduation rate for first-time, full-time students who began their studies in 2006-7 was 56 percent, according to the Education Department.

When it comes to job placement, graduates of some Kaplan programs in Pittsburgh are doing better than others, according to data reported to the state of Pennsylvania. More than three-quarters of recent graduates of the medical-assistant program are employed in their field, but only half of the graduates of the criminal-justice program—the college's largest—are so employed.

Students interviewed outside the Kaplan building on a recent spring evening offered mixed reviews of the college.

Josh Gill, a criminal-justice student who said his cousin had pressured him to enroll, said Kaplan was even better than he had expected. He had just recommended it to two other family members.

"The teachers help us strive for our success," said Mr. Gill, who wore the campus uniform: khaki pants and a polo shirt stamped with the college's name and torch logo. He said he had a 3.98 GPA.

But Dan Bateman and Matt Hale, who are also in the criminal-justice program, said they were disappointed by how "extremely easy" their courses were.

"I should have researched it a little better," Mr. Bateman said. "I'm not getting challenged, and it's too much money."

Mr. Hale said that he left the program last year to enroll at the Community College of Allegheny County, which offers a criminal-justice degree for an eighth of the price, but that he couldn't find classes that fit around his job as a security officer.

Most of the roughly 20 students interviewed said they hadn't heard of instructors' offering lengthy extensions or raising grades. Kiona Germany, who is in the medical-assistant program, said she "wouldn't want a teacher like that."

"There's no easy way out," she said.

But Mr. Bateman said one of his instructors recently complained to him about a student who never showed up for class. "The teacher told me, 'They'll probably make me change my grade again.'"

Consider how Field describes online education. In your experience, is online education the same as face-to-face education? Are students authentically able to succeed in either traditional or virtual classrooms? What factors define whether or not they may succeed?

According to Field, what is wrong with online education—so wrong that it becomes a matter of illegal fraud? How are the problems she identifies with online education different from problems facing traditional educational settings?

In a short essay, describe your own experiences with online learning—either with taking a class in History or with learning something else, such as how to re-tile a floor. Was your learning experience better or worse—terms that need to be defined—online than it might have been in a traditional academic setting? Why? In what ways is an online education more or less passive than a traditional education? Is it possible for an online student to be even more present and engaged in her or his education than a student sitting in a classroom?

John Gravois is an editor at the Washington Monthly, *where he writes on topics ranging from the politics of Google Maps to the marijuana legalization debate in California. In this article, he considers how online education, traditionally the stomping ground of publicly traded companies, is now being threatened from the nonprofit sector.*

THE COLLEGE FOR-PROFITS SHOULD FEAR

BY JOHN GRAVOIS

John Robinson was working nights as an emergency medical technician in Woonsocket, Rhode Island, when he decided to pull his son out of school. David was a second grader with a penchant for acting out, and Robinson, as the parent who stayed home—however groggily—during the day, bore the brunt of the phone calls from the boy's addled teachers. One afternoon in 2008, during a season of endless parent-teacher conferences and emergency midday pickups, Robinson got a call saying that his son had wrecked a classroom in an uncontrollable fit. A short while later Robinson sat in the familiar grip of a meeting with school officials. "Do you have any suggestions?" they asked him. "Yeah," he found himself saying. "How about I teach him?"

The teachers persuaded Robinson to send his son to a school for kids with behavioral disorders. But after David had been there for just a few weeks, Robinson found out that the boy was being physically restrained. So Robinson began homeschooling David, arriving home every morning at seven from his eight-hour shift on the ambulance, making breakfast for the two of them, and then teaching through lunch. After that he would steal a few hours of sleep before heading back to work and starting the cycle all over again. The grueling schedule only accelerated Robinson's growing fatigue with life as a third-shift EMT. "I was starting to feel the burnout," he recalls, citing what is widely held to be an inevitable fact of life for emergency medical workers. He was desperate to climb out of his job. The problem was that there was no clear next rung on the ladder for him to reach for.

Robinson's career had been a series of false starts. After serving as a military policeman during the first Gulf War, he'd studied criminal justice at a local community college for a while, then decided it wasn't for him. He earned his EMT certification—a relatively quick credential—a couple of years later. Fully aware that ambulance work wasn't really "a lifelong career kind of thing," Robinson set his sights on a nursing degree, going so far as to earn all the academic prerequisites. But then, just before he pulled David out of school, Robinson ran aground in the great sand trap of contemporary American public higher education: due to a shortage of instructors, there was a two-and-a-half-year waiting list for the nursing program at his local community college. Other state schools, he heard, had wait lists as well. The system was maxed out.

As Robinson's name inched slowly up the rolls—and as he continued his routine of homeschooling by day and sirens by night—he and his wife started to discuss a new idea. For years, he had been working with kids in his spare time: at a Sunday school, in martial arts lessons, in an afterschool program for children in public housing projects. And now, with his son, Robinson seemed to be making real progress. It was a giant leap—but what if he became a teacher? Better yet, what if he specialized in teaching kids like David, kids who needed special ed? By all accounts, the country was in dire need of such teachers, and the job promised security and solid benefits, perks he had always lacked as an EMT.

With newfound resolve, Robinson began his search for a degree program in special education. And for the first time in his life, he didn't look to a nearby state college. Given his daily commitments, trucking to campus for a normal class schedule was out of the question. His best, and perhaps only, option, it seemed, was to step out into the wilderness of online education.

Robinson had heard of the University of Phoenix and Kaplan University, schools that cater to working adults via a mixture of online courses and classroom facilities in suburban office parks. But he also knew enough, vaguely, to feel he should steer clear of them. ("When you tell people, 'I go to the University of Phoenix,' it's like, 'Haha, that's not a real degree'—you know?")

Robinson doesn't remember exactly how he discovered Western Governors University; he thinks he may have clicked on an advertisement generated by a Google search. He noticed that the school was accredited by the National Council for Accreditation of Teacher Education, a professional oversight body recognized by the U.S. Department of Education; that seemed promising. (WGU happens to be the only all-online school that bears that distinction.) He also noticed that the university was founded by the governors of nineteen U.S. states, which seemed a legitimate, if unusual, provenance. A phone call with an admissions counselor sealed the deal. He enrolled in July 2009.

With that, Robinson stumbled into one of the most unassuming but revolutionary institutions in American higher education. Western Governors differs in several respects from the crush of online schools that have mushroomed in recent years to serve working adults like Robinson. For one thing, unlike the Phoenixes, Capellas, Ashfords, and Grand Canyons that plaster America's billboards, Web sites, and subway cars with ads, Western Governors is a nonprofit institution. That means no $100 million marketing budget, and no 30 percent profit margin. For anyone actually enrolled at Western Governors, the biggest difference is simply its price. The average annual cost of tuition at for-profit universities is around $15,600. Tuition at Western Governors, meanwhile, costs a flat rate of just under $6,000 a year.

The reason Western Governors can offer this kind of tuition (which is often, in practice, even cheaper than it looks; more on this later) is because of its signature twist on the idea of a university—a feature that sets it apart not only from its for-profit competitors, but from virtually every other institution of higher education in the country. This innovation allows WGU to offer its students a college degree that is of greater demonstrable value than what its for-profit competitors offer—and do so for about a third the price, in half the time.

That value proposition is catching on with more and more Americans. With just over 25,000 students today, Western Governors is growing at a rate of about 30 percent a year, and has done so for much of the past decade. That kind of rapid expansion may not have been especially remarkable in the online education sector a few years ago, when the industry was booming, but today it renders WGU a stark outlier. After ten years of breakneck growth, for-profit colleges are in damage control mode, having found themselves the recent target of congressional hearings, scathing news investigations, and a tightening regulatory regime. New enrollments at the University of Phoenix dropped by just over 40 percent in the first part of 2011, while tuition has only increased. At Kaplan new enrollments fell by 48 percent in the same period. These collapsing numbers are not merely the short-term results of bad press. The for-profits are suffering because they have a business model that doesn't quite work anymore; Western Governors is growing because it has one that does.

To understand WGU's big innovation, it helps to think first about the system we have now. In the United States today, a college degree can signal a variety of things. A diploma from an elite school, for instance, broadcasts the culture, prestige, and exclusivity of the institution that stamped it. But as you move down-market into the vast middle range of American schools, those institution-specific signals either become very weak—verging on inaudible—or very geographically specific. (A diploma from Louisiana State University will get you a lot farther in bayou country than in San Francisco.) And yet colleges all across this spectrum produce the same four-year credential: a bachelor's degree. So what is the common denominator between a diploma from, say, Cornell and one from Texas Southern University? Simply put: time. At bottom, every college degree is a blunt, dumb testament to its recipient's persistence. As a recent report from the Center for American Progress put it, a degree means you sat through 120 credit hours of coursework and didn't fail—whatever "fail" may have meant to your given crop of professors.

This way of doing things has two main drawbacks. The first is that for employers a diploma doesn't impart all that much useful information. (What does a C student *know*? Half the material well? All the material by half?) The second major drawback is that for students without a lot of time on their hands—students like John Robinson—it entails a lot of sitting around.

WGU's answer to the status quo is to offer a degree that is based on competency rather than time. By gathering information from employers, industry experts, and academics, Western Governors formulates a detailed, institution- wide sense of what every graduate of a given degree program needs to know. Then they work backward from there, defining what every student who has taken a given course needs to know. As they go, they design assessments—tests—of all those competencies. "Essentially," says Kevin Kinser, a professor of education at the State University of New York at Albany, "they're creating a bar exam for each point along the way that leads to a degree."

Those fixed standards enable a world of variation. At Western Governors, students aren't asked to sit in a class any longer than it takes for them to demonstrate that they have mastered the material. In fact, they aren't asked to sit in a "class" at all. At the beginning of a course, students are given a test called a "pre-assessment." Then they have a conversation with their mentor—a kind of personal coach assigned to each student for the duration of their degree program—to discuss which concepts in the course they already grasp, which they still need to master, and how to go about closing the gap. The students are then offered a broad set of "learning resources"—a drab phrase, sure, but no more so than "crowded lecture hall"—that may include videos, textbooks, online simulations, conversations with a WGU course mentor (an expert in the subject matter who is on call to answer questions), or even tutors in the student's hometown.

If the course material is entirely new to a student, she might make her way through it in eight weeks, or eighteen—or eighty, for that matter. Then again, maybe the student is, say, an ex-pastor who's been selling Nissans in western North Carolina to make ends meet while he earns an MBA in human resources management—and maybe the course is Business Ethics. Ray Shawn McKinnon, the former pastor in question, studied ethics in his early twenties for his bachelor's in ministry and theology, so he nailed the pre-assessment. Given that success, his mentor allowed him to immediately take the final, which he passed. With that, Business Ethics went down on his transcript—and McKinnon moved on to subjects that genuinely terrified him, like math. "If you can prove your competence," McKinnon said, "why pay all of that money to sit through something you already know?"

This is where the real power of the Western Governors economic model comes in. Tuition at the school works according to the "all-you-can-eat buffet" principle: $6,000 covers as many courses as you can finish in two semesters. Given the freedom to move at their own pace, many students can finish more than a standard academic load each term. In fact, according to Western Governors, the average time to degree for people who complete their bachelor's at the school is around thirty months. That's a college degree in two and a half years—for a total of around fifteen thousand bucks.

By comparison, most for-profit institutions—where the average time to degree is fifty-seven months—have simply found ways to shave down the overhead costs of delivering an otherwise utterly conventional college degree. "Ninety-five percent of online education in the country is really classroom education delivered over a wire," Robert Mendenhall, the president of WGU, likes to say. "It's still a professor with fifteen or twenty or thirty students on the other end, and they have a syllabus and assignments." Given the academic industry standard—a hulking research university— it's not particularly hard to find marginal efficiencies in the way higher education is delivered. These institutions are just farmers of low-hanging fruit.

Moreover, while they've lowered the cost of producing an education, they have seldom lowered the price of acquiring one. Many for-profits have simply pegged their tuition at or near the maximum federal loan allowance, which is itself tied to the soaring tuition rates of traditional brick-and-mortar schools. This is a formula that has produced reliably fat profit margins and rising stock prices, if not necessarily high-quality educations. And it has been ripe for a takedown.

Western Governors was always meant to be a revolutionary institution. Its founders simply had the wrong revolution in mind. On a balmy Sunday evening in June 1995, eighteen governors sat down around a conference table in the mountain resort town of Park City, Utah, and began trading war stories about their states' higher education systems. It was a special closed-door session of the annual Western Governors Association meeting, and in the absence of reporters, the state executives vented. They all faced the same awful statistics: growing populations, state budgets failing to keep pace. It was painfully clear that public institutions would need to find a way to scale up drastically, and cheaply, if they were to keep up with demand. But universities were fiercely protective of their inefficiencies—and their worst-performing programs. One governor described catching hell for trying to close a barely functional veterinary school. Others had similar tales. Whenever they tried to intervene in their public higher education systems, the governors agreed, they found themselves rebuffed and ridiculed. So, right then and there, they hit on the notion of starting a new university from scratch.

The chief instigators of the idea were Michael Leavitt, then the Republican governor of Utah, and Roy Romer, the Democratic governor of Colorado at the time. Leavitt was a quintessential 1990s futurist, so steeped in ideas about technology's transformative potential that a Utah student newspaper dubbed him "Governor Leavittate." It was Leavitt who proposed the then-novel idea of launching the university online, thus allowing it to operate across state lines and reach students in the western hinterlands. Romer brought the idea of "competency-based" education to the table, partly as a means to hold institutions accountable—are students learning a commonly agreed-upon set of competencies, or aren't they?—and partly to streamline the college experience. As the former head of a flight school, Romer saw the process of acquiring a pilot's license as a sensible template: if you can demonstrate your abilities, however you came by them, you should receive the credential. (He also liked to evoke the image of Abraham Lincoln studying law out on his own, by candlelight, before being admitted to the Illinois bar.)

That December, the governors organized a conference of state officials, higher education advocates, and technology entrepreneurs at Caesars Palace in Las Vegas. The event was half symposium, half ambush. The organizers asked the hotel to set up its main ballroom as if for a prizefight. Their aim: to stage a showdown between the higher education establishment and the idea that eighteen governors had cooked up excitedly in a hotel conference room a few months before. They called it the "Next Generation Virtual University."

The proposed institution was scarcely more than a vision statement, but it was enough to set off three years of hype surrounding what came to be known as Western Governors University. A series of articles in the *Chronicle of Higher Education* followed, along with a slew of heady pronouncements about WGU and the future of higher education. For traditional colleges and universities, wrote one prominent commentator at the time, "the scare words of choice are 'Western Governors University.'"

In 1999, Kevin Kinser, then a young doctoral student at Columbia, wrote his dissertation about Western Governors. "There are some institutions which have had an enormous impact on American higher education. Harvard stands out as the first college. Cornell is the crown of the land grant movement. Johns Hopkins is America's first research university," he wrote. "Today, like them, the WGU has the potential to set the future direction for higher education."

Not long thereafter, Kinser's dissertation adviser actually apologized for suggesting WGU as a subject for his research. By the start of the new millennium, the project looked like a total flop. When Western Governors began accepting applications in 1998, it received only seventy-five in the first two weeks. The next year, the headline "Virtual U Struggles to Get Real" appeared in the *Salt Lake Tribune*. By the end of 2000, the school had all of

200 students, and a Utah auditor general was officially lambasting it for low enrollments and a failure to compete with other distance education programs. In a year that saw the ignominious collapse of Pets.com, Western Governors was hard to distinguish from all the flotsam sloshing around in the wake of the dot-com bust.

But the school's slow start was no accident. At the Las Vegas meeting, the founders of Western Governors had picked perhaps their biggest fight with the accreditation establishment, the set of powerful nonprofit industry associations that function as the gatekeepers of academic legitimacy, determining which schools are eligible to take part in federal student financial aid programs. Leavitt, who saw the accreditors as a chief barrier to new ideas in higher education, was determined to make Western Governors a kind of test case for the accreditation of geographically dispersed, online, competency-based programs—and was willing to stake his political capital on making it happen. The process took years, and in the interim, students were naturally reluctant to enroll in an unknown, unaccredited school. (As WGU was slogging through its earnest precedent-setting exercise, meanwhile, for-profit schools with online programs discovered a more expedient workaround: they figured out they could gain accreditation simply by acquiring existing but dying traditional institutions—body-snatcher style—and inheriting theirs.)

By the time Western Governors finally secured its accreditation in 2003—from not just one, but four of the major regional accreditors—times had changed. The online education marketplace was an increasingly crowded bazaar. For-profit schools, fortified by infusions of capital from Wall Street and multimillion-dollar marketing budgets, had begun their decade-long boom. No longer a pure symbol of online education's upstart potential, Western Governors was just another player looking for an edge in a competitive field.

Trial and error led the university to a tightly focused approach. Initially, the bulk of the school's offerings had been associate's degree programs aimed at students attending college for the first time. But those students, who were relatively close in age and experience to the traditional college norm, floundered in WGU's online, competency-based program. By contrast, adult students with some college and workplace experience thrived. Ironically, that placed Western Governors squarely in contention not with the entrenched traditional institutions that had so frustrated the school's founders, but with the burgeoning for-profit sector. At Western Governors the average age settled at thirty-six—exactly the same as in University of Phoenix's online programs. Western Governors was not competing with the sun-dappled quad. It was competing with the billboards on Interstate 10.

The school decided on a curriculum offering bachelor's and master's degrees in four "high-demand" areas: education, business, information technology, and health professions, mainly nursing. (Though there are liberal arts components to the school's bachelor's programs, Western Governors professes no interest in churning out philosophy, English, or music history grads.) Those areas of curricular focus, too, put Western Governors on much the same playing field as many of the for-profits. But here again the school could offer something distinct. For-profit universities have often built their businesses around supplying the sort of career training that requires no external validation from a professional body. "They target fields where the credential from the university is sufficient," says Kinser. "So you don't have a lot of nursing programs in the for-profit sector, because there's an external nursing exam. You don't have a lot of law schools, because there's a bar exam. You have legal assistants or medical assistants"—professions defined only by the piece of paper a university hands you. That, of course, frees the for-profits from an element of external accountability—but at a cost to their credibility.

Western Governors, by contrast, found its model particularly well suited to degree programs that feed directly to an official test of proficiency, such as the Praxis national teachers' exams. Such external tests dovetail naturally with the school's system of competency assessments, and in some cases are essentially folded in among them. For example, before he graduates with his MBA in human resources, McKinnon—the North Carolina ex-pastor—will have to pass the national human resources management certification exam. In an online education sector plagued by accusations of low quality, Western Governors can show that its degrees are backstopped by the official guardians of various professions. (It also helps that WGU students tend to score higher than the national average on such professional exams.)

Western Governors attracted students at a steady clip through the mid- and late 2000s—but so did everyone else in the online degree bazaar. The economic crisis of 2008 and the ensuing waves of unemployment were pushing ever more Americans into the market for "retraining," where a gold rush was on. As public television's *Frontline* pointed out last year, some of the for-profits were spending more money on advertising than retail giants like Tide detergent and Revlon cosmetics. Western Governors enjoyed better press than its competitors, but as a nonprofit institution with a modest marketing budget it remained a relatively quiet presence.

Then, in 2009, with the arrival of the Obama administration, the earth began to shift under the for-profits' feet. After a decade of regulatory inactivity under Bush, Washington began to focus a widening beam of scrutiny on the industry, whose business model had increasingly come to consist of vacuuming up federal student loan dollars with little regard for the academic success of the students who brought them. In 2010, for-profit schools derived three-quarters of their revenue from federal grants and Title IV loans. Though for-profits accounted for just 9 percent of the nation's enrollments, they attracted 25 percent of the available federal aid money— and wore out plenty of shoe leather doing it. News accounts, most notably by *Bloomberg*'s Daniel Golden, described for-profit college recruiters bringing their hard sell to casinos, homeless shelters, and military barracks that housed veterans suffering from traumatic brain injury. To many observers, their practices were reminiscent of nothing so much as the tales of subprime mortgage brokers circa 2007, hustling lower-class Americans into adjustable rate loans for houses they couldn't afford. (See "The Subprime Student Loan Racket," November/ December 2009.)

2010 was a year of reckoning for the industry. In April, President Obama's deputy undersecretary of education, Robert Shireman, gave a speech comparing for-profit universities to the Wall Street firms that had brought down the economy, and the stocks of Apollo (Phoenix's parent company), DeVry, Strayer, and others dove promptly. That summer, Senator Tom Harkin of Iowa, the chairman of the Health, Education, Labor, and Pensions (HELP) Committee, called a series of withering hearings stressing the for-profits' dropout rates, their accelerating loan defaults, and their degrees' shoddy performance in the job market. Among those who testified was the hedge fund manager Steve Eisman—who had served as the bluff, de facto hero of Michael Lewis's nonfiction account of the financial crisis, *The Big Short*, because of his prescience about the subprime mortgage market. "Until recently, I thought that there would never again be an opportunity to be involved with an industry as socially destructive as the subprime mortgage industry," he began. "I was wrong."

The chief regulatory threat to the for-profits coalesced in the form of something called the "gainful employment rule." The federal Higher Education Act states that, in order to be eligible for federal aid money, career-oriented schools must "prepare students for gainful employment in a recognized occupation." And so the Education Department set out to define "gainful employment" as a ratio of student loan debt to income. If students weren't earning enough in the workforce to service their debts after leaving a school, the idea went, then the school should not be eligible for aid. The very premise of the rule shook the foundations of the for-profits' business model. Their stocks dropped to four-year lows. New enrollments started to plunge as waves of bad press reverberated through the market, and as schools began reengineering their models away from the old boiler-room recruitment schemes. The entire industry was suddenly pitched against a ferocious headwind.

Western Governors, however, continued to grow. The school's enrollment was verging on 25,000 students— up from just 500 in 2003—and its yearly revenues had climbed from $32 million to $111 million. And if 2010 was the worst of years for the for-profits, it was among WGU's best—not least because of a remarkable announcement made by Indiana's governor, Mitch Daniels, that June. With the stroke of a pen, he declared that he was creating a new state university: WGU Indiana.

With a decimated manufacturing sector, high unemployment, and college completion rates trailing the rest of the country, Indiana was desperate to graduate more students. (Hand-wringing about the value of a college education aside, the numbers are clear: bachelor's degree holders earn $20,000 a year more, on average, than high school graduates, and enjoy 50 percent lower unemployment.) Daniels saw WGU as a way to expand the state's raw higher education capacity, and also to catch Hoosiers who had dropped out of college years ago, giving them a clear route to finishing their degree as working adults. In practice, the creation of WGU Indiana was a wave of the legal wand; it simply meant that students could apply state financial aid toward a degree at Western Governors. But the deal also gave the school the credibility of state backing, along with some free TV spots featuring Governor Daniels himself. Enrollment in the state immediately shot up to twenty times the rate in the rest of the country. And for its part of the bargain, Indiana paid almost nothing. Startup costs for the venture were covered by the Gates and Lumina foundations.

A few months later, the state of Washington signed on to a similar deal, creating WGU Washington. Rumors of talks with more states followed.

Suddenly, WGU had begun playing a role not unlike the one it was designed to play. The economic crisis of 2008 reduced public universities to exactly the circumstances that members of the Western Governors Association had feared in 1995: with state budgets in high distress and populations surging, many universities are capping enrollments, and most are passing more and more of their costs on to students. Western Governors was launched with a set of $100,000 down payments from the states in the Western Governors Association, plus an infusion of $20 million from the federal government and $20 million from industry donors in the private sector. Thus, for a little over $40 million—or the price of a nice new building on a single campus— Western Governors is providing states with a low-cost means to satisfy demand for higher education. "WGU was developed by states, for states," said a very pleased Mike Leavitt in a recent interview, "for just exactly this type of circumstance."

If there is one statistic that should give anyone pause about Western Governors, it is the school's six-year graduation rate as calculated by the federal government: 22 percent. That happens to be the same as the average rate among for-profit colleges, and it is far from heartening. But the statistic comes with a number of caveats. As a matter of policy, the government determines graduation rates by looking only at students who are attending college for the first time and on a full-time basis—in short, the most conventional undergraduates. Like most schools that serve the "nontraditional" demographic, WGU points out that this set of criteria leaves out the vast bulk of its own student body. (The standard retort is that, even if such conventional students make up a tiny proportion of a school's enrollment, they are the ones most likely to graduate in most circumstances.)

In WGU's case, there are more caveats. The school's most recent six-year graduation rate was published in 2010, which means it tracks students who began their studies back in 2004. At the time, most of WGU's current programs didn't exist yet, its enrollment stood at around 3,000, and it was in the process of decommissioning its less-than-successful complement of associate's degrees. In short, Western Governors may simply be too young for this to be a great measure of its success. (Like most schools, Western Governors calculates its six-year graduation rate to include part-time students and those returning to college; that number is 40 percent. But that measure looks back to 2004 as well.)

Another statistic that college watchdogs prize is a school's retention rate, which gauges whether students persist beyond the first year of study. And here Western Governors fares significantly better. This year, 77 percent of its first-year students hung on for a second year, higher than the national average at both for-profits and traditional schools. (According to the Online Education Database, Western Governors ranks fourth among online schools on this measure.)

Moreover, some data suggests that Western Governors does rather well at seeing older students—its target demographic—through to graduation. A 2010 study funded by the Gates Foundation and carried out by McKinsey and Company compared WGU's graduation rate, broken down by different age brackets, to that of an anonymous but typical state higher education system. For students beginning a bachelor's degree in their late twenties, WGU's completion rate was 18 percentage points higher than the control. For students in their forties, it was 28 percentage points higher. Perhaps not surprisingly, only students who entered college in their late teens fared better in the conventional state system.

Those who do graduate from Western Governors credit their mentors with being the single biggest factor in their success. Playing a role with no real analog in the wider world of higher education, WGU's mentors operate from home offices and kitchen tables scattered across the country. (But unlike the armies of adjuncts and graduate students who do most of the teaching at both for-profit and traditional schools, mentors work full-time with benefits.) They might advise a student on time management one day and on finding an attorney the next. McKinnon, the ex-pastor studying for his MBA, was working sixty hours a week at the Nissan dealership earlier this year, and his studies were beginning to crumple under the workload. His mentor, Melissa Prentice, gently raised the issue with him during their regular conversations, and McKinnon started discussing his sense of diminishing returns with his wife. Eventually the three of them—as if in a kind of family meeting—jointly decided that it would be best if he quit the dealership to focus on finishing his degree. Remarkably, given the scope of her role in his life, McKinnon has never actually met Melissa—nor is he exactly sure where she lives. "Melissa, I think, is in Seattle," McKinnon said recently, "or Colorado. She's incredible."

The school's mentors are also in a unique position to survey just how arduous it can be for a grown man or woman in America to finish college and make a fresh start. A few months after John Robinson enrolled at Western Governors in 2009, he lost his job with the ambulance company. His wife had lost her job the year before. In the grim Rhode Island economy, Robinson tried his hand at running a small business, renting a storefront in Woonsocket and opening a martial arts studio. He managed to cultivate enough paying students to cover his overhead, and he started coaching a couple of mixed martial arts cage fighters on the side. But he never cleared much of a profit.

And so, earlier this year, Robinson shuttered his business and moved away from Rhode Island, where he had lived most of his life. He took a job in an auto parts factory in Richmond, Kentucky, where his brother works. These days, Robinson's schedule is more grueling than ever. He works overnight shifts that can last up to twelve hours, painting shock absorbers on an assembly line—then commutes home at five a.m. through a strange landscape of Baptist churches and fields full of cows.

Robinson's load has lightened in at least one respect, however. Soon after the family's move, his son tried going to school for the last part of the year. The experiment went well enough, and David was anxious to play drums in the school band and join the wresting team. So this fall he is entering junior high, and Robinson is putting his homeschooling days behind him. "It had its season," he says.

While Robinson was in the midst of uprooting his life and replanting it in the Bluegrass State, he had to take a few weeks off from Western Governors; he was simply too exhausted to log on. At another school, the semester might have swept past him. But Robinson's mentor told him, "You just do what you need to do." When things had settled back down, he was able to pick up where he had left off. Today he is a little more than halfway through his degree in special education.

Though WGU's brand of competency-based education may sound high concept, Robinson has found it perfectly intuitive in practice. "To me it made more sense than being in a classroom," he says. "As soon as you're done with the work, you get to move on. That just makes more sense." Now, when he looks back at his prior experiences in college, it is with exasperation. "No offense to the younger kids, but you know, I'm in my thirties. You go in there with eighteen- and nineteen-year-olds, and it's more of a social thing for them," he says. "You go sit in a classroom and listen to people ask stupid questions, and the teacher has to go over things, over and over. I was like, oh my gosh, this is just breaking me."

This time, however, he is determined to finish his degree. "I just don't have an option anymore. I'm gonna turn forty next year, and now what? I'm not gonna work a dead-end job," he says. "I'm not a twenty-one-year-old college kid anymore."

No matter how much market share it seizes from the for-profits, Western Governors is unlikely to fire the imaginations of those who like to think of college as a crucible of open-ended inquiry, critical citizenship, and humanistic contemplation. But it's worth remembering that not all crucibles look alike. Before he enrolled at Western Governors, John Robinson says, he had never written a paper in his life. Now he has written more than a score of them, and the experience has given him newfound confidence in his own thinking. "Ideas are flowing, I'm making notes of things," he says. "When I get an idea, I write it down." The other day, he sat down at his computer with his morning cup of coffee after sleeping off a shift at the factory and discovered, via Facebook alert, that an essay he had submitted to a Christian online magazine had been published.

The education of "nontraditional" students has been a subject fraught with cognitive dissonance in America, where much of the discussion surrounding higher education is unduly preoccupied with matters of prestige and exclusivity. In this context, leaders of for-profit colleges have held up their neglected, underserved student populations as a badge of moral seriousness. "What we do is educate people who would never have a shot, thank you very much," a former Kaplan executive said in a recent Washington Post article. In effect, the for-profit schools have accused their prestigious critics of looking at the world of working-class, adult students and saying, for all intents and purposes, "Let them eat cake." And despite their many flaws, the for-profits have a point here. That's why the country needs more institutions like Western Governors— innovative, low-cost schools offering degrees of demonstrable value—that put both the snobs and the profiteers to shame.

Looking forward, all signs point to WGU's continued growth. In a recent interview with the online magazine Inside Higher Ed, Mendenhall was bullish about the template set by the school's deal with Indiana. "Over the next five years we'll aim to do 10, 12 states and then see where that takes us," he said. In early August, Governor Rick Perry announced the creation of WGU Texas, and California's legislature is exploring the feasibility of its own Western Governors subsidiary. Other rumored possible partners include Arizona and Louisiana. Entering into similar agreements with states "would be a rather difficult model for the for-profit sector to duplicate," says Kevin Kinser. Last summer, California's community college system tried to arrive at a similar partnership with Kaplan, but the school's for-profit status made the deal unworkable. (Its increasingly horrible press did not help either.)

In June, the Department of Education handed down the final version of its gainful employment rule. Though more watered down than some reformers had hoped, the new regulation is predicted to render about 5 percent of for-profit programs ineligible for federal aid—effectively shutting them down—starting in 2015. But just as dramatic are the effects the rule is already having on the industry, as schools clamber to reengineer their business models so as not to run afoul of Washington. Last year, 25 percent of students who attended for-profit colleges defaulted on their student loans within three years. In order to survive, schools will have to find some way to bring those numbers down. Phoenix, which not long ago compensated recruiters according to the number of students they enrolled (homeless, addicted, brain injured, or no), has instituted a mandatory three-week student orientation period. The entire sector is grappling with the shock of suddenly having a stake in its students' success.

WGU, whose model needs no overhauling—and whose student loan default rate is about 5 percent—will only benefit from its competitors' time in the wilderness. The demand for higher education, after all, is stronger than ever.

What's more, it may only be a matter of time before the Western Governors model begins to pose its founders' challenge to traditional higher education as well. Consider WGU's college of business, the school's second largest academic program. Business is the most popular undergraduate major in America. But recently, the sociologists Richard Arum and Josipa Roksa found that undergraduate students of business learn measurably less than students in other fields. The scholars examined the results of a national essay-based exam called the Collegiate Learning Assessment, and measured how much students' scores improved over the course of four years in college. Business students' scores improved scarcely at all.

Colleges across the country regularly administer the Collegiate Learning Assessment. But schools closely guard the results—so loath are they to reveal what their students are, or aren't, getting out of their studies. By contrast, a Western Governors degree is a fairly straightforward testament to what a graduate knows. It doesn't seem much of a stretch to imagine that, given the choice, employers might come to prefer the latter.

Earlier this year, the Center for American Progress published a report called "Disrupting College," by the Harvard business school professor Clayton Christensen and three coauthors. Research universities, Christensen argues, simply weren't designed to do what we are increasingly asking higher education to do: educate students from wildly different backgrounds for jobs outside the academy in ways that can be measured and assessed. Christensen and his coauthors describe the for-profit and online schools that have cropped up over the past twenty years as a "first wave of educational disruptive innovation." But that wave arose under a system of regulatory incentives that didn't either reward student success or punish failure, and so it could break up against reforms like the gainful employment rule. Some schools in that first wave will survive, and others won't. Phoenix, with its astonishing enrollment of 438,000 students, is fiercely trying to adapt—and, with its multibillion-dollar revenues, it probably will succeed. Corinthian Colleges, a large chain of schools with an average 40 percent default rate—15 percentage points higher than the average in the sector—might not.

At just over 25,000 students, WGU's enrollment is still a rounding error in the grand scheme of American higher education. The school's curriculum is relatively narrow, and its model may require a degree of discipline and self-motivation that many students don't possess. But perhaps more than any other institution out there, Western Governors is aligned with the new pressures shaping the higher education market. The only question is how big it can get.

Writing nonstop for at least five minutes, consider this: What makes a degree from one school more valuable than the same degree from another school? Why do some people consider a degree from a prestigious, private school more meaningful than the same degree from a large state university? Why do some people consider a degree from an online school to be worth less?

Consider the information provided in this article, and then visit the Web site for WGU. Based on your reading, how is your school different from WGU? Does it, for example, serve different students? Meet different student needs?

Summarize, in a short essay, the arguments Gravois makes about why WGU is superior to other schools—especially for-profit schools. Explain why you agree or disagree with his reasoning and his conclusions. In what ways does this reasoning ask you to consider the idea of an authentic education?

Katie Davis is a 2011 MA graduate of the Harvard Graduate School of Education. Much of her work exists at the intersection of digital media and education in America. Scott Seider is an assistant professor at Boston University (in the School of Education) and author or co-author of several books, including Shelter: Where Harvard Meets the Homeless. *According to his heavily detailed home page at howardgardner.com, Howard Gardner is "The author of 25 books translated into 28 languages, and several hundred articles." He is a prolific writer in fields ranging from education to psychology. In this scholarly article from* Social Research, *this dynamic team of researchers turn their critical eye on the nature of human self-fabrication.*

WHEN FALSE REPRESENTATIONS RING TRUE (AND WHEN THEY DON'T)

By Katie Davis, Scott Seider, and Howard Gardner

In April 2007, Marilee Jones resigned as MIT's dean of admissions after word reached the administration that she had fabricated part of her resume 28 years earlier (Lewin, 2007: A1). When she first applied for a job at MIT in 1979, Jones had claimed to have earned degrees from three colleges in upstate New York. Yet, there was no record of her having earned a degree from any of the institutions she named. The revelation came as a shock to the MIT community and to those who were familiar with her work as dean of admissions. During the 10 years since she had assumed the position, Jones had tried to discourage parents and students from embellishing their resumes in an effort to appear more attractive to colleges. In her 2006 book, *Less Stress, More Success: A New Approach to Guiding Your Teen Through College Admissions and Beyond,* Jones urges students to live with integrity and avoid the temptation to cheat. Her message resonated with parents, students, and college admissions administrators and contributed to her popularity in the MIT community.

Jones's resignation coincided with a course that one of this article's authors co-taught in 2007 at a selective liberal arts college. The course, entitled "Meaningful Work in a Meaningful Life," encouraged students to reflect on their approach to work, including critical issues they will likely encounter and difficult decisions they might have to make. The course aimed to provide students with a "toolkit" of concepts that would be useful as they embarked on a life of meaningful work. At the time, we asked the students participating in this course what they thought of Jones's deception. Most of the students asserted that Jones's fabricated resume did not warrant her resignation. They reasoned that she had done exemplary work while serving as the dean of admissions, and she should not have been punished for an act that has become commonplace. When pressed to explain their perspective, our students argued that everyone misrepresents themselves to a certain extent on their resumes. We had not anticipated this response, and we were disturbed to hear the students' casual defense of Jones's actions. Their attitude did not reflect awareness or concern that the falsification of one's credentials is grounds for immediate dismissal at any place of employment, nor were they struck by Jones's clear, if poignant, hypocrisy.

The disjunction between our own interpretation of the Jones story and that of our students heightened our interest in young people's attitudes toward self-fabrication. We began by asking ourselves whether all self-fabrications are necessarily wrong. According to Goffman's (1959) dramaturgic analysis of social life, self-fabrications are normative, not exceptional. We are all putting on a performance to some extent. However, Goffman distinguished between true and false performances, arguing that a true performance is one that is authorized whereas a false performance is not. Since the self is a "collaborative manufacture" between performer and audience, authorization must be a collective act. Individuals cannot be the sole arbiters of their self-performances. It becomes necessary, then, for interacting individuals to find consensus regarding the parameters of authorization. In this paper we seek to identify these parameters through an examination of the causes and consequences of young people's various self-fabrications. In so doing we explore the individual and societal factors that both compel and sanction these fabrications. We argue that there are circumstances under which self-fabrications may have beneficial effects and are, thus, authorized representations of the self. In contrast, a false, or unauthorized self-representation is one that results in harm to the self, to others, and to society.

THE HUMAN NATURE OF SELF-FABRICATIONS

Goffman (1959) explained that in any given social situation we do not have access to all of the facts, in part because we cannot know another person's innermost thoughts and feelings. We must therefore rely on representations of reality rather than on the reality itself. As manmade substitutes of reality, representations are open to manipulation. Taking a dramaturgic perspective, Goffman argued that we stage our self-performances in order to manage the impressions that others form of us. He described the self as a product, not a cause, of the scene that a performer creates. The self is the character that the performer plays. It arises as the performance is recognized by the audience. Thus, the self does not exist within the individual. It is, rather, a "collaborative manufacture" between performer and audience. Goffman extended his theater metaphor further by distinguishing between the "front region" and the "back region" of a self-performance. The performance takes place in the front region and the audience interprets its meaning. The performer works in the back region to construct the scene, drawing on the tools at his or her disposal to produce the desired impression.

The dramatic aspect of one's self-presentation may be accentuated during adolescence. Erikson (1968) described this stage of the life cycle as a period of identity development. Individuals experience a psychological "crisis" as they begin to reexamine their childhood identifications and contemplate their role in the broader society. During this period, individuals develop the ability to think abstractly, a skill that enables them to entertain and hold onto multiple versions of themselves and to begin developing a self-theory. Harter (1999) notes that this cognitive capacity emerges at a time in individuals' lives when they face an increasing number of potential roles as their social contexts multiply and expand. The transition from middle school to high school tends to bring with it greater autonomy from parents, the experience of multiple teachers and classmates throughout the day, and new and diverse extracurricular options. According to Harter, individuals assume different roles in different situations in order to adapt to the situation at hand.

To resolve the adolescent identity crisis, Erikson (1968) argued that many individuals require a psychosocial moratorium, or a "time out," during which they are free to explore alternate roles and values and evaluate how other people receive them. In this space, consequences may be suspended as adolescents rework and integrate their childhood identifications into an identity that is situated in and recognized by the broader society. Identity experimentation is not simply an expected attribute of the adolescent period; it is a necessary and healthy part of individuals' psychosocial development. Building on Erikson's work, Marcia (1988) elaborated on the centrality of exploration in the identity formation process. He warns that without such exploration, adolescents may experience one of two forms of identity confusion. Either they commit to a rigid and narrowly defined identity without exploring other options; or, they refrain from exploration and commitment altogether and maintain a diffuse identity that may be crippling.

In the contemporary United States, it may well have become more difficult for middle-class adolescents to carry out identity exploration (Turkle, 1999). Their lives are overly scheduled with the academic work and extracurricular activities they need to gain acceptance to college. They are strictly monitored by the adults in their lives, who fear for their safety in this age of "stranger danger" (boyd, 2007). Even if they do manage to escape adult supervision, boyd notes that young people are often regarded as menaces and banned from many public spaces such as shopping malls. Moreover, their recreational activities can have weighty consequences such as the danger of contracting a sexually transmitted disease through unprotected sex or getting into accidents through reckless driving (Turkle, 1999). In this atmosphere, it is perhaps unsurprising that young people tend not to spend time exploring their identities. Indeed, Arnett (2004) goes so far as to argue that the identity exploration phase may have shifted to emerging adulthood (that is, the college years).

THE BENEFITS OF SELF-FABRICATIONS

One space in the twenty-first century United States does seem to provide opportunities to adolescents for identity exploration: online activity. As Turkle (1999) notes, the affordances of digital technology make it easy and appealing to engage in identity experimentation. Unlike offline spaces, where one is constrained by physical characteristics such as age, height, race, and sex, online spaces give individuals virtually complete control over their self-presentation. Thus, the way in which adolescents engage in online identity experimentation is limited only by their software program and technological skill. With online virtual worlds such as *World of Warcraft*, *Second Life*, and *City of Heroes*, players create avatars, graphical representations of their online persona, that might (and quite often) bear little resemblance to their offline appearance. A 16-year-old girl can become an ancient wizard with God-like powers; a boy with cerebral palsy can become a superhero capable of flight. Avatars are used in other online spaces as well, such as social network sites, online chat forums, blogs, and instant messaging. People go to sites like Meez and WeeWorld to create their avatars and attach them to different online environments. Some people attach a single avatar to multiple online spaces, whereas others choose to create different avatars for different spaces.

There are many ways to engage in identity experimentation online besides the construction of an avatar. One study looked at how Dutch youth ages 9 to 18 portrayed themselves when using text-based instant messaging to chat with others online (Valkenburg, Schouten, and Peter, 2005). Of the 600 respondents, 50 percent said they experimented with their identity at least sometimes while online. The most common forms of identity experimentation included pretending to be an older person, an offline acquaintance, a more flirtatious person, or an elaborated fantasy person. Stern's interviews (2007) with young authors of personal websites and blogs revealed the deliberateness with which these young content creators chose to present themselves online. One girl who wanted to project a counterculture, antiestablishment image on her personal website made careful decisions about what music to list on her site. She said that she omitted songs and groups that she enjoyed but did not fit the image of herself she was trying to convey to her online audience. Similarly, a blogger said that he showed only the "deep" parts of his personality on his blog because he wanted to come across as serious and introspective.

Once created, an online self-representation is easy to revise, update, or delete. Adolescents can therefore change the look and content of their blog, website, or social network profiles as frequently as they wish. They might upload new photos of themselves; reprogram the layout of their page with new colors and designs; or update their lists of favorite music, books, and television shows. Notably, the nature of the new digital media allows adolescents to undertake these multiple forms of identity experimentation simultaneously (Turkle, 1999).

Besides the ease with which individuals can manipulate their identities online, digital spaces boast several additional characteristics that make identity experimentation appealing and rewarding. First, the stakes are often perceived to be lower online than offline (Turkle, 1999). Due to the distance from one's audience and the absence of certain visual and auditory cues, it often feels safer to try out different versions of oneself and evaluate their reception by others (Valkenburg et al., 2005). Thus, an individual may feel more comfortable taking certain risks as a Night Elf in *World of Warcraft* than as a tenth-grade student in high school. Indeed, several of the young people that Stern (2007) interviewed said they found it easier in online spaces to confront aspects of their experiences that they had kept hidden offline, such as depression and sexual orientation. They explained that they were unsure how their family and friends would react. It felt safer to tell an unseen audience and gauge their response before attempting to speak face-to-face with their loved ones.

Additional benefits of identity play are illuminated by the example of Heather Lawver and her fictitious school newspaper, *The Daily Prophet* (Jenkins, 2006). At the age of 13, Heather started an online newspaper for the imaginary Hogwarts School for Witchcraft and Wizardry. Writers for the newspaper assumed fictitious personas relating to the *Harry Potter* world. Typically, children created identities that combined elements of their offline selves with aspects of the *Harry Potter* characters. Often, these online personas revealed glimpses of the children's offline difficulties, such as illness or family conflict. Heather's staff of writers eventually grew into the hundreds. The stories they wrote were fanciful and covered the imagined goings on of the fictitious students at Hogwarts.

Heather encouraged her staff of writers to leave the trappings of offline life and enter deliberately into the imaginary world of *Harry Potter*. Jenkins (2006) argues that children and adolescents' participation in this world gave them the opportunity to express their creativity and grow as writers and individuals. Heather assumed a mentoring role and edited every piece herself. In this way, she helped the budding writers to develop their writing skills and discover their authorial voices. Many adults have expressed concern that young people are copying the work of others when they engage in fan fiction writing. Jenkins suggests instead that fan fiction can be viewed as a type of apprenticeship that frees individuals to practice an array of literary skills.

The children who participated in *The Daily Prophet* grew as individuals as well as writers. By writing each other into their fantasies, they experienced personal connections and validation that may have been lacking in their offline lives (Jenkins, 2006). The connections they forged with the *Harry Potter* characters also proved significant. For instance, many of the girls claimed an affiliation to the only central female character of the series, Hermione. Through this affiliation, Jenkins argues, they were able to play out their own "empowerment fantasies." Notably, virtually all of the characters created by the children possessed a special gift or talent. In this way, the writers for *The*

Daily Prophet were able to explore their ideal, or "possible," selves (Markus and Nurius, 1986). In short, role-playing provided these children with a means for understanding themselves in a deeper way. Eventually, individuals must be able to connect their online and offline identities. Self-transformation through identity experimentation occurs when the various elements with which one is experimenting are integrated (Turkle, 1999). In late adolescence, individuals develop the cognitive ability to coordinate abstract representations, including representations of the self. This cognitive skill makes it possible for them to begin the process of integrating their multiple identities. Internet-based activities such as online journaling provide a space for adolescents to do this work. The young people that Stern (2007) interviewed described how they used their online journals to engage in self-reflection and receive feedback from their virtual audience. These adolescents observed how their audience responded to their identity experiments; made adjustments based on perceived discrepancies between their self-perception and others' perceptions of them; and tested out alternate versions of themselves for further feedback. With any luck, through this cycle of experimentation, feedback, and self-reflection, they were able to bring the multiple versions of themselves into alignment and form a coherent identity.

DANGERS TO THE SELF

While identity experimentation can promote healthy development, there are many instances when self-fabrications can prove harmful to the identity formation process. Widespread immersion in the Internet is a recent phenomenon, and it is not yet clear the extent to which online identity play helps or hinders the formation of a healthy sense of self (Buckingham, 2007). Turkle (1995) identifies at least two ways in which computer-mediated identity play can do harm to the self. Fragmentation arises when the different identities that one tries on remain uncoordinated. Turkle observes that "multiplicity is not viable if it means shifting among personalities that cannot communicate" (1995: 258). Fragmentation is problematic because it prevents the formation of a coherent sense of self, the defining characteristic of a healthy identity (Erikson, 1968).

A *Frontline* documentary that aired on PBS in 2008 featured Jessica Hunter, a self-described outcast who had no friends at her high school and endured constant teasing from her classmates. Jessica went online and created a personal website, where she became the Goth model and artist "Autumn Edows" and eventually developed a cult following. Jessica said she loved the positive attention she received online, which contrasted sharply with her offline experience. Since she did not like herself offline, she explained, she enjoyed the feeling of being someone else online. Jessica's transformation from a shy, awkward, and friendless high school student into the popular Goth artist and model Autumn Edows could be considered one example of a fragmented self. Jessica kept her online and offline personas separate and distinct from one another. Unlike the young people interviewed by Stern (2007), she did not attempt to bring the two versions of herself into alignment. As long as the gulf between Jessica Hunter and Autumn Edows remains, her sense of self is likely to remain fragmented and, ultimately, unsatisfying.

Turkle (1995) also distinguishes between "acting out" and "working through" in relation to identity play. Using online activities to recast and work through one's offline challenges can lead to growth and insight. In contrast, acting out involves "fruitless repetition" of ongoing conflicts across settings. Individuals who act out fail to reflect on and learn from past mistakes and their conflicts remain unresolved. *The New Yorker* magazine profiled a young woman whose story of online identity play illustrates this concept well (McGrath, 2006). Offline, Stevie Ryan was a 22-year-old aspiring actress in Los Angeles dating the actor Drake Bell; on YouTube she became Cynthia, or Little Loca, an 18-year-old Latina from East L.A. with a boyfriend named Raul. Ryan's transformation from Stevie to Little Loca took about 15 minutes and involved the application of a fake mole on her cheek, a change of clothes and makeup, and the donning of a more assertive and accented style of speech. Ryan used her Internet persona to act out when she and her real-life boyfriend, Bell, broke up, replaying the conflict online as a dispute between Little Loca and Raul. Little Loca used her YouTube platform to rant against Raul, blaming him for the recent vandalism of her car and accusing him of drug use. While the production of these videos may have been a cathartic exercise for Ryan, they seem more like a repetition of than a resolution to her offline problems. It is unclear how Little Loca's tirades against Raul helped Ryan to gain insight into her failed relationship with Drake Bell.

In addition to fragmentation and acting out, the creation of multiple selves is problematic when the selves one creates are inauthentic. As children move into adolescence their social contexts expand and they must find ways to adapt to the different situations in which they find themselves. They may alter aspects of their self-presentation in order to move more easily across their changing contexts. These alterations can be healthy and adaptive, provided they are done in a spirit of authenticity. Harter (1999) explains that inauthentic selves arise when individuals hide their true thoughts and feelings in order to gain the approval of others. The suppression of authentic parts of oneself is associated with a variety of negative consequences, including feelings of low self-worth, depressed affect, and a weakening of one's close relationships (Gilligan, 1996). Adolescents often expend a tremendous amount of energy promoting themselves online (Stern, 2007). They design their social network profiles, blogs, and websites in a way that will capture and hold the attention of their audience. In the process, they may keep out thoughts and feelings that do not fit with the image they are trying to convey online. To the extent that self-promotion becomes the central focus of attention, the selves adolescents portray online are likely to be inauthentic fabrications. In contrast to the healthy act of using online spaces to explore previously unexamined facets of one's identity, the deliberate suppression of parts of oneself undermines the identity formation process by preventing the construction of an integrated, holistic sense of self.

HARM TO OTHERS

The consequences of self-fabrications cross over into the realm of morality when harm is done to other people. In some cases, the manipulation of one's identity engenders feelings of betrayal among those on the receiving end. When viewers started to notice that Little Loca's mole changed position from one video to the next and that her boyfriend Raul bore a striking resemblance to the actor Drake Bell, Ryan eventually admitted that Little Loca was a fabrication (McGrath, 2006). While many viewers had long suspected the ruse and continued to watch nonetheless, it is likely that others believed Little Loca to be a real person until the moment Ryan confessed. They might have felt deceived when they watched Ryan explain that Little Loca was nothing more than a product of her imagination. It is important to realize that individuals come to online spaces with different expectations and goals (James et al., 2008). Some people approach their online activities in a playful spirit. These people are unlikely to be surprised or disturbed to learn that the people with whom they interact online do not exist in the same form offline. Others, however, enter into online interactions with earnestness and expect others to do the same. When they find out that other users do not hold the same motivations and goals, they may feel disappointed and deceived.

Stevie Ryan had many models of staged performances to follow when she created the character of Little Loca. In the media, "reality" television shows employ diverse strategies to ensure that each episode includes sufficient drama, emotion, and suspense to attract viewers. For instance, the story editors of MTV's *Laguna Beach,* a show aimed specifically at young people, used the popular technique of "Frankenbiting" to create a nonexistent love triangle among two girls and a boy (Poniewozik and McDowell, 2006). With Frankenbiting, story editors manufacture a particular relationship between two people by editing together footage taken in different contexts. Thus, a statement said about one person may be edited to make it seem as if it was said about another, thereby creating a relational dynamic that does not exist.

The public does not appear to be surprised by such tactics. In one survey, the majority of respondents said they expect reality shows to manipulate events in some way (Poniewozik and McDowell, 2006). Other surveys have shown that both adults and young people perceive mainstream news media to be biased (Kiesa et al., 2007; Turner, 2007). In particular, cable television networks such as CNN and Fox are thought to deliver the news with an ideological slant. One experiment showed that viewers detected an ideological bias in television news stories that were assigned either a CNN or a Fox label, irrespective of the content of the story (Turner, 2007). These results were true whether the viewer was a self-described liberal, conservative, or moderate. Briefly stated, both the entertainment and news media provide powerful models of inventive representations of reality.

In addition to examples in the media, deception is also modeled closer to home by the adults in young people's everyday lives. The recent case of Megan Meier is an extreme example. At 13, Megan began a flirtation with a 16-year-old boy, Josh Evans, on the popular social network site MySpace (Maag, 2007). The flirtation continued for a month until Josh suddenly changed his attitude and started to tease and insult Megan. She committed suicide shortly after he wrote to her that the world would be better without her in it. Josh Evans turned out to be Lori Drew, a 47-year-old woman and mother of Megan's former friend. Drew created the persona of a 16-year-old boy to earn Megan's trust and find out what Megan thought about her daughter. While online deception rarely ends in death, Megan's story provides a potent example of the very real harm that self-fabrication can do to others.

Sometimes self-fabrications can harm other people by unfairly denying them certain opportunities. In the early part of this decade, our research team at the GoodWork Project (www.goodworkproject.org) interviewed several high school students who took part in the highly competitive Intel Science Talent Search. The interviews were part of a larger empirical investigation studying young people's approach to work. The rewards of the Intel competition are high and include money, status, social networks, and, in most cases, access to the nation's most prestigious universities. One of the young scientists we interviewed was Allison (a pseudonym), a high school senior who worked as a research apprentice in a university-based neurobiology lab. During her interview, Allison spoke strongly of the values that guided her scientific work. She believed that scientists should never fabricate their data or represent others' work as their own. Yet, when she sat down to write the report of her findings for the Intel judges, Allison deliberately misrepresented the way in which she had conducted her experiment in order to win the judges' favor. She was named a semifinalist and won $2,000 and a college scholarship. She was subsequently accepted at an Ivy League school, where she planned to pursue scientific research in molecular or cell biology. She hoped one day to teach at the graduate level. While Allison benefited personally from her decision to misrepresent the design of her experiment, her actions may have deprived another student from earning $2,000 and a college scholarship. Also, if she continues to deceive in this fashion, she risks harming herself and others, while also undermining the calling of science. Here, again, a false representation "harmed" another individual.

Callahan describes similar examples in *The Cheating Culture* (2004), a book that explores the motivations behind Americans' growing comfort with cutting corners in order to get ahead. With respect to young people, Callahan relates the diverse ways that students at both public and private high schools misrepresent their work, including the use of the Internet to find and plagiarize term papers. Copy-paste functionality and the power of a Google search make it possible for students to "write" papers that lack any original sentences of their own. Callahan notes that parents are often complicit in students' fabrications. For instance, wealthy parents hire private college counselors to write (or at least heavily edit) their children's college essays; employ private tutors to do their children's homework; and ask psychiatrists to diagnose their children with a learning disability so they can take the SAT without time restrictions. Students who are given an academic boost by hired experts enjoy an unfair advantage over students who, through choice or necessity, do not receive such assistance. The help these students receive may secure them a place at a competitive college, but their success comes at the expense of other students.

explain how we live in this such a competitive environment
pressure → competitor

THE ROLE OF MARKET FORCES IN PROMOTING SELF-FABRICATIONS

Callahan (2004) attributes students' willingness to cut corners in part to the intensely competitive atmosphere in which they are raised. Frank and Cook (1995) were among the first to describe the "winner take all" society of the late twentieth century. It is a society distinguished historically by the extreme competition to succeed at all costs. The stakes are high because the difference between winning and losing is so large. Due to modern technology and market globalization, the best performers in any given field attract a wide audience. As a result, there is no audience for the competent, but slightly less-skilled, performers.

Thus, winners are lavishly rewarded, losers receive little compensation, and a middle ground between these two extreme conditions has become rarer. Frank and Cook identified this disparity as the primary reason for the rising income gap, which has only grown in the twenty-first century.

In this competitive atmosphere, Brook argues that young professionals face the unfair choice of being "a sellout or a saint" (2007: 6). He notes that a generation ago the difference in salary between a lawyer and a teacher was not so great as to prevent the two professionals from owning homes and living in the same community. Today, corporate lawyers earn enough to buy large houses in gated communities, while a teacher's salary makes it difficult to buy a house in many communities. Due to this state of affairs, young people who may have been attracted to teaching are looking instead to corporate America and vying for jobs as management consultants and investment bankers (Rimer, 2008). According to Brook, they are not necessarily aiming to strike it rich; rather, they are trying to avoid poverty.

The competition for a job in corporate America begins before college. Most of the leading management consultancy firms and investment banks hire exclusively from elite universities. Faced with unwieldy applicant pools, employers rely on heuristics such as the reputation of one's school in order to reduce applicants to a manageable number. It thus becomes critical for young people to attend a top college if they hope to be considered for such a job when they graduate. And yet, with top colleges and universities in the United States accepting less than 10 to 20 percent of their applicants, it has never been more difficult to gain admittance to these institutions.

From CEO of a Fortune 500 company to high school junior sitting the SAT for the first time, everyone is feeling the pressure to succeed. Callahan notes that, "As the race for money and status has intensified, it has become more acceptable for individuals to act opportunistically and dishonestly to get ahead" (2004: 106). In other words, profitability, not morality, drives people's decisions. In this context, it is perhaps not surprising that so many students and their parents are willing to hire experts to write college essays and complete homework assignments if it means improving their chances of getting into a top college, with the dividends that accompany this status.

Surveys of college and high school students show that young people do, in fact, feel tremendous pressure to gain a competitive advantage over their peers. The college students surveyed across the United States by McCabe, Trevino, and Butterfield (2001) said they often felt compelled to cheat in school because they are competing for a small number of desirable jobs. Since they see their peers around them cheating, they reason they must also cheat in order to remain competitive. The 2006 Report Card on the Ethics of American Youth showed a similar trend among high school students. This national survey found that close to 60 percent of respondents agreed or strongly agreed that "In the real world, successful people do what they have to do to win, even if others consider it cheating."

Young people's focus on gaining a competitive advantage in the workplace is a relatively recent development. The Cooperative Institutional Research Program's Survey of American Freshmen shows an illuminating shift in attitudes towards work and lifestyle (Pryor et al., 2007). This annual survey has tracked the attitudes, values, and goals of first-year college students across the United States since 1966. In 1966, 42.2 percent of the students surveyed said that "being very well off financially" is "very important" or "essential" to them. In 2006, this figure was 73.4 percent. In contrast, 85.8 percent of the students surveyed in 1967 said that "developing a meaningful philosophy of life" is "very important" or "essential" to them, whereas only 46.3 percent of the students in 2006 said the same.

THE INFLUENCE OF CULTURAL ATTITUDES
REGARDING MORALITY

Allison, the young high school scientist described earlier, not only felt immense pressure to misrepresent her experiment design in the Intel competition; she felt completely justified in doing so. Cultural attitudes regarding morality that are distinct to our time and society evidently contribute to young people's comfort with fabricated self-representations. In the United States today, a "culture of individualism" prevails in which the pursuit of the American Dream seems to be the mandate of every citizen (Bellah, Madsen, Sullivan, Swidler, and Tipton, 1996; Kluegel and Smith, 1986). This cultural discourse attributes successes and failures to individual effort alone. The rich are rewarded for being more talented, harder working, and experienced than the poor. In our focus on the individual, we often fail to consider the economic and political forces that have contributed to disparities in wealth and wellbeing in the United States. Instead, we blame the poor for their plight and congratulate the rich for their inherent superiority or their well-earned success.

In its celebration of the individual, our culture is distinct from many others. Shweder, Much, Mahapatra, and Park (1997) describe the moral discourse of the United States as an "ethics of autonomy" that overshadows two alternative moral discourses: the "ethics of community" and the "ethics of divinity." The authors explain that an "ethics of autonomy" is commonly found in individualistic societies such as the United States. This moral discourse places value on individuals' free will to choose and be guided by their personal interests and preferences without interference from other individuals or institutions. Concepts such as individual harm, rights, and justice are central to this discourse.

According to Shweder et al. (1997), different cultures emphasize different moral discourses such that the ratio of the three moral goods varies across cultural traditions. An ethics of autonomy is present in rural India, but it is less salient than the ethics of community and divinity. For that society, the interests of the individual are typically overshadowed by the interests of the community and the sacred order. In contrast, secular societies such as the United States possess a much different ratio of moral goods. Our free market society foregrounds the claims of the individual as it diminishes the authority of community and divinity.

The dominion of the individual has never been as far-reaching in American society as it is in the twenty-first century. Wolfe (2001) claims that we have been accumulating individual freedoms throughout the history of the United States—most recently our moral freedom. Wolfe notes that the right to own property and make and sell goods secured our economic liberty in the nineteenth century. Our political freedom was achieved in the twentieth century upon individuals' acquisition of the right to vote and run for office. According to Wolfe, cultural and political upheavals of the 1960s and 1970s ushered in the final freedom, the freedom to define for oneself the meaning of a virtuous life.

Wolfe's research team asked Americans what it means to lead a good and virtuous life, and probed as well the role that virtues such as honesty, loyalty, forgiveness, and self-discipline play in their daily actions and decisions (Wolfe, 2001). Respondents said they were guided primarily by subjective feelings regarding their own best interest and their desire to avoid harming others. They did not believe they needed to sacrifice their personal needs and desires in order to lead a virtuous life. Nor did they feel that others had any right to pass judgment on their morality or other prevailing community norms. Wolfe's subjects felt beholden to themselves rather than to the authority of tradition. Wolfe observes: "Americans approach the virtues gingerly. They recognize their importance, but since they are wary of treating moral principles as absolutes, they reinvent their meaning to make sense of the situations in which they find themselves" (2001: 223). Free to own property, buy and sell goods, vote, and hold office, Americans also feel free now to define for themselves what it means to be good and virtuous.

The manifestations of moral freedom in American society are numerous. Wolfe (2001) argues that moral freedom stretches the concept of individualism to such a degree that individuals focus almost exclusively on their rights while overlooking their responsibilities. As people assume control over every aspect of their lives, they detach themselves from family, faith, and tradition. Thus, the ambition and competition that characterizes the way so many people approach their work and everyday lives. In this "culture of narcissism," it may seem quite justifiable to present oneself in whatever manner will serve one's best interests.

It appears that today's young people have embraced the concept of moral freedom to a greater extent than any previous generation. Twenge (2006) labels the group of young people born after 1970 "Generation Me" and claims they are more self-centered than young people of earlier generations. Today's youth are less likely to attend church, more likely to value self-love above love for others, and are highly focused on their appearance. Twenge attributes the self-focus of the "GenMe" group to the "self-esteem curriculum" that gained popularity in the 1970s. During this period, parents, teachers, and the broader society began to instill in children the belief that they are unique, special, and worthy individuals. This idea—that people are worthy for who they are rather than what they do and how they do it—has only gained in popularity since the 1970s. As a result, Twenge argues, young people today believe that they can be whatever they want to be and do whatever they want to do. In pursuing their goals, they are answerable first and foremost to themselves.

THE SOCIETAL EFFECTS OF SELF-FABRICATIONS

Ultimately, the prioritizing of self above all else is untenable in any society. As social beings, we are of necessity interconnected and dependent on each other for our well-being (Bellah et al., 1996). Indeed, economists and political scientists argue that a healthy economy and functioning democracy require the cooperation of individual citizens (Fukuyama, 1995; Putnam, 1995). Cooperation occurs when people trust each other to be open, honest, and true to their word. If individuals portray themselves in an inaccurate or misleading light, either to remain competitive in a market-driven society or because they feel entitled to devise their own rules of morality, social trust will diminish over time. Without trust, people become cut off from one another and cooperation ceases, with negative consequences for social life and economic well-being. Putnam (1995) observes that cooperation among Americans has diminished in recent decades due to the fact that we are "bowling alone" rather than participating in bowling leagues and other voluntary associations of the sort French political philosopher Alexis de Tocqueville celebrated during his visit to America almost 200 years ago. Putnam attributes the parallel decline in democratic participation to this diminishment of civic life.

Jenkins (2006) suggests that online engagement has the potential to enhance democratic participation by encouraging cooperation among a wide variety of individuals. The young reporters for *The Daily Prophet* would not have found each other or created the community they did without the ability to transcend geographic constraints through the Internet. In a similar way, Stevie Ryan reached thousands of geographically dispersed viewers through her Little Loca videos on YouTube. Jenkins suggests that engagement in such "participatory cultures" serves as a starting point for engagement in participatory democracy more broadly. Online activities hold the potential, then, to revive the voluntary association model that de Tocqueville first described in the nineteenth century (Gardner, 2007b). And yet this potential is just that, a potential; it is by no means guaranteed. In fact, it may be particularly difficult to establish a cohesive, enduring "participatory culture" when anonymity, fluctuations in group membership, and unclear roles, responsibilities, and norms conspire to reduce feelings of connectedness and accountability among participants of an online community (James et al., 2008). Moreover, the focus on self-presentation, promotion, and validation that seems characteristic of many online activities may overshadow the participatory aspect of "participatory culture" and undermine the integrity of the community.

When individuals put themselves before others and represent themselves in a misleading way, they risk damaging the cohesion and smooth functioning of society by decreasing trust among its citizens. In addition, there is a more abstract way in which self-fabrications can threaten a society. In any given society, people assume various roles, most notably the role of professional worker and citizen (Gardner, 2007a). The adoption of a particular role brings with it certain obligations and responsibilities. In the role of doctor, a person must strive to avoid harming any patient. In the role of journalist, a person must attempt to report the facts of an event in an unbiased and thorough manner. In the role of citizen, a person is expected to vote, pay taxes, and participate knowledgeably in civil society. If individuals place self-interest above the obligations of the roles they assume, they undermine the integrity of society. When an aspiring scientist like Allison misrepresented her experiment design in the Intel competition, she failed to uphold the core values embodied in the role of scientist. Perhaps she succumbed to the pressure of competition, and perhaps she felt justified to do so because the idea of moral freedom pervades today's society. Nevertheless, her behavior was unethical because she pursued her self-interest while undermining her responsibilities as a young scientist.

CONCLUSION

According to Wolfe (2001), the idea of moral freedom is here to stay. It is not a simple matter to repeal a freedom once it has been embraced by the majority of society. The challenge, Wolfe argues, is to strike a balance between the authority of tradition and the authority of the individual. As our discussion of young people's self-fabrications suggests, finding such balance entails considering the consequences of one's actions as they relate to the well-being of the self, others, and society. We—parents, educators, the media, and community leaders—face the task of promoting young people's awareness of the people and institutions that can be affected by their actions. Of course, this effort begins with our own actions. We must model responsible self-representations if we expect young people to exercise responsibility themselves.

Active intervention may well be warranted (Rimer, 2008). With our colleagues on the GoodWork Project, we have devised an educational curriculum that encourages young people to reflect on their roles and responsibilities as they make decisions about the way to conduct their lives in various contexts, including school and work. The GoodWork toolkit comprises several ethical dilemmas that emerged during our interviews with aspiring and young professionals. Allison's story is included as an example of one aspiring professional's decision to postpone ethical considerations until she had "made it" in today's competitive, market-driven environment (Fischman, Solomon, Greenspan, and Gardner, 2004). The toolkit also includes a variety of activities and discussion prompts that educators can use to encourage their students to think critically about the dilemmas and make connections to their personal goals and values.

The toolkit is currently being piloted in a number of high schools and universities in the United States. We are also participating in several college courses, such as the one described at the beginning of this paper, on pursuing meaningful work, meaningful citizenship, and a meaningful life. Through these endeavors, we hope to refine an educational curriculum that encourages tomorrow's citizens and workers to pursue their goals in a way that not only benefits them personally, but also serves the interests of the broader society. An important part of our work involves developing in our students an appreciation for the difference between a self-fabrication that rings true and one that is, quite simply, false.

REFERENCES

Arnett, Jeffrey Jensen. *Emerging Adulthood: The Winding Road from the Late Teens through the Twenties*. New York: Oxford University Press, 2004.

Bellah, Robert N., Richard Madsen, William M. Sullivan, Ann Swidler, and Steven M. Tipton. *Habits of the Heart: Individualism and Commitment in American Life*. Berkeley: University of California Press, 1996.

boyd, danah. "Why Youth (Heart) Social Networking Sites: The Role of Networked Publics in Teenage Social Life." *Youth, Identity, and Digital Media*. Ed. David Buckingham. Cambridge: MIT Press, 2007.

Brook, Daniel. *The Trap: Selling Out to Stay Afloat in Winner-Take-All America*. New York: Times Books, 2007.

Buckingham, David. "Introducing Identity." *Youth, Identity, and Digital Media*. Ed. David Buckingham. Cambridge: MIT Press, 2007.

Callahan, David. *The Cheating Culture: Why More Americans are Doing Wrong to Get Ahead*. Orlando: Harcourt, 2004.

Erikson, Erik. *Identity, Youth and Crisis*. New York: Norton, 1968.

Fischman, Wendy, Becca Solomon, Deborah Greenspan, and Howard Gardner. *Making Good: How Young People Cope with Moral Dilemmas at Work*. Cambridge: Harvard University Press, 2004.

Frank, Robert H., and Philip J. Cook. *The Winner-Take-All Society: How More and More Americans Compete for Ever Fewer and Bigger Prizes, Encouraging Economic Waste, Income Inequality, and an Impoverished Cultural Life*. New York: Free Press, 1995.

Fukuyama, Francis. *Trust: The Social Virtues and the Creation of Prosperity*. New York: Free Press, 1995.

Gardner, Howard. *Five Minds for the Future*. Boston: Harvard Business School Press, 2007a.

———. "The Unlimited Frontiers." The MacArthur Spotlight Blog (April 10, 2007b) <http://spotlight.macfound.org/main/entry/unlimited_frontiers/>.

Gilligan, Carol. "The Centrality of Relationship in Human Development: A Puzzle, Some Evidence, and a Theory." *Development and Vulnerability in Close Relationships*. Eds. Gil Noam and Kurt Fischer. Mahwah, N.J.: Lawrence Erlbaum Associates, 1996.

Goffman, Erving. *The Presentation of Self in Everyday Life*. New York: Doubleday, 1959.

Harter, Susan. *The Construction of the Self: A Developmental Perspective*. New York: Guilford Press, 1999.

James, Carrie, Katie Davis, Andrea Flores, John Francis, Lindsay Pettingill, Margaret Rundle, and   Howard Gardner. "Young People, Ethics, and the New Digital Media: A Synthesis from   the GoodPlay Project." *GoodWork Project Series*. No. 54 (2008) <http://www.pz.harvard.edu/eBookstore/PDFs/GoodWork54.pdf>.

Jenkins, Henry. *Convergence Culture: Where Old and New Media Collide*. New York: New York University Press, 2006.

Jones, Marilee, Kenneth R.Ginsburg and Martha Moraghan Jablow. *Less Stress, More Success: A New Approach to Guiding Your Teen Through College Admissions and Beyond*. Elk Grove Village, Ill.: American Academy of Pediatrics, 2006.

Josephson Institute of Ethics. 2006 Report Card on the Ethics of American Youth. October 2006 <http://charactercounts.org/pdf/reportcard/reportcard-all.pdf>.

Kiesa, Abby, Alexander P. Orlowski, Peter Levine, Deborah Both, Emily H. Kirby, Mark H. Lopez, and Karlo B. Marcelo. "Millenials Talk Politics: A Study of College Student Political Engagement." Center for Information and Research on Civic Learning and Engagement (CIRCLE), University of Maryland, School of Public Policy, 2007.

Kluegel, James R., and Eliot R. Smith. *Beliefs About Inequality: Americans' Views of What Is and What Ought to Be.* New York: de Gruyter, 1986.

Lewin, Tamar. "M.I.T.'s Admissions Dean Resigns; Ends 28-Year Lie About Degrees." New York Times, April 27, 2007: A1.

Maag, Christopher. "A Hoax Turned Fatal Draws Anger but No Charges." New York Times, November 28, 2007: A23.

Marcia, James E. "Common Processes Underlying Ego Identity, Cognitive/ Moral Development, and Individuation." *Self, Ego, and Identity: Integrative Approaches.* Eds. Daniel K. Lapsley and F. Clark Power. New York: Springer-Verlag, 1988.

Markus, H., and P. Nurius. "Possible Selves." *American Psychologist* 41:9 (1986): 954-969.

McCabe, D. L., L. K. Trevino, and K. D. Butterfield. "Cheating in Academic Institutions: A Decade of Research." *Ethics and Behavior* 11:3 (2001): 219-232.

McGrath, Ben. "It Should Happen to You: The Anxieties of YouTube Fame." *New Yorker* (October 16, 2006): 86.

Poniewozik, James, and Jeanne McDowell. "How Reality TV Fakes It." *Time* (January 29, 2006): 60-62.

Pryor, John H., Sylvia Hurtado, Victor B. Saenz, Jose Luis Santos, and William S. Korn. *The American Freshman: Forty Year Trends*, 1966-2006. Los Angeles: Graduate School of Education and Information Studies, University of California, Los Angeles, 2007.

Putnam, R. D. "Bowling Alone: America's Declining Social Capital." *Journal of Democracy* 6:1 (1995): 65-78.

Rimer, Sara. "Big Paycheck or Service? Students Are Put to the Test." *New York Times*, June 23, 2008: A15.

Shweder, Richard A., Nancy C. Much, Manamohan Mahapatra, and Lawrence Park. "The 'Big Three' of Morality (Autonomy, Community, Divinity) and the 'Big Three' Explanations of Suffering." *Morality and Health*. Eds.

Allan M. Brandt and Paul Rozin. New York:Taylor and Frances/Routledge, 1997.

Stern, Susannah. "Producing Sites, Exploring Identities: Youth Online Authorship." *Youth, Identity, and Digital Media*. Ed. David Buckingham. Cambridge: MIT Press, 2007.

Turkle, Sherry. *Life on the Screen: Identity in the Age of the Internet*. New York: Simon andSchuster, 1995.

————. "Cyberspace and Identity." *Contemporary Sociology* 28:6 (1999): 643-648.

Turner, J. "The Messenger Overwhelming the Message: Ideological Cues and Perceptions of Bias in Television News." *Political Behavior* 29:4 (2007): 441-464.

Twenge, Jean M. *Generation Me: Why Today's Young Americans are More Confident, Assertive, Entitled—and More Miserable than Ever Before*. New York: Free Press, 2006.

Valkenburg, P. M., A. P. Schouten, and J. Peter. "Adolescents' Identity Experiments on the Internet." *New Media and Society* 7 (2005): 383-402.

Wolfe, Alan. *Moral Freedom: The Impossible Idea that Defines the Way We Live Now*. New York: Norton, 2001.

Search the Web to locate the resumés of three people who are in the career field you plan to enter. Compare the resumés and consider which person seems to be the most talented and experienced—and why. How does their strength come through in the resumé? Are there places where the wording could be different in order to make the person seem even better? What revisions would you suggest and why?

Consider the arguments made in this article. How much exaggeration is acceptable and how much is too much? Is a certain type of exaggeration expected in a professional setting? What about personal settings? Is a person in an online space, such as *World of Warcraft*, more or less likely to be a true representation of their "real" self? Why?

Working in small groups, locate at least five of the sources used in this article and read them. How does familiarity with these sources change your reading of "When False Representations Ring True (and When They Don't)"?

Locate a resumé online of a person working in the professional field you plan to enter. Using that resumé as a model, draft a resumé of your own—one that highlights your skills, background, etc. How can you authentically represent yourself while still making the most of what you have? How can you tell if you've gone too far in positively representing your abilities?

AUTHENTICITY

Claire McIntosh is a frequent contributor to Ebony magazine, focusing heavily, but not exclusively, on matters of relationships and dating. In her most recent article, "Mama Said: Motherhood Inspired," McIntosh tells the stories of seven exceptional mothers. In the article that follows, McIntosh considers some of the darkness beneath the rosy surface of online dating.

DIGITAL DECEPTION

BY CLAIRE MCINTOSH

Bogus profiles, global grifters, married posers, fake fiancés and even show-throwing spinsters. Singles searching for love online are finding a lot more than they bargained for.

He got the door for her and helped her with her coat. He took her on romantic trips and got along great with her daughters. In just a few whirlwind months, Lisa, a nurse in upstate New York, had no doubt that Donald, a wealthy businessman she had met on an online dating site, was her soul mate. Last winter, when he proposed, she knew that "something special" was happening. They made an offer on a million-dollar home and ordered $30,000 worth of furniture. While on a couple's retreat to a spa last spring, as she lay next to him in bed and anticipated their May ceremony in Bermuda, eight armed S.W.A.T. officers dressed in black rushed into the bedroom and arrested her fiancé on charges of fraud and larceny. The flowers, jewelry, gift cards and other merchandise he'd used to woo her were the ill-gotten gains of check-cashing scams. Through bogus deposits to her accounts and other means, he'd taken her for $12,000.

Welcome to the seamy side of cyberdating. Sites such as Match.com, eHarmony. com and Zoosk.com are now as ubiquitous on the singles' scene as breath mints and condoms. About 30 million Americans say they know someone who has been in a long-term relationship or married someone he or she met online; a majority of online daters say they have had good experiences. The explosion of online options, including BlackPeopleMeet.com, SoulSingles.com and EbonyFriends.com (not connected to EBONY magazine), are a sign that African-Americans are embracing electronic hookups. While 11 percent of Internet users have dated online, 13 percent of Black users have, according to the Pew Internet & American Life Project. Matchmaking sites have gone mainstream, but they are largely unregulated and often poorly policed. Users frequently encounter false statements, fake profiles and even criminal activity—sometimes with devastating results. A Hollywood woman suing Match.com (she says the site is responsible for her being sexually assaulted by a known sex offender) is pushing for tighter screening measures.

Most commonplace are the lies. In a survey conducted last year by Norton, a maker of Internet security software, men were found more likely to lie than women in 13 out of 14 categories, such as name, contact information, income, city of residence and relationship status. Women lied more frequently about weight. According to the 2010 Norton Cybercrime Report, 33 percent of adults have used a fake identity and 45 percent have lied about their personal details.

Usually it's men who lie about age—but not always. Mel, 40, a Pennsylvania bachelor who has since sworn off dating sites, had to put the brakes on what he'd thought was a promising match he'd made on a Black dating site. His cyberhottie said she was in her late 20s—a globe-trotting good-time girl with a love for humanity and kids. In her photo, she was out-of-his league attractive. Ready for a rendezvous, he drove four hours to upstate New York. "When I opened the door, I thought I saw my grandmother. She looked old and tired, moved slowly, wore a hairnet and heavy makeup," he says, recalling his shock and disappointment.

Just as statements can be falsified, so can entire online profiles—a growing concern amid claims that some companies are knowingly posting false information. Match.com faces a class action lawsuit alleging that more than half of the profiles on the site belong to inactive members or scammers. The Dallas-based dating giant will "defend the case vigorously," notes a company spokesperson who says a similar case was dismissed last December. But other industry insiders don't deny that such practices exist.

Rochelle Peachy runs the trans-Atlantic dating site iloveyouraccent.com. "When I began the site on Valentine's Day 2010, I was contacted by someone offering to sell me fake profiles. He told me I could have 10,000 members within 24 hours if I bought them from him. This is such a huge scandal within the dating site world, much more than just the odd male or female thrown on the site to attract members into paying," explains Peachy, who now has 10,000 legitimate members. She learned such operators steal photos off of social networking sites, such as Facebook, to create the bogus profiles.

Stolen photographs are also used by international con artists to convince unwitting singles to wire them money in sweetheart swindles. The practice is so widespread that the U.S. State Department, U.S. Department of Defense and some American embassies abroad have all posted warnings online. LaVonya Reeves, one of the few African-American heads of an online dating company, launched reboundlovers.com, a niche site for the brokenhearted. "Seventy percent of scammers whom we have come across have come from Nigeria and Ghana," she says, adding that not all people from those countries are con artists. Having run into unsavory people herself while online dating, she warns that requests for personal information (address, financial info) are the number one signs of trouble. Mary Leal, a security consultant and former police officer in the Dayton, Ohio, area, is founder of The Predator Project. She began investigating offshore scammers after a friend and colleague was fleeced by her "boyfriend" for $18,000.

Industry leaders and lawmakers are working toward better protections. Many sites themselves are monitoring activities with additional manpower or technology: posting safety rules, asking users to report suspicious behaviors and closing the accounts of members who have committed abuses. But such measures are piecemeal at best. The real power to avoid digital deceivers lies in the hand that is clicking the mouse. Many daters now prefer social networking sites where they can learn more about a prospect's associates and behavior. And others have decided to look for love in a site that, to some, may feel a bit new and unfamiliar: the real world.

Collaborate

As a group, list all of the social media sites and services you can think of—from virtual spaces devoted to discussing a local sports team to national "dating" services that facilitate infidelity for married members. How important are such sites and services to the social fabric of daily life for many people? Are online friendships as valid as any other friendships, even if the friends never meet anywhere except Xbox Live? Is online matchmaking superior or inferior to more traditional forms of meeting potential romantic partners? Why or why not?

In a short essay, consider this: Are the problems with "digital deception" that are defined and described in this article significant, or has the Internet become such a part of society that these problems are normal concerns in modern life?

If people lead lives online that are more interesting or exciting than their day-to-day lives, and they never deliberately harm anyone else, then is their "deception" a real problem? The writer Augusten Burroughs, for example, often writes about how, during his years as an addict, he would write personal ads as something of a hobby: He would "advertise" online for a certain type of date or certain type of mate, but then he rarely met any of the people who would send him email. His pleasure came from creating a false personal ad and reading the responses. Was anyone harmed by his inauthentic approach to dating?

MAJOR ASSIGNMENTS

MAJOR ASSIGNMENT #1
ON MEMORY

BACKGROUND

When James Frey admitted to his readers that he had misrepresented many of the details of his own life in his "memoir" about overcoming addiction, there was a huge outcry. Many critics argued that if memoir was a view of the past dependent entirely on the writer's own recollections, with every detail filtered through his or her lens, then memoir was ultimately nothing but fiction based loosely on events that may (or may not) have once happened—to a character that may or may not resemble the author. If you have not done so already, read the selection in this book from *A Million Little Pieces*. Also read James Frey's note to his readers, where he begins to detail the fabrications and exaggerations present in his book. If possible, you may find it useful to locate the two interviews that Oprah Winfrey conducted with James Frey—when she praised him…and when she excoriated him.

ASSIGNMENT

Choose an event from the past—one that you do not have any memory of. The simplest way to do this is to choose something that took place either when you were a child or even before you were born. Depending on your age and lived experience, this could include an event such as your parent's wedding or the assassination of President John F. Kennedy. Once you have selected an event, ask two people to describe the event to you. With a "small" event from your family, this could be talking to both of your parents—separately, rather than together—about the events on the day they were married. If you choose to focus upon a "large" event, you could interview family members or virtually anyone else. Take notes on how each person describes the event you've chosen. What do they remember first or best? What do they feel or think at the time, and how did these thoughts or feelings compare with those of your other interview subject? In an essay, describe what event you've chosen and explain how each of your interview subjects remembered the event. Focus particularly on those points where the two people you interviewed seem to disagree and consider the significance of these differences in your essay.

QUESTIONS FOR INVENTION AND RESEARCH

1. What is the first major world event you can remember that took place during your lifetime? Describe the event and your memories of it.

2. What are your thoughts on the subject you've chosen? Since you did not witness the event and/or were not alive at the time it occurred, how much do you know? What are your sources for the information you have—that is, how do you know what you know?

3. Depending on the event you've chosen, who are the best interview subjects? If you are writing about a wedding, for example, you might interview the bride and groom—but it might be even more interesting to interview the bride and one of the bridesmaids. If you are writing about a major world event, such as the bombing of Pearl Harbor in 1941, consider interviewing people with very different backgrounds—a neighbor who was born in the United States and served in the military at the time and another neighbor who is an immigrant from Mexico, for example.

4. Consider carefully the questions you will ask your interviewees. The questions should build from the more basic—questions about the facts of an event—to the more complex—questions about feelings, thoughts, etc. Be sure to ask both subjects the same questions.

MAJOR ASSIGNMENT #2
JUST THE FACTS

BACKGROUND

If you have not done so already, read the selections from journalists Stephen Glass, Jayson Blair, and JR Moehringer. Be sure to read the "expose" pieces that follow the selections from Glass and Blair, too. In nearly every case, journalists strive to tell the facts to their readers as best they are able—facts that, unlike those in a memoir, are not filtered through a single writer's interpretation and ideology. They interview multiple sources, perform research, and put every article through a rigorous process of fact checking. Even then, mistakes are made, and virtually all news publications regularly print lists of "corrections"—to set the record straight on facts that were inadvertently misrepresented. Even when everything is thought to be correct, however, not everyone necessarily cites the same facts—and changing the facts that are presented can alter the way the entire story is perceived.

ASSIGNMENT

Record two television news broadcasts simultaneously or view the same news story as it is presented on the Web sites of two different news organizations—FOX and NBC, for example. Watch each news broadcast and make a list of the topics that are covered. Note how much time is devoted to each topic. In an essay, compare the two news broadcasts. In what ways was their coverage of the news of the day similar? In what ways was their coverage different? What might account for the differences in the coverage? To support your argument, use screenshots from the news broadcasts or, if you are composing a multimodal essay using Wordpress or a similar program, insert images and/or complete video clips.

QUESTIONS FOR INVENTION AND RESEARCH

1. How much news do you have access to daily only on television? Make a list of all the news channels available to you in your area, note whether there is local news or only world news, and briefly explain any impressions you have of each channel. Does one network focus primarily on issues through a more liberal approach, for example? A more conservative approach?

2. Where do you get your news about local, national, and international events? What television channels, specific television programs, publications, Web sites, etc. do you consult as you form your view of the world around you? Why do you get your information from these specific sources?

3. Select one television channel that focuses at least part of its broadcast day on the news and visit the channel's Web site (or, if necessary, call its local office). What company owns the television channel? Researching further up the corporate chain, what company owns that company? Considering who owns the news source, can you imagine stories that might not be covered objectively by local reporters?

MAJOR ASSIGNMENT #3
RESEARCHING LOCAL SCHOOLS

BACKGROUND

As the readings by Catherine Rampell, Alfie Kohn, and Jeffrey A. Erickson demonstrate, the issue of "grade inflation" has been present in American education nearly as long as there has *been* American education. Schools are judged by the performance of their students on standardized tests, for example, and the stakes can be very high; often low-performing schools lose a significant amount of their funding from the government if specific educational levels aren't being demonstrated by students. It's a matter of pressure: The government puts pressure on schools to perform better, so schools put pressure on teachers, and the teachers pressure their students to learn...often to learn only what will be on the government's test. Grades may go up within this pedagogical pressure cooker, but does learning occur?

ASSIGNMENT

Consider your own grades in your K-12 educational career. In an essay, describe the kind of student you think you were. What subjects did you study, and how hard did you push yourself? How hard were you pushed by someone else? Were there special challenges you had to confront to achieve your education? Perhaps most important of all, did the grades that you received reflect how much you learned? Consider the data available about your school (most likely at the Web site for the local school district). What is the rate of student success? Failure? What is the percentage of students who drop out? Summarize the information you found and reflect on how it confirms or refutes your own experiences as a student.

QUESTIONS FOR INVENTION AND RESEARCH

1. Jeffrey A. Erickson describes a situation in which a change in grading philosophy made all the difference in his school. How would the change he describes affect your high school? How would it have affected your own education?

2. Kelly Field describes, in part, a situation where faculty at online schools felt pressured to give students good grades. How have the online classes you've taken compared to other classes conducted in classrooms? Do you feel that the grade in the online class was a better (or worse) reflection of your actual accomplishments in the class?

3. Visit the homepage of your high school (or even the high school itself, if this is possible). What data points are reported regarding grading and academic success? How does the information presented there compare with information you can locate (online or at the school) about the school's standing in relation to the No Child Left Behind act? Where does your former school stand in relation to other schools in the district, the state, or the nation?

4. Talk to two or three people in your community who have students at different levels of the local educational system. How do they feel about education in your community? How do their feelings compare with your own experiences? How do their feelings compare with the data that is available regarding academic achievement at your local schools?

MAJOR ESSAY #4
A MATTER OF DESCRIPTION

BACKGROUND

Beginning in the mid-1990s, Internet connection speeds improved dramatically, often because users were no longer dependent on their telephone line to make their connection. The Web became a much more visual place, and video games suddenly pioneered a new frontier. Games from *Doom* to *Duke Nukem* were able to bring players together in virtual space—players from around the nation and around the world. Now, games like *World of Warcraft* allow players to live a virtual existence online. As the Internet has become a more and more integrated aspect of social life, matchmaking sites have become more and more popular, from Match.com, which reminds users that "1 in 5" relationships today begin online, to AshleyMadison.com, which promises its married users a chance at infidelity without consequences. Dating and gaming share one component, however: A real person sits at the keyboard… constructing themselves online in whatever way they might wish, whether the representation reflects the reality of the individual or not.

ASSIGNMENT

Select a place, company, or other organization that you know very well through direct personal experience. Visit the Web site for the subject you've chosen and, in an essay, describe how the subject represents itself. What images are shown? How does the subject you've chosen define and describe what it does? How are visitors to the Web site led to see the subject? In your essay, be sure to go into detail about the information given on the Web site, from things that appear immediately on the home page to things provided in the tiny-font links at the bottom. After you have completed your essay, briefly present it to your peers. Show them the Web site, if this technology is available. Briefly discuss how the web site either reinforces your own knowledge of the subject or contradicts it.

QUESTIONS FOR INVENTION AND RESEARCH

1. How much can an individual stretch or bend the truth as they represent themselves online? Is it inauthentic to show a really good picture, for example, even if that picture is a few years out of date?

2. Talk to a friend who plays—or has played—games online. How did they represent themselves—the same or different from the "real" person?

3. Consider a social networking site such as Facebook. In your opinion, do people represent themselves accurately or inaccurately there? Examine the page of a person you do not know. What things does the person choose to reveal—about likes and dislikes, for example—and what image does that create for you? Are there other representations, such as photographs, that reinforce or contradict the image of the person that you see?

4. Select an energy company, particularly coal or oil, and research that company's Web site. Then research how that company is represented by those opposed to what it does—a national environmental group, for example. Is either characterization an authentic one, in your opinion, or do both have elements of caricature that make them inauthentic?

MAJOR ESSAY #5
A MATTER OF INTERPRETATION

BACKGROUND

Beginning in the 1950s, political advertising was changed forever when Dwight D. Eisenhower ran ads on television as part of his campaign strategy; many of these ads can be located online. In modern American politics, television advertising is a major part of campaigning for office—from mayor to president. As the Internet has become more integral to politics, advertising has steadily moved in that direction, too, largely because the cost of Internet advertising is insignificant in comparison to the cost of television.

ASSIGNMENT

Searching online, find a campaign ad for an American politician and their opponent. Each ad must be at least 30 seconds long, but do not select an ad that is longer than two minutes. In an essay, describe how each ad defines one of the candidates. What images of them appear? What other images are shown and why? How does music and voice-over narration work with (or against) the images being presented? Be sure to consider this: If one ad is a generally positive description of the candidate, and one ad is an attack ad, which makes the best case for its own authenticity and why?

QUESTIONS FOR INVENTION AND RESEARCH

1. Once you have selected an advertisement, watch it several times with the sound off. How does the ad affect you when the audio portion is absent? What images stand out most in your mind? Why? Now play the ad again, this time with your eyes closed. What stands out when only the audio aspects of the advertisement are available to you?

2. Watch "The Bear" (from Ronald Reagan's campaign in 1984) and "Wolves" (from George W. Bush's campaign in 2004). How do these two ads represent the issue of national defense similarly/differently? What accounts for the similarities/differences?

3. Select one specific presidential campaign that has occurred since 1952. Who were the two ultimate candidates? How did each incorporate television into their campaign for office? Which seems most effective?

4. Research the Web site of a candidate from the most recent national election you participated in—presidential, senatorial, or congressional. Just looking at the candidate's Web site, how do you think they wanted to be viewed by the audience? Are there other ways you think viewers might have reacted—ways the candidate didn't intend, necessarily?

MAJOR ESSAY #6
A MATTER OF CREATION...OR REVISION

BACKGROUND

According to Wikipedia, Wikipedia was launched in January of 2001 and, by 2012, contained more than 23 million articles in 285 languages (roughly four million in English alone). The massive site, a collaborative encyclopedia, boasts more than 100,000 active contributors (all volunteers). While recognized, traditional experts will sometimes agree that a given article or group of articles may be as accurate as any other published source, including peer-reviewed scholarship, Wikipedia is far more likely to be considered an illegitimate and unworthy source of information in anything but the most informal of writing.

ASSIGNMENT

Consider your own areas of expertise—from knitting scarves to shoeing horses, from playing rugby to brewing coffee, from the geography of your home town to the social scene at your university. Find the Wikipedia page most relevant to your area of greatest expertise. Review the Wikipedia entry and then correct it. Revise the entry to make it, in your opinion, a more authentic and accurate representation of the place/skill/etc. being described. Add pictures and other visual representations, including video, to make the entry useful and relevant to readers. In an essay, explain what changes you made and why you made them. What visuals were present and why did you remove them? What visuals did you add? Explain what they do to further develop the Wikipedia entry.

QUESTIONS FOR INVENTION AND RESEARCH

1. Searching in your local or school library, locate an encyclopedia entry for a plant or animal native to your area or climate. Copy this article and compare it to the Wikipedia entry on this same topic. How are the two alike? How are they different? What could account for these similarities and/or differences?

2. Review the Wikipedia entry for your school. What does the entry cover in greatest detail? What receives the least attention? Based on your own experiences, how well does the Wikipedia entry reflect the reality of your school?

3. Using an encyclopedia that is at least fifty years old, locate the entry for an event from American history—the assassination of John F. Kennedy, the Battle of Gettysburg, etc. Be sure to pick a specific event—like the Battle of Bunker Hill—rather than a broad, blurry topic, like the American Revolution. Copy the encyclopedia entry that describes this event. Using the resources available at your library, locate a newspaper from the time the event occurred—ideally from the day the event happened or the day after the event happened. Copy this newspaper story. Compare both the newspaper story and the encyclopedia entry. If the event you chose is modern enough to have been filmed in some way, then locate and view any visual resources—from pictures to television news stories archived online. How are these texts all similar to or different from one another? How do they compare to the Wikipedia entry for the event you chose? Where are these texts similar to one another and where are they different?

FILMOGRAPHY

American Beauty
Trapped in a seemingly meaningless life, an entire suburban family struggles to find its true existence—using drug abuse, infidelity, and blackmail.

The Basketball Diaries
Based on the memoir by Jim Carroll, this film follows a young writer as he searches for his authentic self in a world of drug abuse and crime—pulled between the mother who loves him and the streets that feed his art.

Citizen Cohn
Serving as one of the primary prosecutors of alleged communists during the American Red Scare, Roy Cohn ruthlessly pursues individuals whose "weaknesses" he can exploit—even when he shares them or simply fabricates them.

Dances with Wolves
Seeking the authentic American frontier, a Union soldier ultimately finds his true self.

Dead Poets Society
A group of boys fight to define their true identities in the face of parental pressure and the weight of tradition at their exclusive prep school—with the aid of a nontraditional English teacher who has Romantic ideas about self-will and self-identification.

Death of a Salesman
In this drama, adapted many times to both film and television, a family's reality blurs with its fantasy of itself—leaving everyone to face the facts and contend with their fallout.

Enemy at the Gates
A Russian soldier is quickly redefined by propagandists as the sniper-hero of Stalingrad, a symbol of Soviet resistance to the overwhelming force of the Nazi army—only to lose his identity at the hands of a heart-sick, jealous friend.

Europa Europa
To escape the horrors of Nazi Germany, a young Jewish boy assumes not only the role of a non-Jew but that of a perfect specimen of Hitler's Aryan youth.

Fargo
When his wife is kidnapped, a meek salesman is left alone to handle an overbearing father-in-law and a terrified son—tasks complicated by his own complicity in the manufactured crime.

Finding Forrester
A local genius and a neighborhood recluse form an unlikely friendship, which is stretched to its breaking point by an accusation of plagiarism.

Focus
Based on the short novel by Arthur Miller, this film considers what happens in a Brooklyn neighborhood (and beyond) when a man is suddenly perceived to be Jewish. In a world of bigotry and anti-Semitism, he is left to struggle to authenticate his own identity.

Guilty by Suspicion
In Hollywood during the Red Scare, no one wanted to be defined by the company they kept—and everyone's authenticity was open to debate before the House Un-American Activities Committee.

Hoop Dreams
Two boys from Chicago struggle to define themselves as they come of age in an environment so focused on basketball that to pursue any dream other than the NBA is virtually unthinkable. In the end, the authenticity they seek is—and is not—found on the court.

Imagining Indians
Analyzing the classical westerns of Hollywood's Golden Age, this documentary considers just how limiting and damaging such texts were in the creation and recreation of Native American culture.

The Imposter
In this documentary, the case of con man Frederic Bourdin is considered—a man who managed to fool government officials and a grieving family into believing that he was a long-missing boy, despite the fact that he was much older, had the wrong hair and eye color, and spoke with an accent.

Kids
A raw and rambling faux-documentary, *Kids* follows a group of teens defining their internal and external lives in relation to the highly sexualized world around them—with devastating consequences.

Little Big Man
Focusing on a young Caucasian boy raised by Native Americans, this satirical film considers everything from the clashing of equally authentic but oppositional cultures on the frontier to American involvement in the Vietnam War.

The Man Who Never Was
During World War II, in Operation Mincemeat, the British army misdirected Hitler's forces about the upcoming invasion of Sicily, primarily hiding the truth behind a dead man floating in the sea.

Mazes and Monsters
A young man fights to retain his true identity despite the seductive call of role-playing games.

Mortal Thoughts
A murder suspect's story strikes all the right notes but still doesn't find the right tone...until the facts fall into their proper place.

Mother Night
Although he served as a spy inside Germany during World War II, broadcasting propaganda for the Nazis with hidden messages for the Allies, a man learns to his horror that sometimes you are judged according to what you pretend to be.

Our Man in Havana
Hired to be a British secret agent, a salesman sends sketches of vacuum parts as "secret" plans. As his spying operation grows, though, it becomes all too real.

Outfoxed: Rupert Murdoch's War on Journalism
When most Americans get their news of the day from television, argues this documentary, it presents a problem—especially when that source has its own clear agenda.

Page One
In this documentary about *The New York Times*, the struggles of this print-paper in the digital age are considered, along with issues ranging from Wikileaks to the Pentagon Papers to plagiarist Jayson Blair.

Prison Town, USA
When the local industries in Susanville, California, failed, they invited the prison industry to town—and now struggle to maintain small-town identity in a relationship between town and prison that is simultaneously symbiotic and parasitic.

Resurrecting the Champ
When he tells the story of a down-and-almost-out boxer, a sports writer forgets to ask his subject the most important question of all: Who are you, really?

A River Runs Through It
Norman Maclean tells the story of the central tragedy of his life, but only four decades after-the-fact and only by twisting most of the facts into a much more "literate" form.

Shattered Glass
Some stories are just too good to be true, as one Washington editor learns to his shame.

The Shawshank Redemption

A convicted killer maintains his true identity in the face of violent prison guards and a corrupt warden—knowing all along that he neither murdered his wife and her lover nor intends to serve his time.

Six Characters in Search of an Author

When the characters in his television program come to life and confront him, a director is left to sort out six different points of view on the story he was trying to tell.

Storytelling

The members of a writing workshop learn that nothing is true once it's written, just as a young man learns that no one is really who they are after the cameras roll.

The Usual Suspects

A crafty detective drags the truth out of a murder suspect, only to learn that the tapestry of truth can be woven from many broken threads.

AUTHENTICITY

WORKS CITED

Akst, Jef. "When Is Self-Plagiarism OK?" The Scientist. (9/9/2010). Web. 11 December 2012.

Barry, Dan, David Barstow, Jonathan D. Glater, Adam Liptak, Jacques Steinberg. Research support was provided by Delaquérière, Alain, and Wilder, Carolyn. "Times Reporter Who Resigned Leaves Long Trail of Deception." *New York Times* 11 May 2003: 1. *Academic Search Elite*. Web. 11 Dec. 2012.

Blair, Jayson. "Relatives of Missing Soldiers Dread Hearing Worse News." *New York Times* 27 Mar. 2003: 13. *Academic Search Elite*. Web. 11 Dec. 2012.

Dante, Ed. "The Shadow Scholar." *Chronicle Of Higher Education* 57.13 (2010): B6-B9. *Academic Search Elite*. Web. 11 Dec. 2012.

Davis, Katie, Scott Seider, and Howard Gardner. "When False Representations Ring True (And When They Don't)." *Social Research* 75.4 (2008): 1085-1108. *Academic Search Elite*. Web. 11 Dec. 2012.

Erickson, Jeffrey A. "How Grading Reform Changed Our School." *Educational Leadership* 69.3 (2011): 66-70. *Academic Search Elite*. Web. 11 Dec. 2012.

Field, Kelly. "Faculty At For-Profits Allege Constant Pressure To Keep Students Enrolled." *Education Digest* 77.2 (2011): 21-27. *Academic Search Elite*. Web. 11 Dec. 2012.

Frey, James. *A Million Little Pieces*. New York: Anchor, 2003.

Glass, Stephen. "Hack Heaven." *New Republic* 218.20 (1998): 11-12. *Academic Search Elite*. Web. 11 Dec. 2012.

Gravois, John. "The College For-Profits Should Fear." *Washington Monthly* 43.9/10 (2011): 38-48. *Academic Search Elite*. Web. 11 Dec. 2012.

Hamilton, Geoff. "Mixing Memoir and Desire: James Frey, Wound Culture, and the "Essential American Soul". *Journal Of American Culture* 30.3 (2007): 324-333. *Academic Search Elite*. Web. 11 Dec. 2012.

Ketcham, Amaris. "How to Determine Truth." Bark. (9/2/2011). Web. 11 December 2012.

Kohn, Alfie. "The Dangerous Myth of Grade Inflation." *Chronicle Of Higher Education* 49.11 (2002): B7. *Academic Search Elite*. Web. 11 Dec. 2012.

Maclean, Norman. "In Business." *The Norman Maclean Reader: Essays, Letters, and Other Writings by the Author of* A River Runs Through It. Ed. O. Alan Weltzien. Chicago: U of Chicago P, 2008: 55-61.

McIntosh, Claire. "Digital Deception." *Ebony* 66.12 (2011): 75-77. *Academic Search Elite*. Web. 11 Dec. 2012.

Moehringer, JR. "Resurrecting the Champ." *Los Angeles Times* (5/4/97). Web. 11 December 2012.

Penenberg, Adam L. "Lies, Damn Lies and Fiction." *Forbes.com* (5/11/98). Web. 11 December 2012.

Rampell, Catherine. "A History of College Grade Inflation." *The New York Times*. (7/14/2011). Web. 11 December 2012.

NOTES

NOTES

NOTES

NOTES

NOTES

NOTES